DATE DUE

DEC 0 9 1993	
MAY 0 2 1996	

BRODART   Cat. No. 23-221

Getting an Heir

Getting an Heir

Adoption and the Construction of Kinship in Late Imperial China

ANN WALTNER

University of Hawaii Press

Honolulu, Hawaii

90 92 93 94 95 96 5 4 3 2 1

Library of Congress Cataloging-in-Publication Data
Waltner, Ann Beth.
Getting an heir : adoption and the construction of kinship
in late imperial China / Ann Waltner.
p.   cm.
Includes bibliographical references and index.
ISBN 0–8248–1280–8 (alk. paper)
1. Adoption—China—History. 2. Kinship—China—History.
3. China—Social life and customs. I. Title.
HV875.58.C6W35   1990
306.874—dc20   90–43640
CIP

University of Hawaii Press books are printed on acid-
free paper and meet the guidelines for permanence and
durability of the Council on Library Resources.

Contents

Acknowledgments

I would like to thank the many people who have helped me with this project since its inception as a doctoral dissertation many years ago. The members of my dissertation committee—Frederic Wakeman, Wolfram Eberhard, and Tu Wei-ming—provided encouragement and assistance. Suzanne Cahill and Victoria Vernon, then fellow graduate students, made me a better writer and a better critic through our monthly meetings as we wrote our dissertations. Other friends and colleagues have commented on this manuscript in a variety of forms: Charlotte Furth, Robert Hymes, Susan Mann, the late Sharon Nolte, and numerous others. Librarians at the University of Minnesota, University of California at Berkeley, Stanford, Harvard, Princeton, the University of Chicago, and the National Central Library in Taipei all provided assistance. A special word of thanks is due to the interlibrary loan staff at the University of Minnesota for their help during the final revisions. Financial assistance for this project was provided by grants from the University of California at Berkeley and the American Council of Learned Societies. The graduate school of the University of Minnesota has provided, through a McKnight–Land Grant Professorship, extraordinarily generous research support. And finally, I would like to thank my research assistants, Peter Ditmanson and Hsü Pi-ching, who during a summer of careful checking and spirited discussion made this a better book.

Introduction

On the fifteenth day of the seventh month of 1524, several hundred officials, including a number of the most important ministers of the Ming state, demonstrated at the Tso-shun gate to the Forbidden City in Peking to protest the Shih-tsung emperor's refusal to permit himself to be named the adopted son of the Hsiao-tsung emperor. While other residents of the capital busied themselves with preparations for the Ghost Festival, these officials risked careers and lives to protest what Shih-tsung insisted was a private decision. But in the imperial family, especially in regard to succession, there were no private decisions. And so the demonstrators, chanting, invoked the names of Shih-tsung's imperial predecessors, both Hsiao-tsung, his immediate predecessor, and T'ai-tsu, the Ming founder. Court eunuchs, the guardians of peace and propriety in the inner sanctum of the palace, ordered the crowds to disperse. They would not. The eunuchs took the names of the demonstrators and arrested eight of them. As if the arrests were a signal, the remaining officials stormed the gates of the Forbidden City. Confucian decorum vanished as several hundred scholar-bureaucrats pounded on the gates and wailed. The pounding and wailing reverberated throughout the palace. The seventeen-year-old emperor, his patience exhausted, ordered the rest of the demonstrators to be arrested. In all, 134 men were detained. They were sentenced five days later, on the twentieth of the seventh month (August 19, 1524). Eight of the most important leaders were exiled. The remainder were punished according to their rank. The salaries of those whose rank was the fourth degree or above were confiscated. Those whose rank was below the fourth degree were flogged. Sixteen of those flogged died as a result. A week later, punishments were inflicted on a second group of demonstrators. Three more men were exiled for life, and several more were reduced to the legal status of commoner. Another man died as a result of flogging.[1]

1

This episode, known as the *Ta li i,* or Great Ritual Controversy, was a conjunction between public and private interests, between affairs of state and conceptions of family duty. At issue was, on the one hand, the orderly succession to the throne, and on the other hand, the duty owed by a son to his natural parents. The problem arose when the Wu-tsung emperor (r 1505–1521) died in 1521 without an heir. His will named his cousin, who reigned as the Shih-tsung emperor, as his successor.[2] But the Ming rules for succession, spelled out in the ancestral instructions of the founding emperor, did not permit succession by a cousin. The Ministry of Rites, under the leadership of the powerful Yang T'ing-ho (1459–1529), advocated that Shih-tsung recognize Hsiao-tsung (r 1488–1505, the father of Wu-tsung) as his father and assume the role of Wu-tsung's younger brother. Since the succession of a younger brother was permitted in the ancestral instructions, the succession would be ritually correct. And the posthumous adoption of Shih-tsung by Hsiao-tsung (his father's brother) would have fulfilled the requirements of propriety: the adoption of a brother's son was legally and ritually permitted. Indeed, there were precedents from both the Han and the Sung dynasties where adoption had been invoked to remedy a problem in the imperial succession. But were Shih-tsung to permit the adoption, he would be diminishing the honor due his own father, the Prince of Hsing. The ritual status of father of the emperor would adhere to Hsiao-tsung. In the faction-ridden atmosphere of Ming court politics, the emperor's position readily found bureaucratic adherents. Because of the emperor's refusal to follow the recommendation of the Ministry of Rites, the controversy raged at court for three years. Finally, Shih-tsung simultaneously legitimized his succession and honored his father by granting his father the posthumous rank of emperor, with the name of Hsien Huang-ti.

Factionalism, power politics, and self-aggrandizement all played a role in the Ritual Controversy. But it was also a dispute about filial piety and adoption. When the emperor was initially presented with the recommendations that he acknowledge the Hsiao-tsung emperor as father, he reportedly asked: "Can a man change parents so easily?"[3] When Chang Ts'ung (1475–1539) and Kuei O (d 1531), in supporting the emperor's position, cited Mencius as saying "Heaven gives birth to creatures in such a way that they only have one root," they were voicing a sentiment about filiation and about loyalty that found resonance elsewhere. They interpreted this passage as meaning that for Shih-tsung (and by extension, for anyone) to perform rituals to two men as father was an offense against the course of nature.[4] Furthermore, in a memorial quoted in the dynastic history, Fang Hsien-fu (d 1544), a supporter of Chang Ts'ung's position, wrote: "The rituals established by the former kings had their origin in human emotions *(jen ch'ing)*."[5] Thus, Fang implies, a ritual cannot run counter to human nature. A ritual that violates human nature is not a true ritual. Chang Ts'ung went so far as to suggest that the guide to correct behavior *(li)* lay in the human mind.[6]

Yang T'ing-ho, on the other hand, argued that *li* lay not in the minds of men but in the words of texts.[7] A crucial text in this debate is the Kung-yang commentary to the *Ch'un-ch'iu,* a text purportedly from the hand of Confucius himself. Mao Ch'eng (1460–1523), the Minister of Rites, cited a passage from this text saying that he who succeeds (to property or to office) is in effect a son. Mao argued that, according to this principle, the Shih-tsung emperor ought to be adopted by his predecessor's father. Furthermore, he suggested, following the interpretation of the Sung Neo-Confucian Ch'eng I, that one who had been adopted out ought to regard one's own parents as aunt and uncle.[8] To be sure, the Ritual Controversy was politically motivated. But the debate as to how best to resolve the conflict between human emotion and the requirements of classical texts should the two conflict had been a major issue in Neo-Confucianism since the Sung dynasty. Indeed, many of the arguments in the Ming Ritual Controversy were aired during a Sung succession controversy known as P'u-i. That controversy was resolved in a compromise solution when Ying-tsung (r 1064–1067) recognized Jen-tsung as his father. But it was a solution that continued to arouse controversy.[9]

These succession struggles were, in addition to everything else they were, arguments about loyalty, about filiation, and about the unalterable nature of the natural world. These issues found resonance in the wider debate on adoption: How can a man have two fathers? For what reasons may a man abandon the parents who bore him and transfer his loyalties to outsiders? The conflict between ritually correct succession and the duties imposed by blood kinship was acknowledged by private citizens as well as by emperors.

Shih-tsung's adoption, had it taken place, would have been legally and ritually correct. Indeed, a man with no heir was encouraged to adopt a son to continue the line of descent. But these legally and ritually sanctioned adoptions were restricted to persons of the same kin group or same surname. Adoptions that did not meet these criteria were legally prohibited. Yet adoption of persons of a different surname seems to have been relatively common. These adoptions were allowed by neither ritual nor law: custom was their only sanction. But custom is a powerful sanction. And we find an articulated ideology supporting adoption across surname lines, suggesting ways in which the adoptions might be effective.

Adoption, both as a customary arrangement and as a legal institution, mediates an array of tensions within Chinese society. Adoption as a way of getting an heir mediates between the principle of heredity and the principle of merit. Descent is one of the fundamental principles ordering Chinese society. Kinship metaphors assume a primacy in describing ways in which the Chinese state and society are ordered. But merit is another fundamental ordering principle of Chinese society. In the later imperial period that forms the subject of this book, China was governed not by a hereditary aristocracy but rather by a civil service recruited through an examination system. Yao and Shun and Yü, the sage-kings of antiquity, did not transmit the throne to their sons (who were unworthy men), but rather selected men of merit, sages, to succeed them. Sarah Allan has described this as the conflict between the heir and the sage and sees in the myths surrounding China's culture heroes attempts to mediate those tensions.[10] Echoing Allan's argument, Howard Wechsler suggests that rituals of accession to the throne are designed to mediate this tension.[11]

Adoption also raises the question as to how much the natural world is subject to human manipulation. Adoption, as a legal fiction, is a way in which people can tamper with nature, making good a natural deficiency. As Yao Chi sings at the end of act ten of Li Yü's play *Ch'iao t'uan-yüan* (The Amazing Reunion), " 'If a good man has no heir, it can easily be arranged. What need is there for heaven to supervise it?' "[12] A good portion of this book will concern itself with the need for heaven's supervision.

Anthropological Perspectives

The most important work on adoption in China to date has been done by anthropologists dealing with recent and contemporary Chinese societies. They report that adoption across surname lines was practiced relatively freely in the late nineteenth and twentieth centuries in both China and Taiwan. Anthropological accounts abound with references to sons and daughters adopted across surname lines.[13]

The most extensive account of Chinese adoption in a Western language is that of Arthur Wolf and Chieh-shan Huang in *Marriage and Adoption in China, 1845–1945*. Their book clearly demonstrates that many practices that run counter to what we have come to consider appropriate behavior in the "Confucian" family are common in the area they have studied, Hai-shan in northern Taiwan. For example, uxorilocal marriage, minor marriage, as well as adoption across surname lines, were all part of the normal repertoire of behavior. (In uxorilocal marriage the groom joins the family of the bride; he may take her father's surname and his offspring may serve as heirs to her father. "Minor marriage" is what Wolf and Huang term those marriages in which the bride enters the family of the groom as a child and is raised as an adopted daughter, only to marry her "brother" when they reach maturity. She is called a *sim pua* in Taiwanese and a *t'ung-yang-hsi* in Mandarin.) Adoption is an issue that has implications for lineage, but Wolf and Huang find concerns about lineage to be largely irrelevant in Hai-shan. They write that "marriage and adoption are best viewed as the means by which families manipulated their composition to solve immediate problems and to achieve long-term goals."[14] They report that would-be adoptive parents are not pressured to select a member of the surname group as heir. Indeed, informants suggest that adopting a relative could be dangerous, because the child would be more likely to return to the family of its birth. Lineage organization in Hai-shan is relatively weak. Wolf and Huang postulate that in areas where lineage organization is stronger, the capacity of a lineage to enforce rules about adoption (such as the provision that the adopted heir be of the same surname) would be correspondingly greater.[15] Wolf and Huang have found great regional diversity in adoption practices, which can sometimes but not always be correlated to the presence of strong lineages. For example, they find that in Shantung, where lineage organization was weak, adoption practices seemed to have been nonetheless fairly restricted.[16]

James L. Watson, writing about the New Territories of Hong Kong, describes a somewhat different situation. While Taiwan is distinguished by relatively weak lineage organization, lineages are relatively strong in the New Territories of Hong Kong. Watson finds that there are in fact lineage rules that mandate the preference for lineage members as adopted sons. But he finds that the rules are frequently ignored. Despite the fact that choosing an outsider rather than a fellow kinsman required that the adopting father submit to a humiliating initiation ceremony and sponsor an expensive banquet, people frequently chose to adopt strangers. Watson explains this in terms of the potential for segmentary rivalry within the lineage. If an adopted child's father were recognized and resided in the same community, the adoptive father could never be certain of the child's loyalty. Hence, Watson argues, a man without an heir would prefer to adopt an outsider, often a child purchased through an intermediary who would keep secret the identity of the child's birth family. Despite the stigma attached to this form of adoption, people chose it because the child, having made a clear break with the family of his birth, would be a more reliable heir.[17]

Comparing the Ming and early Ch'ing textual evidence with that provided by nineteenth- and twentieth-century ethnographers presents certain obvious methodological difficulties. The nature of the evidence differs: the anthropologist observes and interviews living human beings; the historian reads texts. The level of analysis generally differs: anthropological work typically takes as its focus a single community, while historians (with some exceptions) deal with society at a more general and more abstract level. It is always possible that adoption practices in a sixteenth-century village would demonstrate an attitude as casual as that reported for the twentieth century by Wolf and Watson. Nonetheless, it seems as if Chinese attitudes toward adoption have undergone a sea change in the last hundred years. What was once surrounded by controversy has now become commonplace. The vehemence of the sentiment against adoption that we see in Ming (and earlier) texts seems absent in modern times, at any level of society.

The reasons for this are not obscure. The traditional Chinese family was seen metaphorically, legally, and ritually as the basis of the state. Late nineteenth- and early twentieth-century reformers echoed that linkage when they castigated the traditional family system as a crucial factor in the conservatism of the Chinese state. One key aspect of reform was the rewriting of family law. Legal adoption was no longer restricted to persons among the same surname group.[18] These legal changes, part of the drive to transform the Confucian past and modernize, both reflected social change and propelled it. The delicate dialectic of the interplay between custom and prescriptive law had shifted away from issues such as surname exclusivity. Family and kinship were, to be sure, still issues of interest to the state and to the reformer. But the goals of state policy and the reformers' rhetoric had been transformed. In contrast to other areas of family policy, the legalization of adoption seems to have proceeded in a relatively smooth fashion, doubtless because of a long structure of ideas supporting the practice.

Comparative Perspectives

To someone schooled in the expectations of contemporary Chinese kinship practices, the prohibition of adoption across surname lines seems peculiar. But a cursory glance at the adoption practices of other traditional societies will suggest that what is remarkable is not the existence of the prohibition, but rather its contravention.

Traditional demographic regimes with their high mortality rates abound in children without parents and adults without children. To the modern eye, the two problems seem complementary. The legal fiction of adoption, as practiced in contemporary American society, functions as a solution to these two problems. But modern legal adoption is of remarkably recent origin. The early Christian church condemned adoption,[19] and legal adoption did not exist in British common law. An eighteenth-century French jurist, Prost de Royer, summed up early modern European objections to the institution.

> We believe without a doubt that adoptions are contrary to the laws of nature and those of Christianity, which cause us to regard the rights a father has over his children as sacred rights, and thus inalienable, and the duties

and obligations a father has toward his children as personal obligations which may not be transferred to strangers.[20]

American law of adoption is of relatively recent origin; the first state to pass a comprehensive adoption statute was Massachussetts in 1851.[21] The modern British law of adoption dates from 1923.[22] To be sure, many societies practiced adoption before this time. But the modern conception of adoption as representing the legal dovetailing of the interests of the parents and the welfare of the child is by and large a twentieth-century phenomenon.[23] In most traditional societies, the distinction between adoption and fostering—the one to secure an heir, the other to care for orphaned, abandoned, or otherwise destitute children—was in theory a clear one, though actual practice may have blurred the distinctions somewhat. The private search for an heir and the public need to care for destitute children were discrete concerns. In societies where the purpose of adoption is to get an heir, the kin group might well establish rules to determine who is qualified to join that group. Those rules might be written irrespective of the needs of destitute children. And, as we shall see, it is not only traditional Chinese society that draws a theoretical polarity between the institutions of adoption and fostering.

The definition of adoption itself is somewhat problematic. Anthropologists and legal scholars are not unanimous as to what constitutes a definition. *Black's Law Dictionary* defines adoption as

> the act of one who has taken another's child into his own family, treating him as his son, and giving him all the rights and duties of his own child, in a manner provided by and with consequences provided in statute.[24]

The anthropologist Jack Goody has argued that the term "adoption" should be reserved for those cases where the adopted child is ranked as a child of the adoptive parents and ceases to be seen as a child of his natural parents. Arthur Wolf finds this definition to be too restrictive for the Chinese case, as it would eliminate certain forms of Chinese adoption where the child retains dual family membership. Wolf prefers to follow Ward Goodenough's less restrictive definition.[25] Goodenough sees kinship as a set of rights and obligations, which may be transferred under specific circumstances. Adoption then is seen as being a transaction involving a parent's rights over his child. Goodenough's conceptualization of the transaction perceives adoption as part of a continuum along which are represented varying degrees of alienation from the family of birth and incorporation into the family of adoption.[26] Much of the theoretical work on adoption in preindustrial societies has been done by anthropologists studying Oceanic societies. Goodenough's notion of a continuum has gained considerable currency among these scholars.[27]

Before we delve into the specifics of the Chinese case, let us look at some comparative examples. What are the functions of adoption in some other traditional societies? What sorts of limits are placed on who may be adopted? How do these definitions and restrictions compare with the Chinese case? If surname is not the key criterion for determining eligibility for membership in the kin group, then what is? Let us turn to a brief consideration of adoption in four societies: Rome, India, Oceania, and Japan.

Adoption was widely practiced in Rome, and Roman law concerns itself with the institution. As J. A. Crook has written, "The characteristic remedy for a family in danger of dying out was adoption, and that was the primary purpose of the institution."[28] There were two forms of adoption in Roman law, the first being adrogation, the adoption of an independent adult. A person adrogated was, in principle at least, potentially the head of a family, and he brought with him into his new family not only his property but his descendents. The procedure was intended to be irreversible. This form of adoption, which by its very nature involved an adult as the adoptee, required public approval, because the ancestral cult of the man adrogated would be extinguished. Women were not adrogated.

Roman law also recognized the adoption of individuals. This form of adoption involved the transfer of an individual from the authority of the family of birth to the family of adoption. The transfer was complete and final. The break with the family of birth was a clean one. Roman law of adoption saw a gradual evolution from the early empire, when the basic unit of society was the family, to the time of Justinian (d 565), when the individual had, to a greater extent, become the unit of society. This change was reflected in the degree of alienation of the adopted child from his natal family. During the earlier period, the child's relations with his natal family were severed. Under the code of Justinian, the adopted child usually retained the right to succeed his natal father. In neither form of Roman adoption was kinship the crucial factor in determining eligibility for adoption. Adoption was a legal fiction, and to the Roman mind, the legal construction was adequate to the task. And in neither form of adoption was care for the adopted child the intention of the institution. Other institutions of guardianship protected orphaned or abandoned children.[29]

In Hindu law as well, the chief aim of adoption was the maintenance of the ancestral line. The *Baudchaya,* a commentary to the *Dharmasutra,* cites the following lines from the Hindu adoption ritual:

> I take thee for the fulfillment of my religious duties
> I take thee to continue the line of my ancestors.[30]

There is great diversity in Hindu adoption procedures, and a consequent difference of opinion as to who would constitute an acceptable adopted son. As J. D. Mayne put it, the "fiction of sonship must be as close as possible."[31] According to the *Dattaka Mimasa* and the *Dattaka Chandrika,* the adopted boy should be the nearest male *sapinda,* if possible, a brother's son. If there were no male relative available, then the son of a family following the same spiritual advisor as the adopting family was an acceptable candidate.[32] Thus the spiritual connection stands in the stead of an actual blood tie. The laws of Manu stipulate that a boy must be of the same caste as his adopter, and most writers concur. S. J. Tambiah cites a rule requiring that the adopted son be *putracchayavha,* that is to say one who bears a resemblance to, or is a reflection of, a natural *(aurasa)* son.[33] Thus a commonality of sorts, preferably but not necessarily consanguinity, determined eligibility for adoption. As in Rome, a separate institution of guardianship was instituted for the protection of destitute children.

There are certain general similarities, as we have seen, between Roman and Hindu adoption. The institution in Oceanic societies looks rather different, yet a comparison may be fruitful. Adoption in Oceanic societies is quite common. Although there is a great diversity of adoption practices, the outlines of the institution are clear. There seems to be a preference for adopting the child of a relative or a friend rather than a child of unknown parentage. Reasons given for such a preference vary from the fear that a child of unknown parentage would have inherited character flaws from his parents[34] to the sense that to adopt a child from outside the kin group would be an affront to the kin group as a whole because it would imply that the child resources of the group were incomplete.[35] Adoption did not represent so much the replacement of one set of parents by another as it did the addition of another layer of kinship obligations. Adoption in this context might well be reversible. Orphaned or abandoned children might be cared for by foster parents; again, there would be no necessary connection between the institution of fostering and that of adoption.[36]

Another society where adoption was practiced with relative ease and frequency was Japan. In Japan, adoptions were not restricted to those of the same surname. The concept of the Japanese household *(ie)* as a corporate unit rather than a blood one and the consequences of the extinction of the family in a feudal system doubtless contributed to the prevalence of the institution of adoption. In Japan, promising young men were adopted by families with no sons or by those whose sons possessed only minor talent. Although such adoptions probably did not represent opportunities for large-scale social mobility, to the individuals concerned, adoption by a prominent family was a significant way of bettering one's status.

The prohibition of adoption was one of the key issues in the seventeenth-century Confucian revival in Japan. Reformers wished to eliminate the practice because it violated Confucian norms. But the practice was so ingrained that they met with much resistance. Orthodox Neo-Confucians like Muro Kyūsō argued that adopting an outsider was like grafting a sweet chestnut onto a peach tree. Since the chestnut and the peach did not share a lineage, the graft would not take. But the criticisms of these reformers fell upon an audience largely uninterested in Confucian refinements, whether or not such refinements were couched in horticultural metaphors.[37]

The initial puzzle of Chinese adoption—that one was encouraged, virtually required to adopt an heir if one had none, that such an heir was required to be of the same surname, and that people frequently adopted persons of a different surname—becomes less perplexing if we place adoption in traditional China in a comparative context.

In none of the non-Chinese societies we have examined is surname a key factor in determining who would or would not be an acceptable adopted son. But there are certain general criteria that define the group from whom an adopted son may be taken. The key in all of the cases seems to be the furthering of the interests of the adopting group—whether the crucial factor is kinship, friendship, spiritual affinity, or ability. If we look at the controlling interests of the Chinese kinship group from the standpoint of the official ideology—as portrayed in law codes and clan rules—then surnames are of key importance. In the social world of Ming and early Ch'ing China, order was made possible by distinctions. A world without distinctions was a world without order. Human beings were divided into families, and surname was what distinguished one family from another. Hence one's place in society was determined by membership in a family, signified by surname. Surname was (or ought to be) immutable: granted by the sage kings of antiquity, it fixed one's place in society and the world. Explicit kinship ideology reflects the view that the function of adoption is to perpetuate the family line. The means of perpetuating the line (and the signifier that the line was being perpetuated) was the continuation of the ancestral sacrifices. Hence what qualified one to be adopted was the capacity to participate in the ancestral sacrifices. And direct participation in the sacrifices was restricted to males of the same kin group. Hence adoption was so restricted.

Adoption is a complex topic, and we shall not come to any tidy conclusions. It should come as no surprise to any observer of contemporary debates about family life that Ming and early Ch'ing Chinese did not speak in a single voice on adoption. In the pages that follow, we shall look at a variety of texts, primarily from the Ming and early Ch'ing periods, but drawing on earlier texts that had continuing relevance in the later periods. The use of a variety of genres will enable us to look at the institution of adoption from more than one angle and thereby help us gain a more complete picture of it.

1

Procreation, Adoption, and Heredity

The need for heirs in any traditional society is a compelling one. In traditional China the need was well-nigh absolute. To be without an heir meant that the ancestral sacrifices would be discontinued and that the family property would fall into the hands of strangers. Even in the best of times, biology cannot be counted on to produce an heir. Under conditions of premodern nutrition and hygiene, the problem was intensified.[1] The classical Confucian writer Mencius put the matter bluntly when he said, "There are three things which are unfilial, and to have no posterity is the greatest of these." The injunction is often repeated in Ming and early Ch'ing texts.[2]

The Need for Heirs

That a major function of offspring was to care for one's own (and one's ancestors') needs after death is shown in a story by the seventeenth-century author Li Yü (1611–1680). The only son of Mr. T'u is in a difficult situation, and his father fears that he may die. T'u laments in advance the consequences of the death of his son:

> It seems that my son's life is in jeopardy and that I am destined to become a rambling ghost with no one to make offerings in my afterlife.[3]

Liu Hung-ching, in the twentieth tale of the *P'ai-an ching-ch'i* of Ling Meng-ch'u (1580–1644), laments his childless state while sweeping his ancestors' graves at the Ch'ing-ming festival.

> Have pity on Hung-ching who is very old.
> Among my unfilial acts, the greatest is having no descendants.
> Everyone says that a seventy-year-old man is very rare.

Because of this, my remaining days in this world are few.
Today, my wife and I come to worship at these graves.
But after this, who will approach to honor you?
It is not just that I lament my childlessness,
But always before, there have been sacrifices—
How can I allow them to stop?
Heaven is too high and far away to hear my sighs.
But please, one sympathetic relative, please favor me.
I have emptied my heart and exhausted all my tears.
Ah, ancestors, where are you, righteous and honorable spirits?

Later Liu asks a fortuneteller what crimes he has committed that he has no offspring. Liu attributes his childless state to his misdeeds and ascribes to his ancestors the power to grant him descendants.[4] Thus the failure to produce an heir was a moral problem as well as a religious and social one.

Nor was this merely a private problem. The state recognized the plight of those who died with no descendants and attempted, in establishing *hsiang-li* altars, to offer solace to them. The altars, established one per hundred households by imperial order early in the Hung-wu reign (1368–1399), were for the purpose of worshipping all unconsoled spirits, including persons who had met untimely deaths, as well as those who had no descendants to perform sacrifices to them.[5] We find these altars described in local gazetteers.[6]

Reproduction was not seen as a matter of simple biology. Offspring were granted as a reward and withheld as punishment, not only in response to the acts of the individual concerned, but in response to the acts of his ancestors as well. The transgressions of the ancestors could block the line of descent. The connection between the actions of the ancestors and the production of descendants can be seen in Ming and Ch'ing fiction. In "T'u ou" (The Clay Image), a short story contained in *Liao-chai chih-i* (Strange Stories from the Liao-chai Studio), a collection of tales of the strange and supernatural by P'u Sung-ling (1640–1715), the ghost of Mr. Ma explains to his wife: "It was because of a transgression committed by my father that I died with no son."[7] A similar sense of collective moral responsibility for fertility is shown in Li Yü's short story "Feng-hsien lou" (The Tower of Honoring My Ancestors) in which

Scholar Shu refuses an offer of beef, even though he is starving, because an ancestor had warned that if any member of the family ate beef, the family would henceforth be without male offspring.[8] In the tale "Chüeh-ssu" in the *Lung-t'u kung-an,* a late sixteenth-century collection of detective fiction, Judge Pao is called upon, not to solve a crime, but to explain why Chang (a good man) was childless and Shen (an evil man) had five sons and two daughters. In the complaint addressed to the judge, the questioner states: "The proverb says 'If you accumulate virtue, you'll have many heirs.' The classics say 'If you do good, you'll have posterity.' " Pao, who understands cosmic causality as well as he does human perfidy, explains that their respective fortunes were caused by actions of their ancestors: Chang's misfortune sprang from an evil ancestor and Shen's good luck from a virtuous one.[9]

The belief that children are granted by the will of heaven, even under adverse conditions, is clearly expressed in P'u Sung-ling's story "Nieh Hsiao-ch'ien." The ghost maiden Nieh Hsiao-ch'ien is attempting to convince Ning Ts'ai-chen's mother to allow the two of them to marry. Nieh is a clever ghost and has soon persuaded Ning's mother that she would be an exemplary daughter-in-law, save one thing: she is not human. Ning's mother is worried about the implications this might have for the continuation of the family line, but Nieh persuades her: " 'Sons and daughters are bestowed by heaven. Your son is destined for good fortune, and he is allotted three sons to bring honor to the family. Having a ghost wife will not deprive him of that.' "[10] The marriage takes place and the family line is in fact continued. Similar notions of causality are shown in *Pei-yu chi* (Journey to the North), a novel that Gary Seaman has suggested has its origins as a spirit-writing text. In that text, the Golden Star Venus of the West appears to the daughter of emperor Yang-ti of the Sui dynasty in a dream and tells her, "Your father has no virtue. Therefore his line of descent will be broken with no heir."[11] Sui Yang-ti is the personification of a bad last emperor, a ruler whose perfidy was so great that it destroyed the Sui dynasty. His misdeeds brought about not only the extinction of his dynasty, but also of his line.

It is not just fictional texts that attach extrabiological attributes to fertility. Procreation is a major concern of traditional Chinese medicine, and infertility is attributed to many causes. Medical texts echo the view that infertility might be caused by ritual carelessness on the part of the living. It was essential that the graves of the ancestors (as well as the buildings of the living) be situated according to a complex of principles known collectively as *feng-shui,* often translated into English as "geomancy." The *Fu-jen liang-fang* (Good Prescriptions for Women) lists improper *feng-shui* of the ancestral graves as a primary cause of infertility.[12] Later the same text cites an essay arguing that the ancestors' lack of virtue *(te)* could cause infertility.[13] Another medical text reiterates a moralistic view of procreation. The *Chi-ssu chen-pao* suggests:

> If you ask how this [infertility] can be remedied, I say: "This is not difficult. Only repent your actions in life, eliminate all transgressions and evil deeds . . . If one has done good deeds long enough, then automatically he receives luck and rewards from heaven. Merit does not mean to repair or build Buddhist temples or to read canonical books or to recite [the name of the] Buddha."[14]

Thus merit does not accumulate from the mechanical performance of specific deeds; it has a component of abstract morality.

As infertility might be caused by moral defects, so might children be granted as a reward for virtuous conduct. In a tale by the early Ming author Ch'ü Yu (1341?–1427), the meritorious act is a woman's sacrifice of her flesh (a woman cuts flesh from her thigh to feed her mother-in-law). Although this form of filial self-mutilation was described in the *Hsiao ching* (Classic of Filial Piety), it received no real encouragement in later imperial times. But one does continue to see it mentioned in both fictional and biographical accounts. The divine officials who observed this act of filial piety in Ch'ü's story decreed that as a reward the woman should give birth to two boys.[15] Her symbolic incorporation into the patriline on one level—her flesh sustains her mother-in-law—is rewarded by her incorporation on another level—her flesh produces male heirs.

But in other accounts, the virtuous behavior is described in more abstract ways. Ch'en Ch'eng, in the novel *Hsi-yu chi* (Journey to the West), explains why he calls his daughter "Load of Gold":

> "Since I was childless for many years, I persisted in repairing bridges and roads, in erecting temples and stupas, and in the feasting of monks. I kept a

record of all that I spent—a few ounces here and a few ounces there—and by the time my daughter was born, I had spent exactly thirty pounds of gold. Thirty pounds make one load, and that is how she got her name."[16]

In Feng Meng-lung's (1574–1646) "The Pearl Sewn Shirt," the childless Magistrate Wu performs an act of compassion in freeing his wife San-chiao to be reunited with her former husband, Chiang Hsing-ko. Wu later takes a concubine, who bears him three sons. His peers perceived the birth of his sons to be directly related to his act of compassion: "All agreed that this was a reward for his good deeds."[17]

The mechanism whereby good deeds are rewarded is described in greater detail in another story by Feng Meng-lung. In "The Tattered Felt Hat," Sung Tun and his wife are childless. Sung laments to his wife:

"You know the proverb: 'Bring up sons for your old age and store up grain against famine.' You and I are over forty, yet we have no children. Time flies like an arrow and in the wink of an eye our hair will be white. Who can we rely on to see to our funerals?" Saying this, he shed tears.

His wife assures him that because his ancestors were good men, heaven will not let his line die out. She further suggests that if children are born at an inopportune time, they will cause nothing but grief. Sung Tun soon gets a chance to increase the store of merit left to him by his ancestors by performing a good deed himself. A destitute old monk dies, and Sung provides him with a decent burial. The monk appears to Sung in a dream and says:

"You were fated *(ming)* to have no son, and your span of life was destined to end today. But because you showed such charity, heaven has decreed that you will live another six or seven years, and because we are linked by fate *(yin-yüan)* I shall become a son in your house to repay you for your virtue *(te)* in giving me a coffin."

Sung's wife does subsequently give birth to a son.[18] In a tale illustrating a similar point, this time from P'u Sung-ling's "Lei ts'ao" (The Thunder God), an old friend of the childless Yo Yun-nao appears to him in a dream and says:

"I am the Shao-wei star. Your friendship is still cherished by me, and now you have brought me back from the sky. Truly our destinies are knitted together *(yu yüan)* and I will repay your virtue *(te)* by becoming your son."[19]

In both of these tales, the kindness *(te,* "virtue") of the behavior of one man creates a bond *(yüan)* between the two men. In order to reciprocate the kindness and validate the bond, the recipient of the kindness becomes his benefactor's son. Virtue creates destiny: *yüan* is a function of *te.*

The connection between virtue and offspring is one we have seen expressed in a wide variety of texts in the late Ming and early Ch'ing: fiction, medical texts, and a novel with antecedents as a spirit-writing text. The connection between virtue and destiny and the notion that fate can be manipulated are, as Sakai Tadao and Cynthia Brokaw have shown, themes that emerge in the sixteenth century.[20] Yüan Huang, a crucial figure in the popularization of morality books in the late Ming, made the connection between virtue and offspring explicit in his *Hsün-tzu yen* (Words to Instruct My Sons). A fortuneteller had predicted that Yüan Huang would not pass the civil service exams and that he would have no sons. Yüan initially accepted the prediction. But the monk Yün-ku persuaded Yüan that he was in charge of his own fate. Yüan records Yün-ku's argument.

"As for producing offspring, if you have a hundred generations of virtue *(te),* you will certainly have a hundred generations of offspring to preserve it. If you have ten generations of virtue, you will have ten generations of offspring to protect it. If you have two or three generations of virtue, you will have two or three generations of offspring to protect it. As for those who are cut off with no heirs, their virtue has been exhausted."[21]

Yüan Huang, in an anecdote recounted in his *Li-ming p'ien,* demonstrates the connection between virtue and offspring in a way that recalls the story of Sung Tun in the story by Feng Meng-lung. A man named T'u K'ang-hsi is rewarded for devising a plan for aiding persons unjustly accused of crimes. A deity visits him and says:

"You were fated to have no sons, but now because your proposal for the reduction of punishments was exactly in accord with the mind of heaven,

Shang-ti will grant you three sons, all of whom are destined to wear purple robes and gold belts [as officials]."[22]

In one of the more dramatic formulations of the problem, infertility is described as castration by heaven. The late Yuan writer T'ao Tsung-i makes the point: "There are some men who, although married, never obtain offspring; these are called 'natural eunuchs' (t'ien-yen)."[23]

Childlessness is a consequence of exhausted virtue; it is castration by heaven. It is a sign of heavenly disfavor and a punishment for moral and ritual transgressions. It is a state whose moral consequences can only partly be remedied by the tidy legal fictions of adoption.

Popular religion concerned itself with remedies for childlessness.[24] Rituals and amulets were used in the attempt to produce an heir. In a story by Feng Meng-lung we have already looked at, the procedures taken by Sung Tun and Liu Shun-chuan and their wives to obtain an heir are described.

> Now Sung Tun and his wife, being childless, had been burning incense and offering prayers for a son in many temples, and had made wrappers and bags of yellow cloth to carry the paper cash used in the sacrifice. After each such pilgrimage, they would hang these very reverently at the Buddhist shrine at home. Liu Sun-chuan was forty-six, five years older than his friend, but he had no son either. Recently he heard that a salt merchant from Hui-chou had built a temple to Ch'en-chou Niang-niang [a goddess of childbirth] outside the west gate to Soochow in order to pray for offspring, where the incense smoke was always thick and the prayers never stopped.[25]

Ch'en-chou Niang-niang was not the only deity who might intervene on one's behalf. By the Ming, Kuan-yin was firmly established in the popular mind as the most important of the fertility goddesses. The fertility function of Avalokitesvara, the Indian Buddhist deity of whom Kuan-yin is the Chinese manifestation, is established in the Lotus Sutra:

> If a woman wishes to have a son and worships and pays homage to the Bodhisattva Kuan-yin, she will have a virtuous and wise son. If she wishes to have a daughter, again, she will give birth to an upright and beautiful daughter.[26]

This belief is reiterated in a popular Buddhist tract from the mid-fifteenth century, the "Fo-ting-hsin ta t'o-lo-ni ching."[27] Ming representations of the deity were often of a mother and child or a mother and many children.[28]

Biographical and fictional evidence both confirm the importance of belief in Kuan-yin. The biography of the monk Chih-hsü tells us that his parents had been married for ten years and were childless. After praying to Kuan-yin for a son, his mother gave birth to Chih-hsü.[29] In the novel *Hsi-yu chi,* the lady Yin, having given birth to the future pilgrim Hsüan-tsang, is visited by a spirit. The spirit identifies herself as the spirit star of the south pole and tells the lady Yin that she sent her son by the express command of Kuan-yin.[30]

Just as the cult of Kuan-yin reflects the importance of sons in Chinese society, so do other aspects of mythology reflect a recognition of the fragility of the biological world. Hsieh Chao-che and Hu Ying-lin, both late Ming authors with eclectic tastes and wide-ranging interests, report popular belief in a malevolent deity called the Celestial Hound *(t'ien kou),* believed to cause both sterility and diseases of young children. Hsieh reports that common people said that the Celestial Hound ate small children at night.[31] But the popular pantheon provided the Celestial Hound with a potent enemy: Chang Hsien, the immortal Chang. Chang Hsien immobilized the Celestial Hound by shooting him with a peachwood arrow.[32] Peaches are a symbolically laden fruit, connoting both fertility and immortality. The wood of the peach had apotropaic powers and was used in exorcistic rituals. Indeed, Chang Hsien is here a kind of exorcist. Hu Ying-lin, whose interest in folklore we noted above, also reported belief in Chang Hsien and speculated that the origins of the belief in him lay in the sacrifices to the Kao-mei, an ancient spirit among whose functions was matchmaking. Arrows, the chief identifying feature of Chang Hsien, were offered in a sacrifice to Kao-mei if sons were born.[33] Thus the connection between sons and arrows in the legend of the Kao-mei finds resonance in the Chang Hsien stories: the arrows were used not as sacrificial offerings of thanks but in their more conventional mode as weapons.

The stance of Hu Ying-lin and Hsieh Chao-che toward the beliefs they report is neither skeptical nor credulous. They are in some senses ethnographers reporting on the vast variety of popular beliefs and customs in late Ming China. But we do find skepticism about the efficacy of popular religion in many places, including fiction. Skepticism and satire are rampant in stories dealing with religious beliefs, and it is worth pausing for a moment to consider some of the implications of these viewpoints. Ling Meng-ch'u, in his story "The Revenge of the Baccalaureate Chia," satirizes popular piety. Madame Wu confesses to a nun that she has burned incense daily in front of an image of Kuan-yin, to no avail. The nun responds:

> "You are young and do not know the ways of praying for a child. When seeking children, one must make the request to the White Robed Kuan-yin, from whom came the *White Robe Scriptures*. It is not the ordinary *Kuan-yin*, nor is it the *P'u-men-p'in Kuan-yin Scriptures*. The *White Robe Scriptures* are most efficacious, and the prayers I use at our convent are all recorded at the rear of the book. What a pity I did not bring it for you to see. . . . Whenever I recite these scriptures, there is always a son born. Truly, for every thousand requests there are a thousand replies."

The aim of the nun's rather pedantic solicitude is to lure the lovely young Madame Wu into the convent, so that a priest there can seduce her.[34]

Belief in Chang Hsien is satirized in "Wang Ta-yin huo-fen Pao-lien ssu" (Wang Ta-yin Burns Incense at the Precious Lotus Temple) in Feng Meng-lung's *Hsing-shih heng-yen*. In that story, women went to a temple to pray to Chang Hsien for sons. Their prayers were remarkably effective. Some women reported that they dreamed that the Buddha brought them a child, some said they dreamed they slept with a bodhisattva, and still others would say nothing at all. A magistrate named Wang became suspicious and investigated the strange efficacy of the prayers. He discovered that there was no magic to the enhanced fertility of the supplicants. The priests at the temple to Chang Hsien were seducing them.[35] Late Ming fiction, especially scatalogical fiction, is characterized by its anticlericalism, and licentious monks and seductive nuns are stock figures. But these particular stories provide an added dimension to conventional anticlericalism. Concern for continuing the patriline leads pious women to violate the sanctity of the patriline. And much of the humor is provided by the rather commonsensical suggestion that sex with a mortal is more effective than supplications to a deity at getting a woman pregnant. But the supplications continued.

In addition to entreaties to ancestors and supplications to the gods, fertility potions were used by women who feared that they were barren. In the sixteenth-century novel *Chin p'ing mei,* Wu Yüeh-niang, the principal wife of Hsi-men Ch'ing, is given a prescription to enhance her fertility. The placenta of a newborn child is to be washed in wine, dried, and burned to ashes. The ashes are to be dissolved in liquid and ingested on the forty-ninth day of the sexagenary cycle. The workings of the magic are not obscure; the placenta is to draw forth the creation of new life. When the appointed time comes, Wu Yüeh-niang takes the added precaution of burning incense in front of a portrait of Kuan-yin before taking the potion.[36] Later in the novel, P'an Chin-lien, a secondary wife who is in many respects Wu Yüeh-niang's rival, takes the same potion.[37] Nor are these potions mere fictional creations: prescriptions for fertility drugs are contained in numerous Ming and Ch'ing medical texts.[38]

Supplications to the gods and fertility potions are not infallible remedies for sterility. A man in search of an heir might take a concubine. Concubinage was a legally recognized institution, and the children of a concubine were fully legitimate, though in fact they might be socially disadvantaged. There were, however, some restrictions placed on concubinage. The codes concerning concubinage were interested primarily with maintaining clear status distinctions between a concubine and a wife. One could not make a wife a concubine, nor a concubine a wife. The Ming code stipulated that a man who had reached the age of forty and had no sons by his wife could take a concubine. Commentary suggests that this stipulation prevented a man of any age who had fathered sons or a childless man younger than forty from taking a concubine. The penalty for violating this was forty blows with the light bamboo. While other infractions of domestic regularity required that the situation be rectified (the marriage annulled, the child returned to the family of his birth, etc.), there is no indication that a man was required to dispose of an improperly acquired concubine.[39] It would seem that the law regarding concubinage was soundly ignored, so much so that it is absent from the Ch'ing code.[40]

Even family instructions, such as those of the Cheng communal family, that discouraged concubines on the grounds that they caused "chaos in the distinctions between superior and inferior," urged men who were childless at the age of forty to take a concubine.[41] Family instructions *(chia-hsün)* are a genre that go back at least to the time of Yen Chih-t'ui's *Yen-shih chia-hsün,* which we have already had occasion to cite. The genre flourished during the Ming and Ch'ing periods. Family instructions provide an idealized version of the traditional Chinese family. They are perhaps better guides to aspirations and anxieties than they are to actual behavior, but aspirations and anxieties are a part of the story too.

Fictional evidence provides cases of women not merely permitting their husbands to take concubines, but actually urging them to do so. In the story "Kuei Yüan-wai t'u-ch'iung ch'an-hui" (Kuei Yüan-wai, at Wit's End, Repents), from Feng Meng-lung's *Ching-shih t'ung-yen,* the wife of Shih Chi, Yen-shih, suggests that he take a concubine. Despite the fact that he is over forty and has no children, he refuses.[42] Her lack of jealousy is matched by his fidelity. Other stories show exemplary lack of conjugal jealousy.[43]

But we should not be misled by these tales of communal conjugal bliss. A wife's jealousy might well thwart a man's plans for taking a concubine. The Sung dynasty author Yüan Ts'ai (1140–1190), who rarely minced words on any subject, wrote that "most women are jealous, so men with wives seldom keep concubines."[44] Concubinage seems to have been more common in the Ming and Ch'ing than it was in the Sung; nonetheless, jealousy remained a problem. Indeed, Hsieh Chao-che suggested that jealousy was more of a problem in the Ming than it had been in the Sung because Sung Neo-Confucians had been more successful at family management.[45] The early Ch'ing author P'u Sung-ling, in his story "Heng-niang," writes of Madame Chu, a once happy wife troubled by her husband's obsession with a concubine. She notices that although her neighbor has a concubine, he is utterly devoted to his wife, Heng-niang. Madame Chu asks Heng-niang's advice on how to win back her husband's attentions. The advice is effective, and Chu's husband is once again as attentive as a young groom. But the irony is exquisite: P'u seems to be telling us that such knowledge is not vouchsafed ordinary women. Heng-niang is, we are told at the end of the story, a fox-fairy, a demon noted for its seductive appearance and its skill at bewitching men. It is no wonder that a mortal concubine could not compete.[46]

Female jealousy is dealt with in another way in P'u Sung-ling's "Tuan-shih." Tuan Jui-huan, a man from a wealthy family, was childless. Because his wife, a woman named Lien, was very jealous, he dared not take a concubine. He slept with a serving maid, whom his jealous wife promptly sold. Years later, he died with no clear heir, and endless wrangling over the estate resulted. The problem was solved only when a young man appeared, the son of the brief union between Tuan and the serving maid. As Lien lay on her deathbed, she summoned her junior female relatives and told them: "Pay close attention to what I am going to say. If when you are thirty, you have no children, pawn your jewelry and buy a concubine for your husband. To have no son is hard indeed." The story suggests that a wife must overcome her feelings of jealousy because childlessness is not in her own best interests. It is not only the male members of the patriline who need an heir. P'u Sung-ling, the author of tales of the fantastic, may seem an unlikely moralist, but again and again, we see him reasserting the need for human order according to conventional rules.[47]

To be sure, fear of female jealousy was not the only factor preventing a man from taking a concubine. Supporting a second woman could be expensive. Unless a man were of high social status, he might have difficulty finding a woman willing to marry him as a concubine. Furthermore, the practice of female infanticide meant that there was a net scarcity of women. A man with limited resources might find it difficult to marry one woman, let alone take a concubine. And if a man were sterile, acquiring a concubine would do nothing to remedy the problem of his infertility. In those cases, adoption provided the only solution to the problem of childlessness.

Adoption Defined

What do we mean by adoption? The English term covers several different (though overlapping) Chinese institutions, and the Chinese terms include some arrangements we would not normally call adoption. The first, and most common, form of adoption in China was the perfectly ordinary and legal practice of establishing a related child, preferably but not necessarily a brother's son, as an heir. A child adopted in this manner would be the legal and ritual equivalent of a natural child. There are several Chinese terms used to describe a child adopted as heir: *ssu-tzu, kuo-fang-tzu,* and *kuo-chi-tzu.* A different set of terms was, in theory, reserved for the adoption of a child of a different surname. Such adoptions were more problematic than were adoptions within the surname group. A child so adopted would not necessarily become a full family member. While he might inherit, he was in theory forbidden to change his surname to that of the adopting family. There are several terms used to describe a child adopted in this manner: *yang-tzu, i-tzu,* and *ming-ling-tzu* being the most common. Commentary to the Ming code defines a *yang-tzu* as an *i-tzu* and specifies that his surname differs from the adopting family's.[48] A child adopted by his mother's second husband is called a *lien-tzu.* It is important to note that the theoretically clear distinction among the various forms of adoption does not seem to have been maintained. The various terms were rather loosely applied, and the distinctions among the various forms of adoption were blurred.[49] *Ming-ling* is used in the *P'ai-an ching-ch'i* for a child who quite clearly inherits his father's property. In the same story, the adopting father is variously called an *i-fu* and a *yang-fu.*[50] The term *ssu-tzu* (or simply *ssu*), literally meaning "heir" and theoretically restricted to an adoptee of the same surname, may be used for a child who bears no biological relation to his father.[51] The term *ming-ling-tzu* is used for children of both sexes, related and unrelated, those adopted as children and those adopted as adults. I would suggest that the confusion indicates a general unawareness of the legal distinctions and that it furthermore indicates that such distinctions were marginally relevant to social practice.

The terms *yang-tzu* and *i-tzu* were also applied to arrangements quite different from what we normally think of as adoption. Military men rewarded their subordinates and attempted to insure their loyalty by adopting them.[52] Emperors, prompted no doubt by the same motivations, bestowed the imperial surname on select numbers of their subjects. In a particularly extravagant gesture, the emperor Wu-tsung, who reigned from 1505 to 1521 and whose death precipitated the crisis with which this book opened, on one day in 1511 made 127 men his adopted sons.[53] Private citizens as well made recourse to adoption to solve problems other than the lack of an heir. A sickly child might be given in a symbolic adoption to another family or to a religious institution, with the expectation that the resulting alteration of kinship configuration would better its health.[54] Adoptions might be used to evade the law. During the Ming, commoners were not allowed to own serfs. Persons who were actually serfs might be registered as *yang-tzu* or *i-tzu* to conceal their true, illegal identity.[55] Thus we can see that the institution of adoption had a wide range of meanings—from nearly complete incorporation into the family to little more than a symbolic recognition of merit, a gesture of solidarity, or a ruse to confound the spirits or the state.

It is worth dwelling for a moment on these specific terms for adoption, because they illuminate the nature of the institution. The key element of the English word, derived from the Latin, is "option," or choice.[56] The Chinese words *hou* and *ssu-tzu* are straightforward enough: they mean "successor" and "heir," respectively. *Kuo-fang-tzu* and *kuo-chi-tzu* carry the idea of crossing over *(kuo)* from one branch of the family *(fang)* to another, to continue *(chi)* the succession. Usage extended the meaning to include the adoption of non-kin. *Yang-tzu* and *i-tzu,* frequently used interchangeably, have rather different connotations. *Yang* means to nourish, to educate, to raise. Thus a *yang-tzu* is a child one has raised. *I* means righteousness and appropriateness, with a strong sense of duty. It implies an act of will and a sense of covenant. A relationship infused with *i* will have a degree of reciprocity to it. The Sung dynasty author Hung Mai, in his *Jung-chai sui-pi* (Random Jottings from the Jung-chai Studio), elucidates a further meaning of the word that is relevant here. He explains that "something which enters from the outside and is not original *(fei cheng)* is called *i*" and goes on to list a series of fictive kinship terms to illustrate the meaning: adoptive father, child, elder brother, and younger brother.[57] The Ming author Hsieh Chao-che, in a passage from his *Wen-hai p'i-sha* (Blowing Sands by the Sea of Literature, preface dated 1609) quoted in the Ch'ing compendium *T'ung-su pien* (A Compilation of Customs) writes:

> Hsiang Yü revered the Prince of Huai as an *i* emperor, yet he was a false *(chia)* emperor. In the T'ang people called hairpieces *i* hair. When one strums the *cheng* one calls the pick "*i* fingernails." These are all things which originated outside and have been assimilated. Thus today people call stepfathers *(chia-fu) i* fathers and stepchildren *i* sons and daughters.[58]

I in this sense can be interpreted as meaning "that which has been appropriated." An *i-tzu* is then a child one has made one's own. Another term for adopted child, *ming-ling-tzu* ("mulberry insect children"), is based on a phrase from the *Shih ching* (Book of Songs) and will be discussed in detail below. In brief, the solitary wasp is believed to steal the young of the mulberry insect and transform them into young wasps. Thus a person who becomes the child of someone other than his biological parents is known as a *ming-ling-tzu*. In contrast with the notion of choice in the English term, there are present in the Chinese terms notions of continuing *(hou, ssu-tzu, kuo-chi-tzu)* and of nurturing *(yang-tzu)* and appropriating, perhaps out of a sense of duty, what was not initially yours *(i-tzu)*, as well as the notion of transformation explicitly contained in the term *ming-ling-tzu*.

Let us turn for a moment to the distinction between adoption and fostering, for a clear understanding of the issue is central to the argument of this book. In the Chinese terms for adoption, we see an attempt to maintain the distinction between adoption and fostering we saw earlier for other societies. The purpose of fostering is to care for an orphaned or abandoned child; the purpose of adoption is to get an heir. As we saw earlier, the two institutions might remain distinct. The functions are, in the abstract, unrelated. The mere fact that in each case a child joins a household by some arrangement other than birth should not blind us to very real differences. But it seems to me that, in the Chinese case, the distinctions are less absolute than they might seem at first glance. Family life is, after all, rarely experienced as an abstraction. And furthermore, the centrality of the kinship tie means that other relationships are analogized to kinship. Three of the "five relationships" (ruler-minister, father-son, husband-wife, elder brother–younger brother, and friend-friend), which most Confucian social theorists would regard as the foundation upon which all social order is constructed, are intimately connected with kinship.[59] Other important relations are described by analogy to these five relationships. In politics, a minister's duty to his ruler is explicitly likened to a son's duty to his father, and the magistrate is informally called a "father and mother official." In cosmology, the most famous example can be seen in one of the founding documents of Sung Neo-Confucianism, the "Hsi ming" (Western Inscription) of Chang Tsai (1020–1077). The "Hsi ming" opens: "Heaven is my father and earth is my mother and even such a small creature as I finds an intimate place in their midst."[60] This concept finds echoes in the common saying "Within the four seas all men are brothers." Friends addressed one another using kinship terms, and so forth. Metaphorical extensions perhaps made absolutes more limber. At some levels, kinship may have been conceptualized as an absolute category, but in other respects it was a category to which other categories might be assimilated.

But of course adopting a child is not the same as calling a friend a brother. Adoption is an act with social, legal, and ritual consequences. The available sources seem to indicate that the varieties of adoption in traditional China are not separate, analytically distinct institutions. Goodenough's suggestion that kinship be described as a continuum is useful here. Rather than simply deciding on the basis of imprecise terminology that *yang-tzu, i-tzu,* and *ming-ling-tzu* refer to fostering rather than to "real" adoption, it seems to me that one ought to look at transformations of relations implied by these terms. The ritual and legal obligations of a son in traditional China included the right to property and the duty to mourn the death of the parents and to participate in sacrifices to the spirits of the ancestors. A son would bear his father's surname and would be listed in the family genealogy, if there were such a document. Adoption might change the configuration of rights and obligations around any one (or all) of these issues. Incorporation into the family exists along a continuum; it is conditioned and sanctioned by custom and sentiment as much as it is by law and ritual.

Magic Fungus and Fine Wine: Ideas about Heredity

Kinship is rooted in biology, or more properly, kinship is rooted in ideas about biology. Although the precise nature of the relationship between kinship and biology is of no small controversy among anthropologists, it seems clear that biology distinguishes kinship from all other social relations.[61] In this section I will examine Ming and early Ch'ing ideas about conception and heredity, to see what they can tell us about attitudes toward adoption, and indeed about the nature of kinship itself.

In many societies, including our own, notions of heredity and blood are a factor in inhibiting the willingness of people to adopt outsiders. Fears that a child might have inherited undesirable characteristics from its parents and a concern that a child might pollute the purity of the blood line have both served as potent arguments against adoption in some societies.[62] But did they in China? In Li Yü's *Ch'iao t'uan-yüan* (The Wondrous Reunion), a play that we shall discuss at some length in chapter 4, we see Yao Tung-shan persuading his wife that the fact that a young man is adopted should not diminish his value as a prospective husband for their daughter. He uses a proverb to persuade her: "Magic fungus is without roots, and fine wine is without a source."[63]

It would be anachronistic to look for traces of the modern science of genetics in Ming and early Ch'ing China. Modern Western ideas about genetics and heredity are of remarkably recent origin. In seventeenth-century Europe, knowledge of genetics was so primitive that it was still possible for a writer to assert that an ostrich was a cross between a sparrow and a camel.[64] Mendel's paper on the transmission of characteristics in peas, first published in 1866, was virtually ignored by the scientific community until 1900.[65]

But it is pertinent to ask questions about Ming and early Ch'ing ideas regarding the determinants of human character and personality and the nature of the relationship of a child to his progenitors. Let us first look at some references to heredity in fiction and belles lettres and then move to a consideration of these same ideas as presented in medical texts.

Heredity in Fiction

Early Western thinkers about the roles played by the two parents in determining the characteristics of the child might be divided into two groups: the "ovists" and the "spermists." The ovists held that the characteristics of the unborn child were all contained in the egg and that the sperm merely activated the egg. The spermists held that the sperm was complete and was merely nourished by the egg. Kolreuter first demonstrated in the late eighteenth century that both parents contribute equally to the characteristics of their offspring.[66]

In contrast to the Western division between spermists and ovists, which polarized the contributions of either parent, the Chinese saw conception as the result of the intermingling of *yin* and *yang*. *Yin* and *yang* are of course crucial concepts in Chinese cosmological thinking. *Yin* is the female element, passive and dark, corresponding to the earth and the moon. *Yang* is the male element, active and bright, corresponding to the sky and the sun. Each element contains the seeds of the other; there is constant interplay between them. All creation was seen as the result of interaction between *yin* and *yang* forces. In the *Fu-jen liang-fang* (Good Prescriptions for Women), the term used for the undifferentiated embryo is *hun-tun,* the same term used to describe the cosmos in its primal, undifferentiated state.[67] Medical texts describe conception as a microcosm of the interaction of these cosmic forces, one act of creation parallel to and reflecting all other acts of creation. As N. J. Girardot phrases it, embryology recapitulates cosmology.[68] Male semen and female blood mingle to form a new life.

Although the characteristic element of *yin* and *yang* forces is not their polarity but their interaction, the male force was often seen as dominant. Thus we see Wei Hsi (1624–1680) asserting the transmission of characteristics through the male line.

> Brothers born to the same father of different mothers are, to use a simile, like vegetables of the same seed, planted some in an eastern field, some in a western one. Once they have budded, no one can say they are not the same vegetables because they are growing in separate fields. Brothers born to different fathers of the same mother are like seed of two totally different vegetables planted together in the same field. Once they have budded, no one will call them the same name simply because they are growing in the same field.[69]

Wei Hsi thus denied that the mother had a determining role in the makeup of the child. The mother contributed the vessel in which the child grew and the blood that nourished it, but the essence of the child was provided by its father.[70] This belief is echoed in an anonymous song appended to *Wang Chung-shu ch'üan-hsiao ko* (The Complete Filial Songs of Wang Chung-shu) included in Ch'en Hung-mou's *Wu-chung i-kuei,* which tells us "Your father's semen and your mother's blood formed your body."[71] *Ching,* which seems unambiguously to mean semen in this context, also means (and perhaps always implies) vital essence. Thus the contribution of the father is of vital essence; that of the mother is merely blood.

But conflicting views of the nature of heredity can also be found. The *Sheng yü* (Sacred Edict) of the K'ang-hsi emperor, first promulgated in 1670, inadvertently provides one such example. The *Sheng yü,* a list of sixteen Confucian maxims, was promulgated with the goal of rectifying the behavior of the common people. It was the subject of numerous illustrated editions in the vernacular language and was also the subject of popular lectures. The emperor was concerned that the populace was laboring under misconceptions about the nature of heredity.

> Even if brothers are not born of one mother, yet they are the blood and bones of one father. It doesn't do to say, "They are not of the same mother" and accordingly regard them of a different stock.[72]

The concern of the *Sacred Edict* with arguing that sons of the same father share his blood and bones irrespective of their mothers is a reassertion of the Confucian notion that kinship follows the male line. The edict implies quite clearly that ordinary folk are in fact regarding sons of a different mother as being of different stock.

The connection between notions of heredity and the patriline is made clear in another way in a folk song collected by the seventeenth-century author Feng Meng-lung in his *Shan-ko* (Mountain Songs). Feng Meng-lung shared with his earlier contemporaries Hu Ying-lin and Hsieh Chao-che an almost ethnographic interest in folklore. The songs in this collection present a picture of the family and sexuality sharply at variance with our stereotyped notions of the demands of Confucian morality. In one of the songs, a woman says to her illegitimate child, "You half resemble me, half my lover."[73] Thus patrilineal principles of heredity apply only to recognized members of the patriline.

Lest we conclude too hastily that we are here in the presence of an ideological division between the Confucian state on the one hand and the common people on the other, let us turn for a moment to the *Wu-li t'ung-k'ao* (A Comprehensive Examination of the Five Rituals), a compendium in 262 *chüan* completed in 1761 by Ch'in Hui-t'ien. The *Wu-li t'ung-k'ao* is an example of early Ch'ing evidential scholarship at its best. Although it was not officially sponsored, upon its completion it was copied into the imperial manuscript library, thus granting it a kind of official status. Thus the *Wu-li t'ung-k'ao* can be seen as representing Confucian scholarship and literati orthodoxy. And it argues that a man's sister's sons share his blood and his material force, his *ch'i*.[74] Thus *ch'i*, in Ch'in Hui-t'ien's formulation at least, must be transmitted through the female, as well as the male, line.

Casual statements about the resemblance between parent and child are rare in Ming and early Ch'ing literature, though they do occur. In Li Yü's "Tuo-chin lou," an unattractive and dim-witted couple produce two lovely and intelligent daughters. Li tells us that people often thought the girls were adopted.[75] The supernatural ancestry of the offspring of fox fairies[76] and ghosts[77] is easily discerned from the appearance of the child. In P'u Sung-ling's "Yeh-ch'a kuo" (The Country of the Cannibals), a young man of Chinese descent is clearly distinguished from the cannibals.[78] But these are rather extreme examples.

In "T'u ou" (The Clay Image), when there is some question as to a child's paternity, P'u Sung-ling reassures his readers that the child was "in every feature the counterpart" of his father.[79] In the novel *Hsi-yu chi*, when the young Hsüan-tsang finds his mother, the lady Yin, she is struck by his resemblance "in speech and in manner" to her late husband. She subsequently learns that Hsüan-tsang is her son.[80] When Hsüan-tsang locates his blind grandmother, the old woman immediately notices that his voice is like that of her son.[81] In all of these cases, the strong resemblance between father and son serves to clarify for the reader the murky question of the child's paternity.

A proverb cited in the *Lieh nü chuan,* compilation attributed to Liu Hsiang (79–6 B.C.), is instructive on this point: "I have heard the saying that when one does not understand the child, he may look at the father; when one does not understand the ruler, he may look at the men whom he employs."[82] As the analogy to the ruler-minister relationship makes clear, the resemblance implied in the proverb does not necessarily have its roots in the biological relationship between father and son. It is shaped by training, education, social convention, and hierarchy.

This point is made clear in the Sung author Yüan Ts'ai's discussion of the delicate problem of offspring born to maidservants. In his *Yüan-shih*

shih-fan (Precepts for Social Life), he cautions against sexual dalliance with maidservants (indeed, against laxity that would permit the servants to allege sexual activity) because of the awkwardness that might result from the offspring of such unions, "stupid and vulgar offspring who end up ruining the family."[83] But, as Patricia Ebrey has pointed out, a servant's child is inferior as much because of his education as because of his blood.[84] Thus, Yüan cautions:

> Adopt, raise, and educate from the earliest possible time any child born to women set up in separate households or born after the death of the father. . . . If the boy is left with his mother and by imitating those around him becomes a lowly, uneducated sort of person and then later wants to join your family, the situation will be very troublesome. Daughters can be as much trouble.[85]

Blood then is not the crucial determinant of character. Yao and Shun, the sage-kings of antiquity, chose to pass the throne to men other than their sons because merit and virtue did not necessarily follow blood lines.[86] The idea that heredity should not be a determining factor in judging a man's worth is illustrated in a well-known passage from the *Analects* in which Confucius discusses Chung-kung, the worthy son of an evil man: "The master, speaking of Chung-kung, said, 'If the calf of a brindled cow be red and horned, although man may not wish to use it, would the spirits of the mountains and rivers put it aside?' " The point is that a cow used in the sacrifices had to be red and horned and that the spirits would not reject an appropriate cow because of his brindled ancestry.[87]

European epic abounds in tales in which long-lost relatives feel an affinity for one another before they realize they are related.[88] In *Tristan and Isolde*, Tristan and King Mark are drawn to one another immediately upon Tristan's arrival at Mark's court. Only later do they learn that Tristan is Mark's nephew.[89] The twins Valentine and Orson, in the tale bearing their name, are separated at birth from one another and from their mother, the sister of Pepin. Valentine is raised at Pepin's court; Orson is suckled by a she-bear. The adult Valentine is sent to conquer a wild man who is menacing the countryside. The wild man is of course

Orson; Valentine subdues him by guile and the "force of nature." When the two men discover they have identical birthmarks—the mark of the cross between their shoulder blades—they conclude that they must be brothers.[90] For Tristan and Mark, Valentine and Orson, blood relationship creates an indelible and recognizable bond. Further evidence for the belief in such a recognizable bond is found in an essay by Michel de Montaigne.

> I think that there must be frequent mistakes in that district of Libya described by Herodotus, in which he says the men have intercourse with the women promiscuously but that a child, as soon as it can walk, will find its father in a crowd, natural instinct guiding its first steps toward him.[91]

The passage in question is Herodotus IV, 180. Montaigne's interpretation is based on a misreading of the text by Herodotus' French translator, Saliat. Saliat's error is instructive. The skepticism of Montaigne notwithstanding, Saliat's public was predisposed toward believing that a child's natural instincts would reveal its paternity. The blood bond recognized by Valentine and Orson was apparent even to infants.

There are few instances of the recognition of an unknown relative in Chinese fiction. P'u Sung-ling's tale "Wang Kuei-an" contains one such episode.

> In the course of a year or two, when he (Wang) was on his homeward journey, he chanced to be detained by bad weather at a roadside inn of rather cleaner appearance than usual. Within he saw an old woman playing with a child, which, as soon as he entered, held out its arms to him to be taken. Wang took the child on his knee, and there it remained, refusing to go back to his nurse and when the rain had stopped and he was ready to go, the child cried out "Papa gone."[92]

The child is, of course, Wang's long-lost son. In P'u's "Wang Shih-hsiu" another man named Wang instantly recognizes his long-lost father.[93] But in Chinese fiction, ties of kinship between separated relatives are usually made apparent only after lengthy investigation. Blood does not usually reveal itself in flashes of intuitive insight.

A series of cases involving disputed maternity, reminiscent of the Biblical judgment of Solomon, is instructive here. One case, which a T'ang dynasty text, the *I-lin* (compiled by Ma Tsung, fl 811–822), locates in the late Han dynasty text *Feng-su t'ung-i,* though it is not contained in the text as presently constituted, involves the wives of two brothers who lived together and became pregnant at about the same time. The elder brother's wife miscarried and claimed that the child borne by the younger brother's wife was her own. The dispute continued for three years, until finally Huang Pa (a historical judge of legendary proportions who died in 51 B.C.) had the child brought into court. He informed the women that he would award the child to whichever woman could grasp it. The elder brother's wife grabbed for the child; the younger brother's wife hesitated. Huang Pa, understanding that her hesitation was caused by fear that her child be harmed, judged the younger brother's wife to be the true mother and awarded the child to her. The text is repeated in the *Che-yü kuei-chien* and the *T'ang-yin pi-shih.*[94]

A similar story, though this time the rival women are not sisters-in-law but are rather a human mother and a demon, is contained in the collection of Jataka tales, tales of the former lives of the Buddha. The demon asks the mother if she might play with the child. But then the story turns sour: the demon runs off with the child, insisting that he is hers. The sage Mahosadha responds:

> When he heard the story, although he knew at once by her red unwinking eyes that one of them was a goblin, he asked them whether they would abide by his decision. On their promising to do so, he drew a line and laid the child in the middle and bade the goblin seize the child by the hands and the mother by the feet. Then he said to them, "Lay hold of it and pull; the child is hers who can pull it over." They both pulled, and the child, being pained while it was pulled, uttered a loud cry. Then the mother, with a heart which seemed ready to burst, let the child go and stood weeping. The sage asked the multitude, "Is it the heart of the mother which is tender toward the child or the heart of her that is not the mother?" They answered, "The mother's heart." "Is she the mother who kept hold of the child or she who let it go?" They replied, "She who let it go."[95]

The sage knows in advance which is the demon and which is the mother. The technique is not to demonstrate to him which is the true mother: the red unblinking eyes of the demon have revealed her identity to the sage.

The purpose of the test is to demonstrate to the community which is the true mother.

This theme is echoed in the play *Hui-lan chi* (The Chalk Circle) by the Yüan author Li Hsing-tao. Judge Pao resolved the dispute, this time between a wife and a concubine, by placing the baby inside a chalk circle and telling the feuding women that only the child's true mother would be able to pull him from the circle. Again, the child's mother hesitates, and it is by her hesitation that Judge Pao recognizes her.[96] Judge Pao, Huang Pa, and Mahosadha are all engaged in a complex process of rhetorical double-talk. They state a precept—only the true mother will be able to pull her child from the circle or across the line—that they know to be untrue. The behavior of the true mothers and the pretenders demonstrates the falsity of the precept, and our assorted sages clearly reveal the false claims for what they are.

Not only do concepts of blood affinity seem to have been relatively weak in late imperial China, but concepts of affinity that had nothing to do with blood were significant. Popular notions of reincarnation and retribution assigned children to parents to whom they had a relationship both clear and nonbiological. It is not only Buddhist texts that contain these ideas: they are present in Taoist tracts and fiction as well. The laws of causality could be brutal. Two tracts, one a popular Buddhist text dating from the mid-fifteenth century, the other from the Taoist canon, in addition to suggesting varieties of the karmic connection between mother and child, reflect the dangers of childbirth and the tendency to attribute those dangers to the moral failings of the mother. In the Buddhist text, a tract devoted to Kuan-yin, a woman, pious in this life, had committed murder in a past life. Her former victim enters her womb as an embryo and causes her excruciating suffering.[97] The Taoist text expounds the view that a woman who died in childbirth had been a criminal in an earlier life and that the child who killed her was getting revenge for her past crimes.[98] That these gruesome views had some currency in the Ming is demonstrated in the sixteenth-century novel *Chin p'ing mei,* where Li P'ing-erh is consoled after the death of her baby by being told that he was not really her son at all, but rather a spirit she had wronged in a former existence.[99]

But revenge is not the only motive a spirit might have in seeking rebirth. In "Hua-teng chiao Lien-nü ch'eng fo chi," a story published in Hangchou in the middle of the sixteenth century, an elderly childless couple takes care of a poor woman. To repay them for their kindness, she is reborn as their daughter.[100] Indeed, the Buddhist term for karmic causality, *chung,* ordinarily means "seed." The metaphor is similar to that of Wei Hsi; the concept of generation has in its Buddhist guise taken on both karmic and ethical connotations.[101]

Retribution has many forms. A father's character might adversely affect his sons. The family instructions by the Sung author Ch'en Hsi-i and a short story by Li Yü both warn that a man who is greedy will have prodigal sons.[102] Ch'en also warns that a man who benefits himself to the detriment of others will have rebellious sons and grandsons.[103]

The picture obtained of heredity from fiction is then ambiguous. Although there is a sense of family affinity, the idea of heredity itself does not seem to play an important role. In cases of questionable paternity or supernatural ancestry, the storyteller stresses family resemblance. Sons on occasion recognize their long-lost fathers, and Judge Pao expresses the opinion that there is some sort of instinctive affinity between mother and child. But ideas of rebirth and retribution play an important role in the conceptualization of heredity. Biology is only one determinant of the nature and character of a child.

Heredity in Medical Texts

Let us turn to an examination of the idea of heredity in medical texts. Human development begins, of course, with conception. An essay on the timing of conception contained in the Sung dynasty *Fu-jen liang-fang* states:

> Whoever wishes a child should select an auspicious day for intercourse. If intercourse [occurring on an inauspicious day] results in pregnancy, it will greatly harm the father and mother. The child will be deformed, short-lived, stupid, and unfilial. If intercourse occurs following the regulations, then the child that is born will be virtuous and wise.[104]

The *Fang-nei* section of the *I-hsin fang,* reconstructed in the early part of this century by Yeh Te-hui, quoted the *Ch'an-ching:*

The Yellow Emperor said: "A human being is endowed with life when *yin* and *yang* are united in the woman's womb. At this moment one should take care to avoid the nine calamities. These are the following: (1) A child conceived during the daytime will be given to vomiting. (2) A child conceived at midnight, when the interaction of Heaven and Earth is at a standstill, will be either mute, deaf, or blind. (3) A child conceived during a solar eclipse will be either burned or wounded. (4) A child conceived during thunder and lightning, a time when Heaven in its anger displays its might, will easily develop mental troubles. (5) A child conceived during a lunar eclipse will be persecuted by an ill fate and so will its mother. (6) A child conceived when there is a rainbow in the sky will be exposed to ill fortune. (7) A child conceived during the summer or winter solstitium will bring harm to its parents. (8) A child conceived on nights of the waxing or waning moon will be killed in war or blinded by the wind. (9) A child conceived during intoxication or after a heavy meal will suffer from epilepsy, boils, and ulcers.[105]

Lu Ts'an (1494–1551) records cases of congenital deformity resulting from conception occurring during a thunderstorm or under the sun or moon. Lu writes of one child, conceived in broad daylight by a mother jealous of her husband's concubine, whose head was covered with meaty scales, whose face was blue, and whose cry resembled that of a ghost.[106] These cautions are repeated in the seventeenth-century *Chang-shih i-t'ung* (Master Chang's Comprehensive Medical Compendium), to be discussed at some length below.

But the dire warnings of Ch'en and Lu notwithstanding, their contemporaries did not believe that the form and development of a child was fixed at the moment of conception. A pregnant woman had the responsibility not only for the physical nurturing of her unborn child, but for his moral development as well. The *Lieh nü chuan,* attributed to the Han dynasty author Liu Hsiang, reports in the biography of the three Chou mothers on the principles of prenatal education.

T'ai Jen understood prenatal instruction. In ancient times, a pregnant woman did not lie on her side as she slept; neither would she sit sidewise, or stand on one foot. She would not eat dishes having harmful flavors; if the food was cut awry, she would not eat it; if the mat was not straight, she would not sit on it. She did not let her eyes gaze on lewd sights or let her ears listen to depraved sounds. At night she ordered the blind musicians to chant poetry. She used right reason to adjust affairs, and thus gave birth to children of correct physical form who excelled others in talent and virtue. When a woman is pregnant, she must be cautious about what influences *(kan)* her. If she is influenced by good, then the child will be good. If she is influenced by evil, then the child will be evil. People resemble the myriad things *(wan wu)* because their mothers are influenced by things. Therefore in form or in sound they resemble it.[107]

The influence *(kan)* that a thing has on a pregnant woman calls forth a response: the child resembles *(hsiao)* it. This is an interesting variation on the ideas about the contribution of the mother we have seen thus far. The woman may indeed be seen as the vessel for the nurturing of the child. But she is also the mediator between the natural world (the *wan wu)* and that child. This view depends on a particular view of causality: things influence the pregnant woman and her child responds to those things. This view of causality is a part of what is frequently called correlative thinking. The natural world takes cognizance of (and responds to) actions in the human world. Portents, for example, are interpreted as indicating heavenly approval or disapproval of events. This mode of thinking was developed in the Han dynasty and saw its heyday in the Sung dynasty.

The T'ang pharmaceutical writer Sun Ssu-miao (581–682) cites the above passage, adding that if a pregnant woman wants a wise child, she should observe carp and pheasants. If she wants a beautiful child, she should observe pearls and gems. If she wants a strong child, she should observe flying falcons and running dogs. Sun goes on to enumerate an extensive list of dietary prohibitions for pregnant women, which are repeated by the Yüan author Hu Ssu-hui in his *Yin-shan cheng-yao* (Correct and Important Principles of Nutrition), written in the early fourteenth century but not published until 1456.[108]

The *Tung-hsüan-tzu,* a text attributed to Li Tung-hsuan, emphasizes the moral aspects of the duties of the expectant mother.

After a woman has conceived, she should engage in good works. She should not look upon bad scenes; she should not hear bad words; she should suppress all sexual desire; she should not vituperate or quarrel. She should avoid becoming frightened and not overtire herself. She should not engage in idle talk nor let herself become depressed. She should avoid eating raw, cold, sour, or peppery foods. She should not ride in a cart or on a horse. She should not climb steep hills or go near a precipice. She should not go down steep descents nor walk fast. She should take no medicine nor subject herself to acupuncture or moxibustion. In all respects her thoughts should be correct, and she should continuously listen to the classical books being read aloud. Then her child will be clever and wise, loyal and good. This is called "educating the unborn child."[109]

Rules for prenatal education were contained in family instructions, such as the *Yen-shih chia-hsün* (Family Instructions of the Yen Clan), written by Yen Chih-t'ui, who flourished late in the sixth century. That text informs us:

> The ancient kings had rules for prenatal training. Women, when pregnant for three months, moved from their living quarters to a detached palace where sly glances would not be seen or disturbing sounds heard, and where the tone of music and the flavor of food were controlled by the rules of decorum. The rules were written on jade tablets and kept in a golden box. . . . The common people cannot follow such ways.

Yen continues that the postnatal education of the child should begin as soon as he is able to recognize facial expressions.[110]

Thus it was believed that the behavior of a pregnant woman affected not only the physical well-being but also the moral and intellectual development of her child. The *I-shuo* (Medical Theories), compiled by Chang Kao, who died sometime after 1224, says that women of antiquity could cause a child to be "good, long-lived, loyal, moral, intelligent, and without defect" by observing what was good and distancing themselves from what was evil.[111] An appendix to the *Nü-k'o pai-wen* (A Hundred Questions on Gynecology), a text compiled by the Sung dynasty author Ch'i Chung-fu, says that if the unborn child is exposed to gentlemen *(chün-tzu)* and sages *(sheng-jen),* he will become a gentleman and a sage.[112] The *Fu-jen liang-fang* says that if a woman wishes her unborn child to be wise *(hsien)* and capable *(neng),* she should read books and poetry.[113] Wang K'en-t'ang's *Nü-k'o chun-sheng,* whose preface is dated 1607, describes the principle behind all of these effects in the phrase "external phenomena having internal influence" and suggests that a woman who wants a beautiful child regard jade.[114]

Later texts continue to show concern with the behavior of a pregnant woman, although the precise nature of the concern (indeed, of the texts themselves) differs. Paul Unschuld has suggested ways in which the eclecticism of Ming medical texts replaces (or adds to) the correlative thinking so dominant in Sung medical texts,[115] and Charlotte Furth has applied this insight to medical discussions of women and reproduction.[116] Fetal education *(t'ai chiao)* as such ceases to be a category in texts such as the *Nü-k'o chun-sheng,* though of course the proper nourishment of the developing fetus remains a fundamental concern of the text.[117] And the section on fetal nourishment *(t'ai yang)* suggests, as we have seen above, that in the womb, the child is subject to external influences.[118] Other works, such as the seventeenth-century *Chang-shih i-t'ung,* do have short sections on fetal education. These texts draw on the classical sources cited above, though they modified them. In the *Chang-shih i-t'ung,* Chang Lu begins his section on fetal education by stating that techniques were not well known in his time. But he underlines their significance by saying that "if a pregnant woman follows them and carries them out, not only will she be able to avoid the problems of a difficult birth, but moreover, the child born will rarely suffer the calamities of fetal poison or early death." He says that once forty days have passed since a woman's last menstrual period, she should remain quietly in her rooms. Specific foods are listed as taboo, and the negative effects of maternal stress are outlined. Although specific examples are given (if the pregnant woman is frequently angry, her child will be cruel), the principles of fetal education are abstracted quite succinctly: "To cause the *ch'i* of the fetus to be calm and harmonious: this is what is called fetal education." Chang too is interested in the conditions of conception. For example: If intercourse occurs while the partners are very drunk, the semen will contain alcohol, and a child engendered will not survive. Intercourse occuring after great anger will result in semen containing excessive amounts of "angry fire," and the child will be perverse and obstinate. If the husband uses an aphrodisiac (literally: hot drugs as an aid in combat), then his semen will be "poison and violent," and the child born will be strange and idiotic *(i-ch'ih)*. This list (not here given in its entirety) closes with the following injunction: Continuing the ancestral hall is a great duty—how can it be regarded as a pleasurable game?[119]

According to traditional medical opinion on the development of the embryo, the child's physical form was not fixed until the third month of pregnancy. The *Ch'ien-chin yao-fang* of Sun Ssu-miao says:

> Because the blood is not yet circulating, the fetus changes in response to form. Because it is not yet fixed, when the woman sees an object *(wu)* then the fetus changes. At this time, male and female are not yet differentiated. Therefore, prior to the end of the third month, one may, according to the following prescription, change it and cause a male to be born.[120]

Drugs were not the only therapy available. The general principle of the various therapies, explained by the *Nü-k'o pai-wen,* was to use *yang* objects to call forth the *yang* principle and produce a male child and to use *yin* objects to call forth the *yin* principle and produce a female child.[121] Thus a woman desiring a son might put an axe[122] or three rooster tail feathers[123] under her bed. Or she might eat a rooster,[124] thereby calling forth his *yang.* The *Fu-jen liang-fang* and the *Wan-shih yü-ying chia-mi*[125] provide guidance to those women who would prefer to have daughters—they should look at earrings and bracelets—but, as one might expect, most of the texts provide suggestions to aid in producing male offspring. Chang Lu's *Chang-shih i-t'ung* suggests drug therapy for those who have borne daughters but no sons, but does not suggest that the gender of the fetus might be changed.[126]

The *Fu-jen liang-fang,* a Sung text, provides suggestions as to how one might change the gender of the fetus. Although the *Fu-jen liang-fang* does not cite the *Ch'ien-chin yao-fang,* the language and line of argumentation are similar to Sun's text. The *Fu-jen liang-fang* admits the possibility that a reader might be skeptical that the gender of a fetus might be changed: "I am afraid you will not believe this. Perform an experiment: when a hen is sitting on her eggs, follow my instructions and place [an axe] under the nest. The nest will produce only roosters."[127]

In his extensive commentary on the *Ch'ien-chin yao-fang,* the seventeenth-century author Chang Lu (whose *Chang-shih i-t'ung* we have seen above) continues the tradition of skepticism. He writes that "one cannot help doubting the theory that a female can be changed into a male. But since it came from the *Ch'ien-chin* I thought that it could not be nonsense." He then goes on to analyze various ingredients in the prescription

Sun provides, which includes such ingredients as dried dog testicles. He comments that the ingredients "summon forth *(kan)* their own kind." He then performs the experiment recommended in the *Fu-jen liang-fang:* "Once when I noticed that a hen was brooding on her eggs, I placed an axe under the nest, with its blade facing down. And sure enough, the chicks all turned out to be roosters. This marvellous and mysterious method—I could not help but believe it." The analysis of the prescription, coupled with the experiment, have overcome Chang's initial skepticism. One is left to marvel not only with him, but at him. Scientific curiosity, coupled with male narcissism and a reverence for texts, seems to have momentarily caused Chang Lu to forget why it is people keep chickens in the first place.[128]

Fictional texts corroborate the importance of the prenatal instructions to the development of a child noted in the medical texts while also indicating that they have fallen into disuse. The narrator of the novel *Chin p'ing mei* recites the methods used by women of antiquity to insure that their offspring would be wise and healthy and proceeds to criticize Wu Yüeh-niang for listening to the recitation of Buddhist sutras during her pregnancy. As a result of Yüeh-niang's behavior during her pregnancy, the author implies, the son she bore grew up to be a monk.[129]

Fictional sources also corroborate the existence of the belief that the sex of the fetus could be changed from female to male. Li Yü, in his short story "Feng-hsien lou," expresses such a view. The family of Scholar Shu had for generations produced only a single male heir. When his wife became pregnant, his relatives prayed, saying: "We beseech you to be mindful of the fact that our line of descent is weak. If the fetus is female, change it into a male."[130]

The tenth tale of Li Yü's *Wu sheng hsi* (Silent Operas), entitled "Pien nü wei erh p'u-sa ch'iao" (By a Strange Bargain a Bodhisattva Transforms a Daughter into a Son), recounts a postnatal sex transformation. A wealthy merchant contracted with a Tantric Bodhisattva to dispense four-fifths of his wealth in exchange for a male heir. When the merchant learned that a concubine was pregnant, he reneged on his promise. As a result, the child was born a "stone maiden" *(shih-nü),* a girl with no vagina. The merchant, alarmed at this turn of events, completed the disbursement of the funds, and the child became male.[131]

The child's development was greatly influenced by its ingestion of milk, whether from its mother or a wet nurse. Children of the upper classes were frequently nursed not by their mothers but by wet nurses, who were generally called in to live with the family. The relationship between a child and the woman who nursed it was intimate. The milk not only provided nourishment for the child: it transmitted characteristics as well. A T'ang encyclopedia, the *T'ung-tien,* says that children resemble the women who nurse them. It cites as evidence for this a line from the *Shih ching:* "Caterpillars resemble the grain they eat."[132] The Ming medical text *Ku-chin i-t'ung* (Compendium of Medicine, Old and New) echoes this, saying that great care must be exercised in the choice of a wet nurse because the child who drinks her milk will closely resemble her.[133] The mechanism whereby this occurs is made clear by Li Shih-chen (1518–1593) in *Pen-ts'ao kang-mu,* an important compendium of pharmaceutical knowledge. Li describes breast milk as "transformed *yin* blood" and goes on to say that "before pregnancy it appears as menses below; during pregnancy it provides nourishment of the fetus, and after birth it ascends as milk. The subtleties of these creative transformations are nature's marvels."[134] Family instructions argue against hiring a wet nurse, not so much because of the fear that her milk would pollute the blood of the children she nursed, but because she would neglect, possibly fatally neglect, her own children.[135]

Fiction echoes the belief that characteristics are transmitted through milk. In Li Yü's story "Ho-ying lou," two sisters exchange their nursing babies, and as a result the children greatly resemble one another. Li explains:

> There is an appropriate saying in the *Book of Songs:* "Caterpillars resemble the grain they eat." And it has been established that babies generally resemble the mothers who nurse them because they somehow become related by blood.[136]

In the eighteenth-century novel *Hung lou meng,* Pao-yü, the spoiled scion of the house of Chia, berates his wet nurse for having eaten a treat that was intended for someone else. She accuses him of ingratitude, ingratitude compounded by the fact that she had nursed him with her milk, which was her own blood, transformed and thinned.[137] A mother's (or wet nurse's) milk is thus an important vehicle for transmission of characteristics.

Metaphors of assimilation are expressed in terms of blood and bone in an appendix to the *Hsi yüan lu* (Washing Away of Wrongs), a work of forensic medicine dating from the Sung dynasty. The *Hsi yüan lu* sets forth techniques for establishing the identity of a corpse. If a drop of a child's blood were placed on the skeleton of his parent, the blood would sink in. If the skeleton were that of a stranger, the blood would remain on the surface.[138] Although the primary tie that the test could verify was that between parent and child, it was also believed to be effective between spouses and siblings. The test could also be used for living persons: drops of blood from two people could be put in a basin of water. If the drops mingled, this proved that the two were related. If they did not, this was taken as evidence that there was no tie of blood between them. Commentary to the *Hsi yüan lu* directly addresses the question of whether a son's blood will sink into the skeleton of his stepmother. The mere fact that the question is posed suggests a sense of the permeability of blood boundaries, but the answer suggests that the boundaries nonetheless persist. In posing the question, the text points out that a stepmother nurses her stepson and that he grew up under her tutelage. He owes his very character to her blood and her *ch'i.* Taking all of this into consideration, would his blood soak into her skeleton? The text informs us: "I fear it has never been the case."[139] Thus there is an actual physical barrier to the assimilation of an outsider into the family, metaphorically expressed by the barrier between blood and bone.

The belief in the efficacy of this test as a proof of identity was not limited to coroners, as shown by its appearance in the popular "Ballad of the Lady Meng-chiang," a ballad dating from before the tenth century. The lady is searching for the bones of her husband, Fan Chi-liang, a conscripted laborer who had died while working on the Great Wall. She says of the bones:

> One by one, I'll take them in my hand to look hard at them.
> Then I'll bite my finger and draw blood to put them to the test.
> If it is my husband, the blood will sink deep into the bones.
> But if it is not Chi-liang, blood will remain apart.[140]

We have already had occasion to remark upon the nature of skepticism in medical texts and upon the reflexive nature of commentary in deflecting that skepticism. That the blood of a child would sink into the bones of a parent seems self-evident. As the text itself states: "The bones of the mother and father exist in another form as son and daughter."[141] The blood of the child sinks into the bone of the parent because they are of the same substance. The reason why the blood of spouses would comingle is less self-evident. Indeed, commentary to a nineteenth-century edition of the *Hsi yüan lu* cites the story of the lady Meng-chiang and adds that the story is scarcely credible: it "approaches the unfathomable and is hard to believe." The commentary goes on to cite several Ch'ing dynasty examples where a wife's blood did not sink into her husband's bones.[142] Again, in this controversy we see evidence of the permeability of boundaries of blood and bone.

The blood test plays a crucial role in P'u Sung-ling's tale "T'u ou" (The Clay Image). A man named Ma dies young, with no children. His wife, a woman of the Wang family, vows to remain faithful to his memory, in spite of the urging of her family that she remarry. She has a clay image of him made. She offers the image food, just as if it were alive. One night, the image comes to life and tells her that because of her virtue, officials in the underworld have given him permission to return and engender a son. Wang does in fact become pregnant and gives birth to a son. The local magistrate, informed of the widow's suspicious motherhood, investigates. He interrogates the neighbors, who have nothing suspicious to report. The magistrate tells us that the son of a ghost will not cast a shadow. This child, placed in the sun, casts only a faint shadow. A further test of his paternity is made by putting a drop of his blood on the clay image of his father. The blood soaks in. A drop of the boy's blood is placed on another clay image, but that drop remains on the surface of the clay. The tale concludes: "Thus he [the magistrate] believed her. And in a few years the child's features, speech, and behavior in every respect resembled those of Ma. It was only then that the doubts of the crowd were dispelled."[143]

In conclusion, ideas of affinity, reincarnation, and retribution all influenced thinking about the relationship between a child and his progenitors, but the linkages were complex and were not perceived to be strictly biological in nature. Although the timing of a child's conception was of the utmost importance, its nature was not irrevocably formed at that moment. The behavior of a woman during pregnancy was believed to affect the development of her child—its sex, moral nature, intelligence, and character, as well as its physical health. The process of development continued after a child's birth, when the child inherited more characteristics from whoever nursed it and when it began to learn from its surroundings. Indeed, as the following quotation from Yen Chih-t'ui's *Yen-shih chia-hsün* (Family Instructions for the Yen Clan) demonstrates, education was believed to have the capacity to supplant nature: "Confucius was right in saying: 'What is acquired in babyhood is like original nature; what has been formed in habit is equal to instinct.' "[144] An essay contained in the T'ang dynasty encyclopedia *T'ung tien* voices the opinion that although an adopted child receives his four limbs from his biological mother, he grows his hair and skin under the care of his adoptive mother.[145] The importance of the nurturing function is thus reaffirmed.

The prominence given to notions of blood affinity in early modern Europe has no Chinese counterpart. The twelfth-century expert on canon law Gratian (Decretal LVI) argued that the horror with which God viewed the children of adulterous unions was fundamentally the fear that they would themselves grow up to be adulterers.[146] The sins of the fathers were inherited by the children. In the Chinese moral landscape, though retribution was sure, the children did not inherit the failings of their fathers. Where habit was equal to instinct, and early childhood education could supplant nature, we hear no such arguments against caring for children of uncertain parentage. The arguments and the fears lie on other grounds.

2

Attitudes toward Adoption

The central paradox of adoption in traditional China is that adoption across surname lines was prohibited and that the prohibition was ignored. The previous section described the context in which that paradox existed: subsequent sections will delineate ways in which the paradox is played out (and occasionally resolved) in biography and fiction. This section will confront the paradox directly.

The Prohibition: Law and Ritual

Chinese law is profoundly concerned with marriage, the family, and the transmission of property. The interest of the legal code in the domestic is closely allied with ritual concerns. Indeed, it has been suggested that family law is a codification of ritual.[1] The continuation of the ancestral sacrifices is one of the central concerns of Chinese domestic ritual. Proper continuation of those sacrifices in the absence of a blood heir is a concern of both ritual and law. Furthermore, adoption, especially adoption across surname lines, involved the interests of more than one kin group. The law served to mediate among these competing interests.

The roots of the prohibition of cross-surname adoption lie in ritual texts. The *I-li,* a pre-Han ritual text, specifies that an adopted heir *(hou)* must be of the same lineage as the family that adopts him.[2] *Hou* means literally "one who comes after." The implications of *hou,* of heirship, are not without ambiguity. But access to property and participation in the ancestral sacrifices are central to the concept.

The T'ang code, the earliest code in which mention of adoption survives, states that the adopted child must be from the same lineage and must be of the proper generation (that is to say, one generation younger than the adopting father). A man who adopted as an heir a child of a different lineage was to be banished for a year. The child's natural father was to be beaten fifty strokes, and the adoption was to be annulled.[3] The T'ang code explicitly prohibited the adoption of a male child of a different lineage; commentary interpreted the passage to mean that one was not to be punished for adopting a female child.[4] The notion that kinship proceeded through the male line implied that the adoption of a female was of less ritual significance than that of a male: hence it went unpunished. The code prohibited the adoption of persons of low status *(tsa-hu)*. Adopting such a male child would result in banishment of a year and a half, a female, a hundred strokes. If the adopting family was of official status, the punishment would be made a degree more severe.[5] The implication is clear: A stranger of lower social rank is more of a stranger than one of equal social status.

These injunctions about gender and class are repeated in the *Sung hsing-t'ung,* a collection of law first promulgated in 963 and issued in revised editions in 966, 1071, and 1094. Indeed, commentary to the text explicitly states: "Adopting a male is serious; adopting a female is trivial."[6] The penalty in the *Sung hsing-t'ung* for adopting a male of *tsa-hu* status is one and a half years of exile; for adopting a female, a hundred strokes. If the adopting family was of official status, the penalty was one degree more severe.[7] Whereas the T'ang statute had prohibited the adoption of someone of a different lineage *(tsung),* the Sung statute prohibited the adoption of someone of a different surname *(hsing).*[8] The assumption is that persons of the same surname are ultimately descended from the same ancestor. This is a significant modification—it greatly increased the pool of legally acceptable adoptees—and is retained in later formulations of the law. Kinship has become rarified and abstracted.

Ming law follows earlier law in general form. The statute reads:

> He who adopts a child *(i-tzu)* of a different surname, thereby causing chaos in the lineage, is to be beaten sixty strokes. He who gives a person of a different surname as heir is to suffer the same punishment. The adoption is to be annulled.[9]

The Ch'ing statutes on adoption are taken verbatim from those of the Ming. The substatutes, however, are not. When the Manchus conquered

China in 1644, they adopted to an astonishing degree the code of the Ming. The statutes of the code *(lü)* are regarded as timeless, representing absolute and unalterable principles. Substatutes *(li)*, however, can change and reflect changing principles. And particularities of Ch'ing social structure are reflected in the substatutes. For example, a substatute originating in 1740 states that a bannerman who adopts a child of a different surname is to be demoted a degree, beaten a hundred strokes, and exiled for three years. Bannermen were a legally constituted political elite, comprised of Manchus, Mongols, and Chinese who had declared their allegiance to the Manchus prior to the conquest of China in 1644. The political status of bannermen meant that orderly succession in the banner ranks mattered more than that of ordinary people. The Ch'ing substatutes dealing with the establishment of an heir also show a dramatic increase in explicit concern with property.[10]

While particular statutes and substatutes varied somewhat over time, as long as the child adopted was from within the lineage group and was of the proper generational order, there was considerable latitude as to who could be adopted. An edict of the Hung-chih era (1488–1505) argues that if the adoptee was of the same surname, the adoptive father's kinsmen *(t'ung-tsu)* could not raise objections to the adoption. An edict of the Chia-ching era (1522–1566) repeats the warning, adding that the adopted child must be of the proper generational order, that is to say, a generation younger than the adopting father.[11] Kao Chü (1533–1624), in his commentary to the Ming code, asserts that a man need not choose his closest relative, but might instead choose someone wise *(hsien)* or capable *(neng)* or someone of whom he was particularly fond as heir. As long as the proper generational order was followed, his kinsmen ought not interfere.[12] While these stipulations state that the choice of an heir rested with an individual rather than with the kin group as a collective, they imply that it was a choice in which the kin group might intervene. The perception that close relatives were more appropriate candidates for adoption remained in an edict of the Wan-li era (1573–1619) in which the preferred order of precedence for adoption is outlined in some detail.[13]

Adopting a child from the same lineage who was not of the proper generational order was regarded by the law as being an infraction almost as serious as adopting a child from outside the surname group.[14] Commentators stress that such practice causes chaos *(luan)* within the lineage; it is the same term used to describe the consequences of a cross-surname adoption.[15]

During the T'ang, the penalty for adoption within the lineage but violating the proper generational order was fifty blows for both the adopting and natural fathers and the annullment of the adoption.[16] Yüan Ts'ai's *Yüan-shih shih-fan* explicitly states that one may not adopt someone who is of the same surname but not of the proper *chao-mu* order. (*Chao-mu* refers to the placing of the ancestral tablets; it means proper generational order.) Even geese, so Yüan Ts'ai argues, maintain a proper order in their lines as they fly; how much more should human beings maintain a proper order in their affairs.[17] Wang K'en-t'ang, an authority on law as well as on medicine, concurred in arguing that an adoption in violation of the *chao-mu* order was as bad as an adoption involving members of a different surname group.[18] And a regulation issued during the Wan-li era makes explicit the analogy between adoption within the surname group in violation of the proper order and adoption of those of a different surname. Adopting those of another surname causes chaos within the lineage *(tsung-tsu)*; adopting in improper order creates chaos among the generations.[19] The *Wu-li t'ung-k'ao* stresses the importance of maintaining the proper order, while conceding that many people violated it.[20] From these various commentators, we can see that the proper ritual relationship was a concern as significant as proper blood relationship. Propriety was almost as much the point as was kinship.

The state was not simply concerned with protecting the interests of the lineage. It was also concerned with protecting the interests of a legally adopted heir. The law protected a child adopted from within the surname group from expulsion. For example, a couple who had adopted a child might subsequently bear one of their own. What then became of the child who had been adopted? According to T'ang law, a legally adopted heir could not be expelled simply because of the birth of another heir.[21] But the *Sung hsing-t'ung* states that a child adopted by a childless couple who later gave birth to a child of their own might be permitted to return to the family of his birth.[22] The Ming and Ch'ing codes concur. According to Ming law, if a son was born later, he would inherit equally with the legally adopted heir.[23] But the codes are clear that an adopted child of a different surname could not take property with him if he returned to the family of his birth. (For the sole exception to this, see p. 56.) The early Ch'ing administrator Huang Liu-hung (c 1633–after 1705) echoes these concerns when he writes in his magistrate's manual *Fu-hui ch'üan-shu* (A Complete Book of Happiness and Benevolence) that there should be no discrimination between a natural and a legally adopted son in the matter of inheritance. He reiterates that if the adopted son returned to the family of his birth, he could not take property with him.[24] His status as a property holder was contingent upon his status as an heir.

Both the code and its commentaries contain important qualifications to the general prohibition of the adoption of children across lineage lines. It is at this point that definitions become complex and boundaries blurred.[25] The commentary to the code compiled by Kao Chü says that the code does not prohibit the fostering *(yang)* of a child of a different surname as a *yang-tzu* as long as his surname remains unchanged.[26] The commentary by Su Mao-hsiang, who received his *chin-shih* degree in 1592, concurs, adding that the child may not inherit. Su's commentary uses the term *i-nan* rather than *yang-tzu*.[27] Commentary to the Ch'ing code agrees. The commentary there uses the term *i-tzu*.[28] The *Fu-hui ch'üan-shu* concurs, saying that even though an *i-tzu* might have changed his surname and mourned the death of members of the adoptive family, he still had no rights to inheritance. Huang stresses that although a family might well give such a son a share of the property, such a bequest was a gift rather than an inheritance.[29] And the eighteenth-century ritual expert Ch'in Hui-t'ien cautions in his commentary to the *Wu-li t'ung-k'ao* that if one permitted one's sons-in-law or one's daughters' sons to inherit property, it would then be impossible to prevent them from participating in the ancestral sacrifices. Hence a concern for maintaining the purity of the sacrifices is a reason for vigilance about inheritance.[30] Sacrifice and property might be intimately connected, but one did not lead inevitably to the other.

Another qualification to the general prohibition of adoption has existed within the code itself since the T'ang. An abandoned child younger than three years old could be adopted, and his surname could be changed to that of the adopting family.[31] A Ming commentator tells us that this is because the surname of an abandoned child is not known.[32] But again, the degree to which a child so adopted was incorporated into the family is not clear. A case from the Sung dynasty legal casebook *Ch'ing-ming chi* indicates that a household with a child adopted in this manner does not become extinct *(hu chüeh)*, even though there be no other heirs. Thus the child has in fact become the heir.[33] But a Ming commentary on the law offers a strikingly different interpretation.

> Although they take the surname, they are still *i-nan*. They are not permitted to succeed as heirs, nor are they permitted to inherit the *yin* privilege. Adopting them is the benevolence of nurturing an *i-nan*. It is nothing more.[34]

Kao Chü's commentary, too, asserts that children adopted in this manner could not be made heirs.[35] The commentary to the Ch'ing code makes the same prohibition.[36] The "Shih huo chih" (Treatise on Economics) of the Ch'ing dynastic history states: "An *i-nan* may not be an heir."[37] Huang Liu-hung explicitly states that a child adopted as an *i-nan* could not inherit (though he might be granted property as a gift), even if there was no other heir.[38] The commentaries to both the Ming and Ch'ing codes specify that an abandoned child four years old or older is to be treated under the statute "keeping lost children."[39] The statute specifies that lost or abandoned children are to be turned over immediately to a magistrate. It explicitly forbids the keeping, and presumably therefore the adoption, of such children. The legal commentaries notwithstanding, in actual practice children so adopted did often succeed as heirs and did participate in the ancestral sacrifices.[40]

Consequences of Adoption in Legal and Ritual Texts

We have looked at how adoption is defined in legal texts. Now let us look at the legal and ritual consequences of adoption.

That legal adoption was intended as a transfer of membership in one family to another is indicated by the change in mourning relationships that accompanied it. Mourning regulations, laid out in great detail in classical ritual texts such as the *I-li,* specify with great precision the obligation of each relative to mourn the deceased. These mourning relations prescribe the behavior of the living toward the dead and mediate relations between the spirit world and the human world. Taken in the collective, these mourning regulations form a map delineating degrees of kinship and the obligations thereof. And they indicate that the adoptive son's primary mourning obligation lay with his new family. The *I-li* comments that "he acts as if he were the son."[41] The three years of untrimmed mourning, the deepest degree of mourning, normally worn for a father and by a father for his heir (but not for his other sons) was worn by a father for his adopted heir. The commentary to the *I-li* explains: "This is because he has received a place in the succession and so is entitled to have the deepest grade of mourning worn for him."[42] At the same time, a man who had been adopted out would diminish his mourning for his own parents and blood brothers by one degree.[43] The commentary to the *I-li* explains why the adopted heir wore only the diminished *ta-kung* mourning for his blood brothers: "Because, when he became the successor, he diminished the honor due to his own brothers, whose circle he has left."[44] From the standpoint of ritual, a legally adopted son then is completely allied to his new family. But he has not completely left his old one. They continue to mourn him as if he had not been adopted out, and he continues to mourn them, though in a diminished manner.[45]

Like ritual, Chinese legal codes provide a detailed map of status relationships. In the traditional Chinese legal system, the severity of a crime and the punishment appropriate to it were determined by the status of both criminal and victim and by their relationship to one another. Striking a servant and striking one's father were crimes that differed not only in degree; they represented fundamentally different threats to the social order. Striking a servant was a reprehensible act of violence; striking one's father was a challenge to hierarchy and authority and threatened the very roots of the social order. The Ming and Ch'ing penal codes provide great detail as to the varying legal consequences of domestic violence. The following statute appears in the Ming code and is repeated verbatim in the Ch'ing code.

> If a son or grandson is defiant, and his parents or grandparents in violation of all reason beat him to death, they shall be beaten a hundred strokes. If

they intentionally kill him, they shall be beaten sixty strokes and banished for one year. If he is killed by his stepmother[46] the penalty is a degree heavier. If she causes the line of descent to be broken, then she shall be strangled. The penalty for beating in violation of all reason either the wife of a son (or grandson) or an adopted son (or grandson) of a different surname to the point of injury is eighty strokes. If the injury is severe, the penalty is increased one degree. Moreover, the wife of the son (or grandson) is to be sent home with her dowry and with ten *liang* as compensation. An adopted son is to be given his share of the property as compensation. If death results, the penalty in each case is beating a hundred strokes and exile for three years. If it is a case of intentional killing, in either case the penalty is a hundred blows and exile to a distance of two thousand *li*. If the woman involved is a concubine, then the penalty is reduced two degrees.[47]

This statute is of interest to us for several reasons. If Chinese law were concerned merely with hierarchy, one would expect that killing a son would be a more serious crime than killing an adopted son or a daughter-in-law. But the law is concerned with social order as well as with hierarchy; indeed, it mediates between the principles of social order and those of hierarchy. One has a degree of power over one's own children that one does not have over other people's children. Both an adopted son of a different surname and a daughter-in-law have kinsmen who might be expected to resent their injury or death and to act on that resentment. In clarifying the limited nature of the rights one has over these two categories of people, the law attempts to minimize conflict. The law is not especially interested in the rights of the individual per se. If it were, why would an adopted son receive more protection than a biological son? Rather, it is interested in mediating the competing interests of the two kin groups. Furthermore, both adoption and marriage are legal, contractual relationships. The law can make them and the law can break them. If the adoptive parents or in-laws injure the adoptee or daughter-in-law, they have broken the contract and lost the right to power over the adoptee or wife. A term used to describe the situation in commentary to the Ch'ing code is *i-chüeh,* which literally means breaking the bond of *i,* of righteousness.[48] The same term is also used to prescribe conditions for divorce. Acts that bring about a state of *i-chüeh* include either spouse committing acts of physical violence upon members of the other's family or either spouse having sexual relations with a close relative of the other. If conditions of *i-chüeh* existed, then divorce was obligatory. (*I-chüeh* was the only circumstance under which a wife might divorce her husband.)[49] Both marriage and adoption depend to a degree on the existence of *i;* when that bond of righteousness is broken, the relationship may be said to exist no more.

An act of parental violence not only annuls the marriage or adoption, the injured party has the legal right to property. An injured wife may take not only the dowry she brought into the marriage, but an additional sum in compensation. One is punished for injuring or killing a woman who is merely a concubine of a son (or grandson), though the penalty is one degree less than it would be if she were a wife. This is one more indication of the inferior status of concubines. One should note that an adopted child of a different surname could take property with him only if he was injured by his adoptive parents or grandparents. Thus, in injuring the child, the offending parent forfeited not only his right to a child but also his right to property. But children of one's body could not be forfeited. There is no mechanism for dissolving the relationship even if the parent is abusive. And so the law is silent on the issue of merely injuring one's own child. If a woman other than the child's natural mother kills the child and thereby breaks the line of descent, she shall be strangled. Once again, the penalty is more severe for non–blood relatives. Finally, we should note that in this statute adoption and marriage are seen as parallel categories. The obligations that are incurred by (and to) in-laws and adoptive parents are identical. The analogy is reinforced by the ritual rules regarding mourning. According to the *T'ung-tien,* a T'ang dynasty encyclopedia: "One who has been adopted out, or a daughter who has married, diminishes mourning."[50] We shall see additional reinforcement of this analogy later.

Marriage is not the only kinship relation to which adoption is analogized. The *Ta Ming lü chih-yin,* published in 1526, says that one who kills an *i-tzu* should be punished as if he killed the child of a brother; that is to say with a hundred strokes and three years banishment. If it were intentional murder *(ku-sha)* then in addition to the hundred strokes, the penalty would be exile to a distance of three thousand *li.*[51] At another point the same text reiterates that killing an *i-tzu* is like killing a younger brother's son.[52] Adoption is a relation that mimics kinship, even if it does not duplicate direct filiation.

But in other formulations of the law, the punishments vary, as does the conceptualization of the role of adopted son. The degree to which an *i-tzu* approaches equivalence to a natural son in the criminal code depends on two factors: duration of residence and inheritance of property. For example, if a stepfather or stepmother killed the *i-tzu*, either accidentally or intentionally *(ou-sha* or *ku-sha)*, the punishment would vary according to the condition of the adoption. If the *i-tzu* had been adopted when he was younger than fifteen *sui*, and he had been benevolently nurtured *(en-yang)* for a long time, or if he had been adopted when he was more than sixteen *sui* and had received property *(fen-you ts'ai-ch'an)*, then the adoptive parent was to be punished according to the statute pertaining to adopted sons of a different surname.[53] That statute provided a penalty of a hundred strokes with the bamboo and three years banishment for beating that resulted in death *(ou-sha)*. For murder with intent *(ku-sha)*, to the penalty of a hundred strokes was added banishment to a distance of two thousand *li*.[54] But if adoptive parents killed a child who had neither been adopted long nor received property, they would be punished as if the victim were a hired laborer, incurring a lighter penalty.[55]

If an adopted son committed a crime against his stepparents, the same qualifications pertained, but with slightly different results. If the criminal had been adopted before he was fifteen and nurtured long, or adopted after sixteen but inherited property, then he would be punished as if he were the biological son of the victim. If neither of the two above conditions were met—if the adoption had been of short duration and no property transfer was involved—then the *i-tzu* would be punished as if he were a hired laborer.[56] A stepfather who, in the quaint euphemism used by Alabaster, "unreasonably corrects his charge" would be subject to a more severe penalty than a biological father would be.[57] Biology granted rights to both father and son that legal fiction could only approach. If an adopted son offended the cousins of his adoptive father, he would be punished as if he were a servant, rather than a son; that is to say, he would be punished more severely.[58] By offending the cousins of his adoptive father, or so it seems, the adoptive child diminished his rights to family membership.

The limits to the adoptive relationship are further clarified in marriage law. The law surrounding marriage ritual demanded that both parties to the negotiation be forthcoming with information about both bride and groom. Withholding information that either party was deformed, excessively old or young, the child of a concubine or adopted, either from within the agnatic group *(kuo-fang)* or from outside it *(ch'i-yang),* was against the law in the Ming and Ch'ing dynasties. Commentary states that although being adopted (or being the child of a concubine) was not the same as being deformed or elderly or immature, still, such people did not have the same status as the offspring of a principal wife.[59] The nature of the distinction remains amorphous, but in this formulation, even a child adopted from within the kin group was not like a child of his parents' body. Implied in the law are both the sense that a prospective spouse had the right to know that his or her intended was adopted and the fear that matchmakers (and adoptive parents) would conceal the fact.

The Prohibition: Some Interpretations

If the prohibition against adoption across surname lines were contained only in the legal codes, one might be tempted to conclude that the prohibition was an attempt on the part of the state to limit the capacity of lineages to reproduce themselves. But the concern with restrictions is not limited to the legal codes. The importance of the distinction between fostering and adoption is stressed in popular religious texts such as the eighteenth-century ledger of merits and demerits *Pu-fei-ch'ien kung-te-li* (Meritorious Deeds Which Cost No Money), which cautions: "Do not obscure the family names of children entrusted to you."[60] Many clan rules expressly forbid the adoption of outsiders into the clan and forbid the adoption out of clan members.[61] The K'uai-chi Ch'in clan, in the instructions at the end of its genealogy, echoes the concerns of the legal codes when it asserts that adopting those of a different surname causes chaos in the clan.[62] Clan rules commonly specify that neither a member who is adopted out nor an outsider who is adopted in will be recorded. Frequently, a genealogy that makes such an assertion records both kinds of adoptions, though doubtless many more did go unrecorded.[63] In addition to clan rules found in genealogies, family instructions, such as the *Yao-yen* (Medicinal Words) of Yao Shun-mu (1548–1627), forbid the

adoption of children of different surnames.[64] Clans that establish chari-
table estates for the benefit of their members may specify that those who
adopted a child of a different surname not receive an allowance for that
child.[65] Thus the articulated interest of the state and the lineage in the
matter of cross-surname adoptions seem parallel.

The Sanctity of Surnames

We have seen both legal codes and family rules argue against adoption
across surname lines because the practice will cause chaos in the lineage.
The chaos is not merely a matter of inconvenience: it is disorder with cosmic consequences. The sage kings of antiquity, culture heroes who
brought to humankind such marvels as agriculture, fire, and writing,
established surnames.[66] The Sung Neo-Confucian Chang Shih (1133–
1180) describes their motivation and suggests some implications.

> The sages became active and established surnames to distinguish lineage;
> they made strict provisions for the clans in order that they should be cau-
> tious over their inheritance. This was also in accordance with the properties
> of men's nature and was simply an unalterable principle. If man forces him-
> self from his natural lineage and unites himself with that with which he
> should not be united, he is surely denying his nature.[67]

Surnames, artifices granted by the sages of antiquity, have become markers of nature.

The importance of the knowledge of one's line of descent and the lines
of descent of one's associates is stressed in the preface to the genealogy of
the Shang-yu Shih clan. Citing a line of argument used in both the Han
dynasty *Po hu t'ung* and the classical *I-li*, a preface dated 1051 says:

> Animals know their mothers but don't know their fathers. Rustics *(yeh-jen)*
> say—father and mother, how do you reckon who they are? Now, to know a
> person and carelessly not know who his ancestors are is to be no different
> from wild beasts.[68]

The *Lü-shih ch'un-ch'iu* (Spring and Autumn Annals of Mr. Lü) and the
Shang-chün shu (Book of the Lord of Shang), two pre-Han texts, both

posit a deep antiquity where people in a precivilized state recognized their mothers but not their fathers.[69] The connection between patriline and political order is made clear in the *Lü-shih ch'un-ch'iu:* in the days of high antiquity, when men recognized their mothers but not their fathers (and when there were no distinctions between men and women), there were no rulers and no hierarchical distinctions.

Thus the idea of the patrilineal line of descent is one of the features that distinguishes civilized men from rustics and wild beasts. The passage from the *Sang-fu* section of the *I-li* that the genealogy is quoting continues:

> The minor officers *(shih)* in the cities know to respect their fathers' ancestral tablets. Greater officers *(tai-fu)* and scholars *(hsüeh-shih)* know to respect their grandfathers. The feudal lords *(chu-hou)* extend it to their great grandfathers. The son of heaven extends it to the origins of his ultimate ancestor.[70]

Thus one's responsibility to know and serve his ancestors varied with his social position. The higher one's social position, in the *I-li*'s conceptualization of the cosmos, the greater were one's social responsibilities. The more exalted one's position, the more precise should be his knowledge of his descent and the more reverent his fulfillment of the ritual obligations that the knowledge of the descent implied. Adoption might interfere with the clarity of these distinctions and was hence to be shunned.

The irrevocable gulf between persons of different surnames is demonstrated in two different classical texts. The *Kuo yü* asserts:

> Those of a different surname have a different virtue *(i-te)*. Those of a different virtue are of a different category *(i-lei)*.[71]

The *Tso chuan* expresses a similar sentiment: "If he be not of our kin, he is sure to have a different mind."[72] Kinship represented then an ultimate category, a category that humans had not the power to alter. Surnames represented the efforts of the sage kings to fix that category in terms useful to ordinary people.

But the categories are not infallible. As another Sung Neo-Confucian, Ch'en Ch'un (1153–1217), writes:

Family names originated in antiquity. The sages created them primarily to differentiate how people were born into different groups. Later there were family names bestowed by the emperor and there were concealed names, so that many were mixed and confused. Therefore people wanting to establish the continued family line should not depend on the same family name as evidence. One must carefully select a near kin whose background is clear and put him in the line. In that case there is only one material force *(ch'i)* to be communicated, and the deceased father and grandfather will not be missed in the sacrifice.[73]

The purity of names bestowed by the sages has been polluted by the passage of time. Thus one ought not to rely on them as sole authority, but should select an heir from those one actually knows to be related.

The socially and ideologically significant lineage was that of the father, not the mother. We have seen above notions that kinship was passed through the male line and that the marker of this was surname. A passage contained in Chu Yu-tun's (1379–1439) play *Fu-lo chang* makes this clear. The scene in question impugns the respectability of actors. The specific insult that makes the point is a contrast drawn between families "where there is lineage, and traits of the fathers [and] the standing of the family is right" and families, like those of these actors, who take the mother's surname, "where the seed is not true."[74] The seventeenth-century writer Ku Yen-wu (1613–1682) notes the tendency of his contemporaries to take their mothers' surnames, a tendency he deplores as debasing human ethics.[75]

In the Ming, all children, including those born of adulterous unions, were legally regarded as the offspring of their fathers.[76] But under the T'ang, this was not the case. If both parents were of free *(liang)* status, then the child belonged to the father. But if the father was semiservile (for example, of *tsa-hu* status) and the mother free, the child would be free and would follow the mother. If both parents were semiservile, the child would belong to the mother. If the father was of full servile status (a *nu-pi*) and the mother was free, then the child would be enslaved *(mo-kuan)*.[77] These regulations are indicative of the highly stratified society of the T'ang dynasty. One was assigned to a family based on the conditions of one's conception and the status of one's parents. With the T'ang-Sung transition, the old aristocracy all but vanished. Indeed, the Sung dynasty author Shen Kua wrote that the society of the Six Dynasties and T'ang China more closely resembled the caste system of India than it did the society of Sung China.[78] Thus that the Ming code is less concerned with matters of status than is the T'ang code should come as no surprise.

The prohibition of adoption across surname lines finds an interesting parallel in the prohibition of marriage within the surname group. Like the adoption regulation, the marriage rules find their earliest expression in ancient ritual texts. The *Li-chi* specifies that people of the same surname may not marry one another and further states that if one buys a concubine and is unsure of her original surname, one must divine *(pu)* to determine it.[79] But the pre-Han *Tso chuan* suggests that an illness suffered by the duke of Chin is due to his having not one but four concubines who share his surname. The duke is urged to avoid the four offending concubines.[80] That the offspring of a couple who are of the same surname will not thrive is given in the *Tso chuan* as a criticism of a same-surname marriage.[81] The *Kuo yü* also counsels against marrying someone of the same surname.[82]

The T'ang code proscribed such marriages and attached to them a penalty of two years banishment. The Ming proscription provided for sixty blows with the heavy bamboo and dissolution of the marriage.[83] A regulation in the twenty-sixth year of the reign of the Hung-wu emperor (1393) reiterated the prohibition.[84] That same-surname marriage continued to be an issue is indicated by the persistence of essays condemning it. Ku Yen-wu discusses the significance attached by men of antiquity to the maintenance of surname lines and laments that in the previous hundred years, customs had changed.[85] He argues that surnames were granted by the sage kings of antiquity in accord with the five phases *(wu hsing),* which are, along with *yin* and *yang,* the principal generating agents in Chinese cosmology.[86] Ku argues that the union of people of like surname does not produce dynamic interaction. If two persons had the same surname, the dynamic forces of generation would not operate: their progeny would not thrive. Ku is connecting procreation with cosmology, just as did the medical texts such as the *Fu-jen liang-fang,* which we discussed above.

A Ch'ing official in the Ministry of Justice commented on violations of surname exogamy in marriage: "But since ignorant people are unaware of this prohibition, it often happens that in the isolated countryside, women of the same surname but different *tsu* [lineage] are taken as wives." He counselled that such marriages that had taken place be allowed to stand.[87] The disorder caused by improper blending of surnames was nothing compared to the disorder caused by human divorce.

Property

Cosmic generation is a rarefied and abstract concept. Adoption is also a practical matter, and one of the crucial components of the search for an heir is the problem of inheritance. Adoption of an outsider would mean that property would devolve to that outsider rather than to a kinsman. Family property is not merely wealth; it is the product of the labor of one's forebears and should be transmitted, intact if not enhanced, to one's descendants. Property is the tangible evidence of the corporate existence of the kin group. Thus alienation of property represents not only a diminution of wealth; it is also a dissipation of the collective labors of the kin group and a diminution of the respect due one's ancestors. Property and ancestral sacrifices were intimately connected; access to one implied participation in the other.

Although abstract arguments against adoption prior to the mid-Ch'ing are rarely phrased in terms of property, evidence of such concern is not hard to discern. Legal casebooks contain numerous examples of disputes about property caused by adoption. Evidence from biography also indicates that a desire to maintain control over property was one of the primary reasons for objecting to specific adoptions. Fictional texts also demonstrate a concern over property, as we shall see demonstrated at some length in chapter 4.

The Return of the Adopted Son

An adopted son who returned to the family of his birth was legally prohibited from taking with him property he had inherited from his adopted family, but the fear that he might abscond with property persisted. Ming and Ch'ing law prohibited a *yang-tzu* from taking property with him if he left his adoptive household.[88] Yüan law, however, had suggested that an adopted son who had been with his adopted family for ten or more years and had no family to return to might be permitted to retain a portion of the property if he left. But Shiga Shūzō stresses that this retention of property is more in the nature of a gift than of true inheritance.[89] Legal codes reflect the fear that a child might abandon his adoptive family. A child adopted from within the lineage who abandoned his adoptive parents was to be beaten a hundred blows.[90] A commentary to the Ming code explains that the penalty is due to the child's "turning his back on the benevolence of nurturing."[91] The family instructions compiled by Hsü San-chung, who received his *chin-shih* degree in 1577, caution against adopting an heir of a different surname precisely because he might desert the household.[92] The *Yü-li ch'ao-chuan,* a popular religious text dating from the nineteenth century but probably containing earlier strata, graphically illustrated the fear that property would devolve out of the family. In that text, the inhabitants of the fifth court of hell are condemned to observe for all eternity that "strangers are in possession of the old estate; there is nothing to divide among the children."[93] Another text in the *Yü-li* tradition illustrates the fear that greedy adoptive sons might appropriate family property and then neglect the sacrifices. The text tells of Mr. Chia who had two wealthy but childless uncles. The young man was named heir to them both. After their deaths, he neglected his ritual duties to his adopted fathers. The spirit of one of the uncles took possession of the young man. In a frenzy, the wayward adopted son took a knife and cut flesh from his body. He subsequently died, as did his own son. The family property, which he had inherited from his uncles, was divided.[94]

A kinsman from the child's natal family, it was feared, might use force to try to get him back. A case cited by the seventeenth-century author Li Yü (whose fictional treatments of adoption we shall discuss at some length in chapter 4) shows in his magistrate's handbook *Tzu-chih hsin-shu* (New Writings on Political Affairs) a magistrate ruling that such force was unjustified, punishing the offending kinsman and allowing the adopted child to remain with his second family.[95]

A child who returned to his natal family was not only depriving his adoptive family of property, he was engaging in an even more serious form of neglect—he was depriving the ancestors of his adoptive family of the sacrifices that were their due. The *Tung-ming pao-chi,* another popular religious text, describes a subhell, the "piercing bones" hell, reserved for adopted children who deserted their adoptive families and caused the sacrifices to be terminated. According to this text, a person deserting his adoptive family could expect to be hung on a hook to await iron dogs who would come and devour him.[96] The *Yü-li ch'ao-chuan* describes the third court of hell, among whose denizens are numbered those who fail in their duties as acting sons.[97] The mention of desertion in popular religious tracts and the vivid horror of the penalty indicate that the problem preyed on the popular imagination.

Yet though the descriptions of punishment for the returning son in the *Tung-ming pao-chi* seem unambiguous, there was some ambiguity about the best course of action for a man who had been adopted out of his natal family. The *Sung hsing-t'ung* recognizes this. Commentary to the provision permitting the adoption and change of surname of a child younger than three years old stipulates that if the child had been lost (rather than abandoned) and his original parents located him, then he was to be returned to the family of his birth. They must, however, pay a compensation to the family that raised him.[98] A lost child may be reclaimed; an abandoned child may not be. The implication is that parents who abandoned a child thereby forfeited their parental rights and could not reclaim the child.

A considerable body of opinion advocated that a person who had been adopted return to his natal family. The Sung dynasty Neo-Confucian Chu Hsi (1130–1200) wrote: "There may be difficulties over one's natural sense of obligation and gratitude, but the priorities and the principles of the matter are very clear."[99] But, as we shall see later, Chu Hsi was in some instances willing to be flexible. A fellow Sung Neo-Confucian, Chang Shih, praises one Hsü Heng-chung, who returned to his natal family.[100] Wu Hai, a late Yüan Confucian reformer, takes a rather harder line. In an essay entitled "Fu Te-ch'ien fu shih ming tzu hsü" (An Essay on the Return of Fu Te-ch'ien to his Surname, Given Names, and Bynames), Wu writes:

In Kuei-hsi there was a family named Ni, and in Chin-hsi a family named Fu. They lived very close together, and for generations had intermarried.

When one branch of the Ni family died out, they did not establish a member of the lineage as heir, but rather adopted a Ni. So the Ni had been the heirs of the Fu for five generations. There was one Hui, also known as Po-wen, who was distressed and worried about it. He presented the case to the Min magistrate Wu Hai, saying: "My ancestors were originally Fu, but since the time of Kao-tsu we have been heirs to the Ni. We are not Ni, yet we pose as Ni. We are originally Fu, yet we do not act as Fu. Of the two, which should I follow?" I responded, "According to the *Ch'un-ch'iu,* 'Chu extinguished Tseng.' The Ku-liang commentary says 'They took an heir from the Chu. It was not a military extinction. They established a person of a different surname to supervise the sacrifices. That was the road to their ruin.' Now, surnames *(shih)* are to distinguish lineages *(tsu),* and may not be changed. In order to succeed to a family *(tsung),* you must belong to it. You should return to them." He said: "Since the time of Kao-tsu, it has been more than a hundred years. Were I suddenly to return, it would cause confusion. Moreover, my kinsmen are not willing. Might I alone return?" I said: "If you today rectify a former error, how can people be confused? If your kinsmen are not willing, then why not return alone?" He said: "If I return, later generations may not follow me. What should I do about that?" I said: "Keep a genealogy. Narrate events from the time of Kao-tsu in a private genealogy. In the future, there will be those who understand ritual and esteem origins, who will follow you and return." He said: "Formerly the Ni entrusted me to be their heir. If I leave, it will cut off their line. What can I do?" I said: "When you return, establish an heir for the Ni, and marry him to a girl from the Fu family. Even in distant generations, the line will not be broken. Even though the surnames *(shih)* are distinguished, the ghosts will find rest. Have no doubt about it—ritual does not permit a person of a different surname to be heir. If later generations find fault with you, I will accept the responsibility."[101]

Several points in this passage are worth reiterating. First, Fu Te-ch'ien is approaching the magistrate not for legal advice, but for moral advice. He is not asking Wu Hai what he must do; he is asking what he ought to do. And the role of moral counselor is one that Wu Hai takes to with great relish. We should also note here that the Fu and the Ni are related by both marriage and adoption: both marriage and adoption are mechanisms of artifice that can be used to create kinship networks. We shall see further evidence of this in chapter 3. Wu finds the solution to Fu's problem in a classical text: the passage from the *Ch'un-ch'iu* he cites is one we shall discuss in more detail below. Wu is able to counter each of Fu's objections and concludes by invoking the ultimate authority of ritual texts. In his preface to the genealogy of the Hsüeh family, Wu Hai argues that adopted sons of a different surname should not be recorded, not even in an appendix, because they are unfilial and inhumane.[102] The moral opprobrium of the institution attaches itself to the individual. Individual moral action—the return to the family of birth—could correct the status irregularity. The moral universe of Wu Hai is simpler than that of Chu Hsi: since ritual does not permit cross-surname adoption, the adoptee is unfilial, inhumane, and ought to return, even after an interval of five generations.

Sacrifice and Efficacy

The need to maintain proper distinctions, concern with family property, and fear of desertion are all significant components to opposition to adoption across surname lines, but their significance is secondary. The most significant factor leading to the prohibition of cross-surname adoption in law, ritual, and clan rules was quite simply the conviction that it would not work. From the standpoint of law and ritual, the chief point of adoption was the continuation of the ancestral sacrifices. The ancestor would inevitably recognize the adopted heir as an outsider and refuse his sacrificial offerings. The clearest and most often cited classical formulation of this sentiment appears in the *Tso chuan*: "The spirits do not receive the sacrifices of those who are not of the same category *(fei lei)*, and people do not sacrifice to those who are not of their clan *(fei tsu)*."[103] This passage is often quoted by later writers on adoption in their arguments against cross-surname adoptions. A similar warning against sacrificing to spirits other than one's own ancestors is contained in the *Analects* of Confucius: "The Master said: 'For a man to sacrifice to a spirit which does not belong to him is flattery.' "[104] The *Li chi* reinforces the prohibition: "To offer sacrifices to those whom you ought not to offer sacrifices is called an abusive cult. An abusive cult does not bring happiness."[105]

The passage from the *Ch'un-ch'iu* cited by Wu Hai above, "The people of Chü extinguish Tseng,"[106] is more obscure in its reference to adoption, but the passage is frequently cited by later writers in their arguments against the practice. There is some ambiguity as to who the inappropriate heir was. The Ku-liang commentary to the *Ch'un-ch'iu* says: "They were not [literally] extinguished. They established a man of a different surname to oversee the sacrifices. That is what is meant by 'extinguished.' "[107] Fan Ning, a Chin dynasty commentator to the Ku-liang commentary, suggests that the boy was a nephew: "Tseng established a Chü nephew as heir. He was not of the same clan. The spirits would not accept his sacrifices. Therefore [the text] says 'extinguished.' "[108] The Kung-yang commentary adds: "A woman of the Chü family who was married to a Tseng wanted to establish one of her own *(li ch'i ch'u).*" A commentator to the Kung-yang named Ho Hsiu (129–182) explains: "At that time a woman of Chü was married as a concubine to Tseng. The principal wife had no sons, but had a daughter, who was married to a man of Chü, and they had a son. Because Tseng loved his concubine and had no sons, he established his daughter's son."[109]

Thus the Kung-yang and Ku-liang commentaries disagree as to who the heir was: but there is no disagreement that he was inappropriate and that the sacrifices were cut off because of him. Another commentator adds further that the heir should have been of the same surname.[110] Chang Shih writes that the Tseng were extinguished because their ancestors no longer had blood to eat because the sacrifices were not being received.[111]

The strictures against cross-surname adoption find vivid expression in a pair of stories purportedly dating from the Han dynasty. A story from the *Feng-su t'ung-i* corroborates the view that the ancestors would not receive the sacrifices of those who were unrelated. (This account, like the one discussed above about the two women quarreling over which was the true mother of a baby, is not contained in the *Feng-su t'ung-i* as it is presently constituted, but has been transmitted in the *I-lin* and the *T'ai-p'ing yü-lan.*) The wife of a man named Chou Pa gave birth to a daughter at the same time that a butcher's wife gave birth to a son. Chou's wife, unbeknownst to her husband, paid the butcher's wife to exchange children with her. Eighteen years passed, and Chou's official career flourished. He had an assistant named Chou Kuang, who had the ability to see ghosts. Chou Pa had long been away from his native place, and when an errand happened to send Chou Kuang in the vicinity of his home, he asked him to accompany Pa's son to perform the winter sacrifices to the ancestors and to take particular notice of whether the ancestors enjoyed the sacrifices. The text continues:

> So they went to the graves. The young man made the libations. Chou Kuang concealed himself in the back. He saw a butcher, in tattered clothing, his hair in a spiral knot, sitting crosslegged. He held a knife and was cutting meat.

When he returned home, Chou Kuang told Chou Pa what he had seen. Chou Pa responded by saying:

> "Go away and don't say anything." Then he grasped a sword and went into the hall. He asked his wife, "Why did you raise this son?" His wife fearfully said, "But you have often said 'This child in his features, disposition, and love of study resembles me!' Old man, are you tottering on your deathbed that you say such nonsense?" Weng-chung [Chou Pa] told her everything. He said: "If the sacrifices were like that, then he will not wear mourning for us. The ties between mother and son must be broken." His wife was at wit's end, and so told the story.

After Chou Pa's wife tells him of the switched children, the son is sent away, the daughter is found, and a cousin's son is adopted as heir. The text concludes by quoting and affirming the statement from the *Tso chuan* that we saw above: "That the spirits do not enjoy the sacrifices of those who are not of their kind is clear. What good does it do to adopt someone else's child?"[112] Chou Pa's wife switched babies with the butcher's wife because she clearly understood the need for a son. But she did not understand that not just any boy would do. She got her son, but the ancestors did not get an heir. The expulsion of the boy is dramatic proof of whose needs took precedence in the eyes of the *Feng-su t'ung-i*.

The Sung Neo-Confucian Ch'en Ch'un recounts a similar tale, which he writes is from the *Ch'un-ch'iu fan-lu* (Luxuriant Gems of the *Spring and Autumn Annals*), compiled by Tung Chung-shu (176–104 B.C.), although it is not contained in the text as presently constituted. A man reported on odd occurrences during his performance of sacrifices to his ancestors.

"What I have seen is very strange. There was a government official elaborately dressed in an official robe who hesitated and dared not come in. But a spiritual being *(kuei)* with disheveled hair and stripped to the waist, a butcher knife in hand, came forth bravely to accept the sacrifice. What was this spiritual being?" The master of the family did not understand the reason. An elder said that the family originally had no heir and adopted the son of a butcher from a different family as the heir who is now the master of the sacrifice. This was the reason why he could only influence and invite the heir of the butcher family to come.

Ch'en Ch'un goes on to explain the reason for this.

The ancestors of the family which he continued were not of the same kind of material force and of course there was no possibility of their interaction or influence and response.[113]

Neither Han dynasty text is compelled to explain why ancestors could not accept the sacrifices of those who were not related. But Ch'en Ch'un is so compelled. *Ch'i* (material force) is an important concept to Sung Neo-Confucians. Chu Hsi explains it as follows:

At death material force *(ch'i)* necessarily disintegrates. However, it does not disintegrate completely at once. Therefore in religious sacrifices we have the principle of spiritual influence and response. Whether the material force of ancestors of many generations ago is still there or not cannot be known. Nevertheless, since those who perform the sacrificial rites are their descendants, the material force between them is all the same. Hence, there is the principle by which they can penetrate and respond.[114]

Thus, continuity of *ch'i* is what enables the spirits of the ancestors to accept sacrifices. *Ch'i* is not solely a metaphysical concept; it is also a biological one. Metaphysics is firmly grounded in the physical world. *Ch'i* is a concept of prominence in both philosophical and obstetrical texts. As we saw in chapter 1, *ch'i* is physical substance, obtained only from one's biological father.[115] There can be no substitutions; the spirits of the ancestors cannot be fooled. From the standpoint of the ancestral spirits the requirement that the sacrificant be a kinsman is absolute. From the standpoint of legal and ritual texts, it is to appease these spirits that adoption exists. Variations of the institution that prevent the appeasements of the spirits may not be permitted.

The question of why adoption across surname lines is illegal in traditional China might be recast into the question of why the state has an interest in the naming of an heir, and, more particularly, why the state's interest lies in restricting adoption to those of the same surname. The answer lies in the state's identification of its own interests with those of the ritual foundations of Chinese culture. But the issue is far more complex than that. Chinese family law, if case law is included (and it must be), represents an amalgam of prescriptive law and custom. The battle between custom and prescription is perhaps in no case a fair one: in this particular case, over this particular issue, custom seems to have triumphed. But it is not a triumph without ambiguity, as we shall see in the pages that follow.

Adoption across Surname Lines: The Evidence

Despite the injunctions—legal, classical, and ghostly—against adopting across clan lines, people persisted in adopting children of different surnames as heirs. It is impossible to state with any certainty how common such adoptions were, but contemporary observers found the practice distressingly frequent. The late Yüan author Wu Hai, in the preface to a genealogy for a family named Wei, estimated that nonagnatic adoptions muddied the line of descent in fifty to sixty percent of all descent groups.[116]

The Chia-ching era edition of the Yung-chia county gazetteer says that those without heirs secretly (ssu) adopted persons of a different surname. The secrecy implies a consciousness of the illicit nature of the transaction. The Chinese word ssu implies that the adoption was done for the private gain of the adoptive father, that the adoption of an heir of a different surname was a pitting of private interests against the more general interests of the kin group. From what we have seen above, the disapproval of the gazetteer writer should not surprise us. What is of note here is that he records the practice.[117]

A Ch'ing edition of the T'ai-ts'ang gazetteer records that adoption of sons of a different surname as heir was especially common in Chia-ting. These sons were called kuo-fang, the adopting parents, hsüeh-pao. (For a discussion of hsüeh-pao, see chapter 3.) The gazetteer essay goes on to say that there are people who take their sons-in-law as sons, casting aside legitimate heirs and causing quarrels. Officials are urged to educate the people as to the error of their ways to prevent the practice.[118] Again, that adoption across surname lines is seen as objectionable and disruptive comes as no surprise. Yet the practice, according to the gazetteer writer, persisted.

Other indications of the frequency of adoption may be seen in administrative law. A regulation dated 1488 contained in the *Ta Ming hui-tien* spells out who was allowed to inherit the license permitting a merchant to participate in the government-run salt monopoly, should its holder die without a living son.

> His father and mother, if they are still living; his brothers, if they maintain a common residence and common stove and have not divided the property; his widow, if she has maintained her chastity and not remarried; his grandsons, if they are not adopted *(ch'i-yang kuo-fang).*[119]

The text goes on to specify that a remarried widow, uncles, concubines, nephews, as yet unmarried daughters, as well as any distant relatives who did not share a common residence were prohibited from inheriting the license. In addition to providing a kind of minimalist definition of the Chinese family, this regulation is of interest to us here for two reasons. First, the existence of the prohibition implies that adoption was fairly widespread. Second, even an adopted heir from within the surname group (a *kuo-fang* adoption) was prohibited from inheriting the license. Cross-surname adoptions appear in local gazetteers fairly frequently, and in genealogies. Adoptions across surname lines occur in countless stories and plays from the period. Thus it seems safe to say that cross-surname adoptions were neither rare nor exotic.

Adoption across Surname Lines: The Explanations

Why did people persist in adopting children of a different surname? In some cases, the families who adopted children of different surnames may have been unaware of the prohibition. We saw above a Ch'ing official commenting on ignorance of the prohibition of marriage among persons of the same surname. People who were ignorant of the prohibition of marriage within the surname group might well have been ignorant of the prohibition of adoption outside that group. But ignorance is of limited value as an explanation of the phenomenon of cross-surname adoption. Most of the cases on which information has been preserved involve the social and economic elite, who certainly would have been aware of the prohibition. Ch'in Hui-t'ien, the commentator to the *Wu-li t'ung-k'ao,* wrote that everyone knew that adopting as heir a son of a different surname diminished the adoptee's status *(shih-jen),* and there was no need to waste words on it.[120]

But ancestor worship made it absolutely mandatory that a family have an heir. A family with no heir, and with no possibility of adopting a related child, might ignore the prohibition and adopt an unrelated child to serve as heir and continuator of their ancestral sacrifices. Such a ruse might, after all, work just this once. The spirits could be fooled occasionally.

The sacrificant must be related to the ancestors to whom he sacrifices. But mere blood relation is not sufficient to insure that the ancestors will accept the sacrifices made to them. The *Shang shu* (Book of Documents), a pre-Han Confucian classic, tells us: "The spirits do not always accept the sacrifices which are offered to them; they accept only the sacrifices of the sincere."[121]

The notion that sincerity is an essential aspect of ritual is elaborated upon by Sung dynasty Neo-Confucians. Chu Hsi discussed the importance of sincerity on the part of the sacrificant and explicitly related it to adoption. Much Neo-Confucian philosophy is cast in the form of answers to practical questions posed by specific people. Hsü Chu-fu, perplexed by adoption, consulted Chu Hsi. Hsü began:

> "People frequently establish people of a different surname as heirs. I myself know of a family in the countryside, where there were two brothers. After the elder brother died with no heir, a person of a different surname was established as his heir. Later, the younger brother had a son, who carried out the sacrifices."

Hsü goes on to explain that the sacrifices should in fact have been carried out not by the heir of the younger brother, but by the heir of the elder brother. But in this case, the heir of the elder brother was an adopted son

of a different surname. Hsü suggests that in a case like this one, the son
of the younger brother and the adopted son of the elder brother share the
sacrificial duties.

Chu Hsi replied:

> "The setting up of heirs of different surname is indeed an abuse on the part
> of our contemporaries and is nowadays difficult to correct after it has hap-
> pened. However, it is all right if, when participating in the sacrifices, the
> adopted man has a totally sincere attitude of respect and filial piety."[122]

The moral world of Chu Hsi is more complex than that of Wu Hai,
whose response to Fu Te-ch'ien we saw above (pp. 65–67). Chu Hsi condemns cross-surname adoptions. But he is not an absolutist. Wu Hai is
adamant that the letter of the ritual be followed. But for Chu Hsi, sincerity *(ch'eng)* mediates between the prescriptions of the sacred text and the
exigencies of the actual situation. Sincerity matters more than does the
letter of the ritual. Thus filiality is not determined by biology, and the
family is not limited by constraints of blood. Sincerity of attitude must
supplement and might supplant kinship.

Traditional Chinese ideas about mutability may have influenced willingness to adopt children. The capacity of creatures to transform themselves from one species to another is posited in Chinese nature lore. The
Taoist classic *Chuang-tzu,* for example, opens with an account of the
transformation of the mythical *k'un* fish into the *p'eng* bird.[123] The
potential for transformation is demonstrated by a common term for
adopted child: *ming-ling-tzu.* A *ming-ling* is a mulberry insect. The
source of this odd nomenclature is a passage from the *Book of Odes:*
"The mulberry insect has young ones. / The sphex carries them away. /
Teach and train your young ones / And they will become as good as you
are."[124] The sphex *(kuo-luo),* also known as the solitary wasp, was
believed to be sterile. According to the *Fa-yen* (Model Sayings), a Han
dynasty text compiled by Yang Hsiung:

> The *kuo-luo* entreats the offspring of the *ming-ling:* "Resemble me! Resem-
> ble me!" After a while, they take him as a model *(hsiao).* It is like the seventy
> disciples of Confucius taking him as a model.[125]

The analogy of the disciples of Confucius adds a moral dimension to the metaphor. The transformation of the *ming-ling* into wasps is not merely an anomaly of nature: it is a transformation to which one might aspire. Li Kuei, a Chin dynasty commentator on the *Fa-yen,* elucidates the process of transformation.

> The *kuo-luo* bears no offspring. He takes those of the mulberry insect. In concealment he buries them. In darkness he nourishes them. He entreats them, "Resemble me! Resemble me *(lei wo)!*" After a while, they are transformed into wasps.[126]

The *T'ai-p'ing yü-lan* tells us further that the *ming-ling* is green and tiny, that it lives in grass and trees, and that the *t'u-feng* (a wasp) places the *ming-ling*'s offspring in a hole in wood. He entreats them, saying "Resemble me! Resemble me *(hsiang wo)!*"[127] This story of the transformation of caterpillar to wasp and the use of the term *ming-ling-tzu* for an adopted child quite clearly implies the transformation of the child's membership from one family to another. If an insect can change species, surely a child can change families.[128]

The functionalist approach to legitimacy may be seen operating in several realms. The concept of *cheng ming* (the rectification of names) suggests that a ruler may best attain legitimacy by acting in accordance with his role as ruler. In a passage from the *Analects,* when Duke Ching of Ch'i asks Confucius about government, Confucius replies that good government obtains "when the prince fulfills the role of prince, the minister fulfills the role of minister, the father fulfills the role of father and the son fulfills the role of son."[129] In other words, legitimacy is assured through the proper fulfillment of roles. The primary interpretation of this notion is that a father should act as a father ought and a son should act as a son ought. But the logic of the formulation might run in the other direction: he who acts as a son is a son; she who acts as a mother is a mother. We see Chinese ritual commentators applying this interpretation. As we have already seen, the Kung-yang commentary to the *Ch'un-ch'iu* states that he who succeeds (to property or to office) becomes in effect a son.[130] The *Han shu* cites the earlier formulations: "Ritual tells us that one who is chosen to succeed a man becomes in effect that man's son."[131] The *Hou*

Han shu biography of Hsieh Pi repeats the injunction.[132] Ssu-ma Kuang reiterated it during the Sung dynasty succession crisis known as "P'u-i," as did Ming writers during the Ritual Controversy.[133] As we have seen Minister of Rites Mao Ch'eng used the passage to urge the Shih-tsung emperor to have himself posthumously adopted by his predecessor's father.[134] One attains legitimacy as a ruler by acting as a ruler; one attains authenticity as a son by acting as a son. Succession, to property or to office, is one of the attributes of a son. As kinship implies inheritance, so inheritance implies rights of kinship.[135]

Earlier in this chapter, we cited evidence from classical texts to substantiate and explain the opposition to adoption. But the Chinese classical tradition is a rich and complex one, and references that may be interpreted as legitimizing adoption of persons of a different surname can be found as well. In a series of legends that Sarah Allan has described as myths reflecting the fundamental tension between the principle of merit and that of heredity, the sage-kings of antiquity, Yao, Shun, and Yü, chose men other than their sons to be their heirs.[136] The *Yao tien* section of the *Shang shu* explains Yao's motivations.

> The emperor said: "Who will search out for me a man according to the times, whom I may raise and employ?" Fang Ts'e said: "There is your son, Chu, who is highly intelligent." The emperor said: "Alas! He is insincere and quarrelsome—can he do?"[137]

The choice of merit over blood in these important myths demonstrates the limits of biological filiation.[138] The enduring significance of these myths for attitudes about adoption is clear in the early Ch'ing historian Ku Ying-t'ai's discussion of the Great Ritual Controversy. He argues that since the sage kings of antiquity felt no compunction to honor their biological fathers, Shih-tsung was wrong to insist on honoring his.[139]

Legal adoption practices may have encouraged the adoption of persons of different surnames. That unrelated persons with the same surname could legally be adopted must have had an enormous effect in ameliorating harsh attitudes toward the adoption of unrelated children. The presence, legally and ritually sanctioned, of these relatives within the household must have blurred any neat distinctions as to who was and was not a family member.

Rivalries within a clan may have facilitated acceptance of outsiders. James Watson has argued that twentieth-century families in the New Territories of Hong Kong preferred adopting an unrelated child to a distantly related child. Rather than consign property and the fate of the ancestors to the offspring of a rival segment of the clan, whose loyalties to his own family would never be totally obliterated, Watson found that people preferred to adopt complete strangers, who would be expected to make a clean break with their families of birth.[140]

There is some evidence that tension about adopting within the lineage did exist during the Ming and Ch'ing. The Ch'eng clan genealogy (which we shall examine in some detail in chapter 3) lists several cases in which a man could have adopted a nephew or a cousin's son but nonetheless adopted a child of a different surname.[141] The concern with adoption in other texts indicates that it was problematic. The *Yüan-shih shih-fan*, a Sung dynasty work, says that family discord is often caused by the refusal of people who have no sons to take their nephews as heirs or the unwillingness of others who have many sons to give them to their brothers.[142] Another indication that adoption was seen as problematic is found in the sixteenth-century author Yüan Huang's *Kung-kuo-ke* (Ledger of Merits and Demerits), in which serving as someone's heir accumulates fifty merits, whereas saving a life, preserving a woman's chastity, keeping someone from drowning a child, and preventing someone from having an abortion all are worth a hundred merits. Breaking off someone's line was a fifty-demerit offense, as was breaking up someone's marriage or abandoning someone's bones.[143] The eighteenth-century *Pu-fei-ch'ien kung-te-li* counsels that people in general should help others to preserve their family succession.[144] That popular texts were giving rewards and punishments for participating in adoptions indicates that there were occasionally problems with the institution.

Anecdotal evidence corroborates that there were disputes about adoption within the lineage. The Sung-chiang gazetteer tells of one Ch'in Hsi-chi, who had no sons and wished to adopt his poor nephew Ch'in Kuo-shih. Kuo-shih, for reasons the gazetteer does not specify, was unwilling to be adopted and continued to live modestly. When Hsi-chi died, the family members quarreled over who should inherit his property. Ultimately, the property was divided.[145] The T'ai-ts'ang gazetteer contains another anecdote indicating that merely because a procedure is legal does not mean it is without difficulty. Ch'en Hsi was rich and childless. He named his *tsu-hsiung*'s son as heir. (*Tsu-hsiung* may refer to a third cousin, or it may simply refer to a senior kinsman of one's own generation.) His relatives objected to the adoption, but Hsi overcame their objections.[146] Another edition of the T'ai-ts'ang gazetteer tells of Wang T'ao, who lived during the Wan-li era in K'un-shan. He was orphaned young. When he was nine, he was adopted by an uncle. There were relatives who plotted against him to obtain the property. T'ao was frightened and ran away. The adoptive grandfather solved the problem by dividing the property.[147]

An essay contained in a Ch'ing genealogy deplores the contemporary hesitation to adopt. The essayist quotes the *Shih ching* passage on the transformation of *ming-ling*s into spheges and adds, "If creatures *(wu)* are like this, how much more are people." He paints a desolate picture of childless old age and ancestors bereft of sacrifices. Why does this happen? Because women are not virtuous *(pu hsien)* and don't understand the greater good *(ta-i),* they object to adoption. Husbands would rather let their hands and feet to be cut off than speak harsh words to their wives. The essayist concludes that this is a ridiculous state of affairs and goes on to chronicle numerous adoptions that have occurred in his own family.[148]

Ch'in Hui-t'ien, the compiler and annotater of the *Wu-li t'ung-k'ao,* is equally hard on women. He blames the succession disputes that occurred in the Han and Ming dynasties on the jealousy and ambition of women. He argues that women use their private feelings of anger to cause chaos within the clan and cause the ancestral sacrifices to be broken off.[149] Nor is this a new development. The Sung author Yüan Ts'ai clearly implies that the difficulties in adoption he describes are a result of female intransigence,[150] and the late Yüan author Wu Hai complains that nonagnatic adoptions (among which he finds *wai-tsu* to predominate) are common because men "cannot overcome their wives' viewpoints."[151] And in the *Feng-su t'ung-i* account discussed above, Chou Pa's wife violates the rules of patrilineal descent, perhaps innocently, perhaps not, when she appropriates the butcher's son as her own.

The *Feng-su t'ung-i* does not castigate Chou Pa's wife. But Ch'in Hui-tien, Yüan Ts'ai, and Wu Hai all clearly regard women as a thorn in the side of the patriline. Dismissing for a moment the possibility that they are simply misogynists willing to attribute all manner of social irregularity to the selfish and unenlightened machinations of women, let us look at their statements. Margery Wolf has suggested, based on field work in Taiwan, that the way one perceives the structure of the Chinese family varies depending on one's point of view. She does not deny the centrality of the patriline. But the patriline is the Chinese family constructed from the male point of view. Wolf suggests that from the standpoint of its female members, the Chinese family can be seen as a "uterine family," composed of a woman and her children. While male family members might be expected to subordinate the interests of the conjugal unit to those of the patriline, women would be less likely to do so. This is not because women are unenlightened, but rather because such subordination is not in the best interests of what they conceive of as their families.[152] Adoption demands sacrifices in the uterine family for the benefit of the patrilineal clan. The greater good that Ch'in Hui-t'ien criticizes women for ignoring is the good of the patriline.

Although the adoption of a child of a different surname was illegal, violations of the law were rarely prosecuted. Although suits about property division and adoption are not rare, the guiding principles in their resolution were more complex than merely declaring the adoption illegal and dissolving it. The magistrate ruled on the case, often not even commenting that adopting an heir of a different surname was illegal. In a case brought before the magistrate Chu Wen, a man adopted the only sons of two different families. The magistrate reprimanded him for selfishly causing two family lines to be cut off to insure the perpetuation of his own family but did not condemn him for adopting across surname lines.[153] Custom was too deeply ingrained. Magistrates' reluctance to become involved in family matters doubtlessly compounded the problem. A proverb often quoted in Ming and early Ch'ing fiction says that even the wisest magistrate finds it difficult to arbitrate family disputes.[154] But nonenforcement is related to noncompliance; the law had, in large part, simply ceased to be relevant.

Contemporaries perceived this divergence between the ideal and the actual. Wu Hai (d 1387) deplored that in his native Fukien, the rules of adoption (as well as other familial relationships and burial practices) bore very little relationship to the formulations of Confucian orthodoxy. Wu believed that reform, led by men such as himself, was necessary to correct the lax practices.[155]

Furthermore, law and other normative texts give a particular refraction of social reality. Chinese family law and the normative texts that deal with the family are particularly interested in maintaining the patrilineal family structure. It is a view of the family that the patriarchal state and the patrilineal clan have an obvious interest in maintaining. But it is only one version of the truth about the traditional Chinese family. When individual families decided whom to adopt, the values of the state and of the clan were just one set of factors that contributed to the decision.

A related problem in our interpretation of the legal sources and in our assessment of the significance of the divergence between legal and normative texts on the one hand and actual practice on the other hand is the fundamentally conservative character of Chinese law.[156] Adoption was not the only family practice in which law diverged widely from custom. Ming and Ch'ing law both explicitly prohibited a son from establishing an independent residence (and dividing the family property) while his parents or grandparents were still alive.[157] Yet separate residence, as the seventeenth-century author Ku Yen-wu noted, was common.[158] And, as we saw in chapter 1, the practice of concubinage was often at odds with the laws that purported to regulate it.

Although each dynasty compiled its legal code anew, that code was firmly based on that of preceding dynasties. The Ming founder ordered scholars to review the T'ang code, in preparation for the writing of the Ming code.[159] Two modern Chinese scholars, Tai Yen-hui and Liu Ch'ing-po, writing on the subject of the history of adoption in China, posit that in antiquity the sole purpose of adoption was to maintain the ancestral sacrifices. Therefore it was essential that the adopted child be of the same surname. But, these scholars argue, as the motives for adoption became more diverse, it was less important that the child be of the same surname.[160] Meanwhile, the legal and ritual structure remained, on paper, the same. The divergence between law and custom is at least partially an artifact of the change in custom in light of relatively stable law.

By the Ming, the aristocracy of blood and birth had almost completely disappeared. The expansion of the examination system, the growth of urbanism, and increasing commercialization contributed to a more fluid society. The blood lines of one's father were less significant than they had been during the T'ang. Growing acceptance of adoption across surname lines is evident. The Grand Secretary Hsü Hsüeh-mo (1522–1594) wrote in a short text on family management:

> All babies know to love their parents. But if you send them out to be nursed by another, will they recognize their real mother? And when they grow older, all children know to respect their brothers. But if they are adopted out at an early age, will they be able to tell who are their real brothers?[161]

Hsü seems neither to be praising nor blaming the phenomenon he is commenting on: he is simply reporting that perceptions of kinship are contingent upon coresidence.

The Ming writer Ch'en Chi-ju expresses the concept of assimilation of the heirs of a different surname by quoting a proverb:

> If a yellow chicken lays an egg, and a black chicken hatches it, you know that it is the child of the black chicken. You do not know that it is the child of the yellow chicken.[162]

Confucianism is concerned with order and with symbols. It is a hierarchical social system in which everything has its place. Opponents of cross-surname adoption were arguing for an abstract sense of order and for a system of values in which the wishes of the dead ancestors were a driving force. They inhabited a symbolic world in which the perceived wishes of the dead ancestors would transmute themselves into ghosts. They are powerful images, and it is a potent ideology. But it is not the only ideology. The potential for transformation from outsider to insider, from stranger to kinsman, which was denied in the *Kuo yü* and the *Tso chuan,* is affirmed by the mythology of the *ming-ling* and the aphorism of Ch'en Chi-ju.

3

Case Studies

We have thus far dealt chiefly with abstractions, with ritual codified into law, with symbolic systems that conjure ghosts and permit insects to change their species. These abstractions have as their point of departure (and point of return) actual behavior and concrete events. This section will begin with a discussion of adoption procedures. Before moving on to a discussion of a series of actual adoptions, we will briefly discuss the practice of registering bondservants as adopted children. Although the primary focus in this chapter will be on adoption across surname lines, some attention will be paid to adoption within the surname group. Adoptions recorded in the genealogy of a family named Ch'eng from Hsin-an will be looked at in some detail. Then we will look at adoptions of *wai-tsu* (relatives through a female line), uxorilocal marriage, and finally, the adoption of non-kin.

Adoption Procedures

Although adopting an heir was an act that had implications for the entire kin group, the authority to make the decision was restricted. An edict issued in the Hung-chih era (1488–1505) forbade relatives *(tsung-tsu)* from interfering in the choice of an adoptee of the same surname. An edict of the Wan-li era (1573–1619) repeats the injunction, adding the stipulation that the adopted child must be of the proper generational order.[1] But the repetition of the injunction may well indicate kinsmen with a propensity to interfere.

In adoption, as with virtually all important transactions in Chinese society, there was a go-between. There seems to have been no shortage of children available to these go-betweens. Traditional sources are replete with references to conditions so bad, poverty so dire, that people sold their children.² A regulation of 1281 contained in the *T'ung-chih t'iao-ko*, a Yüan collection of administrative law, notes that it had been the custom of people in Wu and Yüeh (classical names for the Chekiang area) for people to pawn their wives and sell their children. The children might be adopted, or they might be resold. The custom was to be strictly prohibited.³ A century later, in May of 1385, the Ming founder ordered the repurchase at government expense of the sons and daughters sold by the starving people of Honan.⁴ But the practice of selling children persisted. In the mid-Ming, the official Hai Jui (1514–1587) reported that the poor people in his district were forced to sell their wives and children.⁵ The scholar and official Feng Ying-ching (1555–1606) reported that in 1594 during a famine in T'eng-hsien in Shantung, people sold their daughters to be concubines or slaves of the rich for one *ch'ien* of silver or a hundred copper coins. Others, starving, gave away their wives and children in exchange for a meal.⁶ The catastrophic social conditions, famine and warfare, of the early seventeenth century made the situation even worse. Liu Mao reported that during a severe drought in Shensi in 1628, people sold their wives and abandoned their children.⁷ An edict of 1632 forbade Buddhist and Taoist monks from purchasing persons to serve as their pupils.⁸ The English traveler Peter Mundy reported in 1637 in the area north of Macao that poor people were selling their children into servitude "to pay their Debtts or to Maiynetaine themselves."⁹ The 1641 edition of the T'ung-hsiang gazetteer reports the "sale of child slaves and women for not more than 2,000 cash apiece; abandonment of little children; active infanticide; cannibalism."¹⁰ In the seventeenth century, Ku Yen-wu quotes the report of the sixteenth-century author Lao K'an that the residents of Peking "pawned their wives and sold their children to flatter the Buddha with an offering of incense."¹¹ Ku also reports that because people in Sung-chiang were not able to earn enough to pay their taxes, many of them sold their children.¹² Thus we can document that children were on occasion sold.

A Ch'ien-lung era gazetteer from Hsiang-shan in Chekiang indicates the extreme reluctance of people to sell their children, but confirms that children from impoverished households might be adopted by those better off.

Even if they suffer from extreme poverty, they are not willing to sell their sons and daughters to be serfs and maidservants. Sometimes there are years of bad harvests and they do sell their sons. The rich families may also bring them up as adopted sons.[13]

We should note that this gazetteer maintains a distinction between the sale of children and their adoption. Although it seems clear that there was a market in children, the Ming evidence does not permit us to draw firm conclusions about its extent or functions.

A child might be kidnapped for later sale. The Sung author Yüan Ts'ai advocates care in ascertaining the origins of servant girls. He warns: "There is always the danger that she is a commoner's daughter who was kidnapped."[14] James Watson and Arthur Wolf each report modern tales of dealers in children who were possibly also tea or salt merchants.[15] The prevalence of the custom is not verifiable, especially for earlier time periods. Kidnappers rarely leave account books. But there are references to the practice that confirm its existence. Lin Hsi-yüan, who received his *chin-shih* degree in 1517, defended the Portuguese against charges that they trafficked in children. Besides, he added in an aside that undercut his defense, the Chinese who kidnapped and sold the children were more to blame than were the Portuguese who merely bought them.[16] A popular religious text, the *Yü-li ch'ao-chuan,* condemns to the seventh court of hell those persons who kidnapped human beings for sale.[17] Legal texts also indicate that children who strayed from their parents were in a potentially dangerous position. Ming and Ch'ing law both stipulate that lost, strayed, or fugitive children were to be turned over to a magistrate immediately.[18] The Ch'ing code explicitly prohibits the adoption of such children, specifying a penalty of ninety blows and exile for two years.[19]

Adoptions, even those within a surname group, frequently involved a monetary transaction. The monetary aspect was generally more significant when the adoption was contracted between two unrelated parties. The money was sometimes called *p'in-chin,* the same term used for brideprice.[20] Herbert Giles has reported that the money paid for the purchase of a child for adoption was called "ginger and vinegar money," because a dose of ginger and vinegar was customarily administered to a woman who had just given birth.[21]

The *p'in-chin* paid in adoptions had the utilitarian function of compensating the family that bore the child for expenses incurred while raising it and for the future loss of the child's labor. But the transaction also had a symbolic effect, marking the ritual transfer of the child from one lineage to another or from one branch of a lineage to another. V. R. Burckhardt observed that in Kuangtung province in the nineteenth century it was customary for the adopting father to give the go-between a gift of a kitten or puppy or a mug or vase along with the payment for the child. The small animal symbolized the exchange of a life for a life, the crockery of a mouth for a mouth.[22]

That a monetary transaction was involved does not mean that all adoption was equivalent to purchase. Marriage, after all, involved a reciprocal exchange of wealth in the form of dowry and brideprice. But there was a degree of fluidity between the status of adopted child and that of bondservant. The ambiguity is compounded by the fact that bondservants were often called *yang-tzu* or *i-tzu* and that the contracts for adoption were often identical in form to those for the sale of people.[23]

Let us digress a moment to address the problem of bondservants directly. Under Ming law, commoners *(min)* were not permitted to own bondservants *(nu-pi)*. The 1397 code specified a penalty of a hundred blows for the illicit ownership of *nu-pi* and provided for their manumission. The commentary to the code explains the reason for the prohibition: if commoners owned bondservants, the distinction between noble *(kuei)* and base *(chien)* would be muddied.[24]

But during the course of the Ming it was common for poor peasants to join the households of their better-off neighbors as bondservants, thereby obtaining protection and escaping taxation. To conceal their illegal status, persons in the households of wealthy commoners who actually had the status and function of bondservants were often known as *i-nan* and *i-fu* (adopted men and women).[25] That these *i-nan* and *i-fu* were commonly granted their masters' surnames was reported by Tu Mu (1460–1525).[26] The practice is shown in a song collected by Feng Meng-lung in his *Shan-ko* (Mountain Songs): "The master is named Chi / Older sister is named Chi / They've even bestowed the maid *(ya-t'ou)* with the surname Chi."[27]

Mi Chu Wiens has convincingly argued that the granting of surnames to bondservants was not an empty gesture and demonstrates that this category of "adopted sons" did fit into the broad family structure.[28] Ming writers corroborate that limited kin ties (or at least kinlike obligations) could be established with *nu-pi*. According to Chang Lü-hsiang (1611–1674), a scholar from T'ung-hsiang, families were obliged to treat their bondservants well and select spouses for them.[29] Wang Meng-chi went a step further in describing his relationship with his bondservants: "Because of mutual reliance, we are one family."[30] The modern scholar Oyama Masaaki agrees that the bestowal of surnames on one's bondservants was an act of significance, but differs in his interpretation of that significance. He suggests that the paternalism implied by the bestowal of surname led to a greater degree of control over the *nu-pi*.[31]

Some Ming writers perceived this assimilation into the family to be real and sharply attacked it. The practice of bestowing one's surname on one's bondservants attracted the particular ire of Shih T'ien-chi.

> Bondservants and family servants each have their own surnames. Despite differences between the eminent and humble, each lineage has its main and branch families, and servants should never be permitted to adopt our surname; not only would it end their line of descendants, but it would cause the false to be mixed with the true. Our lineage would be thrown into disorder as the years pass, and the children increase in number.[32]

Shih's argument echoes those about the sanctity of surnames we saw in chapter 2.

That bondservants occupied a middle ground between family members and hired labor and that such bondservants could use their position to achieve extraordinary power has been amply demonstrated elsewhere. Perhaps the most notorious example of powerful bondservants is those of the family of Tung Ch'i-ch'ang, whose rapaciousness precipitated a revolt among his ordinary tenants.[33] What is of primary interest to us here are the statements by reformers and observers that comment on the implications of calling a bondservant an adopted son. Chang Lü-hsiang has recorded a story showing that genuine family feeling did occasionally exist between bondservant and master. One of Ch'en Ch'ien-ch'u's field hands died. Ch'en wept in deep mourning, ate his food without tasting it, and when he spoke to people, tears fell. He reportedly said: "Bondservants *(chia-p'u)* are called adopted sons and they should act according to moral obligation between father and son."[34]

But other writers inform us that Ch'en's solicitude was unusual. Hsiao Yung wrote that because the law prohibited commoners *(min)* from owning bondservants, the servants were called adopted sons and daughters. He wrote that bondservants looked on their masters as parents. That being the case, how could the master fail to reciprocate and regard the bondservant as a child? But, he continues, women are deluded *(mi)* and treat their bondservants with little benevolence. They make their bondservants sit by the heat of fire in the summer and cause them to suffer from the cold in winter. If they cooked badly, the women would beat them, smashing their faces and breaking their skin. Hsiao ends by recommending that husbands be more vigilant in the supervision of their wives, so that virtue might accumulate and the family would continue to have bondservants for generations to come.[35]

Hai Jui was also concerned with the welfare of *i-nan*. He wrote that unregistered *i-nan* accounted for a significant portion of the population, a phenomenon in Chiangnan that had been noted more than a century earlier by Chou Ch'en (1382–1435).[36] While Hai Jui was magistrate in Ch'un-an (Chekiang) between 1558 and 1562, he wrote:

> As regards bondservants: everyone everywhere is a commoner of the empire. The law limits the bestowal of bondservants to the families of meritorious officials. The other ordinary families have only hired laborers or have adopted *i-nan*. Hired laborers only work for a term of months and days. Those called adopted sons are like a person's own sons. They are therefore assigned seniority among the elder and younger brothers, according to age, and rank as uncles with respect to the grandsons. They provide labor and are provided for, which is a natural principle. Although it is impossible for them to be loved equally with the others, yet their clothing, food, marriages, and mourning should not be very different from one's own sons and grandsons. I have heard that in Chien-te county (in Chekiang) the people treat their adopted sons more or less in conformity with the law. Customs are not thus in Ch'un-an. Here they treat them simply as bondservants, and this needs to be reformed.[37]

In 1588, the legal status of bondservants was modified. A *nu-pi* who had been bought before he was fifteen and who had been fostered with benevolence *(en-yang)* for a long time, or one who had been bought after the age of sixteen but who had been given a wife by his master, was to assume the status of his master's child. If these conditions were not met, then the status of the former bondservant depended on the status of the former master. If the master was a commoner, then the status of the former bondservant would revert to that of a hired laborer. If the master was an official, then the bondservant would remain a bondservant.[38]

I do not mean to suggest that bondservants who were called *i-nan* were in fact treated as family: the evidence clearly indicates otherwise. But the way in which late Ming thinkers wrote about the problem of *i-nan* and the degree to which they might be incorporated into the family shows one way in which the issue of the incorporation of outsiders into the family might be viewed.

Let us return to adoption. Striking symbolism is reported in a practice known as *hsüeh-pao,* reported in a Ch'ing dynasty edition of a gazetter from T'ai-ts'ang and described in some length in the *Ch'ing-pai lei-ch'ao,* a text containing all manner of information on customs and practices during the Ch'ing dynasty.

> I have heard that there are those who in advance seek out pregnant women and then themselves feign pregnancy. When the time to give birth comes, they are also present at the birth-mat and are attended by a midwife. As soon as the pregnant woman has given birth, they take the child and go home. As soon as the midwife receives the child, the woman who has feigned pregnancy cares for it and hires a wetnurse to feed it. This is commonly called *hsüeh-pao.*[39]

Hsüeh-pao literally means "bloody embrace." The feigned pregnancy conceals from the community the knowledge that the child is adopted. But the mimicry of birth, the adopting mother on the birthing-mat, attended by a midwife, does more than that: it is an attempt to deny the artifice of adoption.

More ordinary adoption rituals might include a ceremonial banquet. Banquets were often ceremonial markers of transitions, such as weddings, in traditional China. Hugh Baker has reported that the adopting father in the New Territories of Hong Kong was obliged to give a banquet for his relatives and friends to mark formally the entry of the child into the family.[40] Banquets to mark the adoption of a child are also recorded in the Ming novel *Chin p'ing mei*.[41] And we shall see more evidence of adoption banquets in fiction in the pages that follow. Judicial intervention was sometimes invoked. In the *Lung-t'u kung-an*, a sixteenth-century collection of crime fiction, Chao Chih-chun asks for approval from a magistrate before approaching Shen Tai about adopting him.[42] Another case where judicial intervention is sought is to be found in the *Hao ch'iu chuan*. Kuo wants a judge to name him the adoptive son of Shui Chu-i. The judge is initially willing to help, but when he learns that Kuo has designs on Shui's daughter, he refuses the request.[43] The ceremony for formalizing an adoption might be as simple as performing respects to the father and might include the exchange of gifts. Or the procedure might be more elaborate, as was the adoption of Ni T'ing-hsi in the eighteenth-century novel *Ju-lin wai-shih*. That adoption involved a contract, the exchange of money, and the selection of an auspicious day for the child to change households.[44] We will examine some procedures in fictional adoptions in some detail in the next chapter.

A magistrate named Teng from Ch'ang-ping hsien in southern Fukien described the adoption procedure there at the beginning of this century.

> It does not matter if a man adopts a person of the same or different surname as heir. In either case, he has to pay a substantial sum of money to the boy's natural parents. This money is known as *p'in-chin*, and the person who arranges the adoption is called a matchmaker. Generally speaking, the amount paid is larger for a boy of a different surname, but in some cases amounts as large as five hundred *yüan* are paid for boys of the same surname who are less than eight years old.[45]

The similarities with the marriage transaction are striking. The term used for the adoption payment is the same as that used for brideprice; the go-between is referred to in the same way. We have already discussed the ways in which criminal law treats adopted sons of a different surname and daughters-in-law as analogous. Here again we see how the ritual and symbolism of adoption more closely suggest the entrance into the family via marriage than they do entrance through birth.[46]

The Ch'eng Genealogy

Genealogies have increasingly been used by social historians of traditional China as sources of information on kinship and demography.[47] Genealogies are ideological documents, documents through which the kin group both defines its membership and delineates relationships among members. The overt ideological predisposition of the genealogy is patrilineal. Consequently, adult males are the members of the kin group who are of the most interest to the genealogy. Persons who are peripheral to the genealogical construction of the patriline, such as males who die young and all females, are less likely to be entered in the genealogy than are males who lived to adulthood. Adopted sons, likewise peripheral, may not be fully entered in the genealogy. Indeed, we have already noted statements that adopted sons should not be entered into genealogies. Nonetheless, some genealogies do yield information about adoption.

Let us turn to one such genealogy. The genealogy of the Hsin-an Ch'eng lineage compiled by Ch'eng Hui-min in the last decade of the sixteenth century records more than 280 adoptions. Fifteen of these adoptions involve persons with surnames other than Ch'eng; the remainder are from within the surname group. Hsin-an, in Anhui province, was a relatively highly commercialized area, and merchants there may well have followed kinship practices that deviated from established legal and customary norms.[48] Indeed, it seems likely that adoption may have been used as a way of acquiring heirs to set up branch houses: an adopted son is more reliable than an ordinary employee, yet more expendable than a biological son. Despite the possibility that this particular genealogy reflects information on practices that deviate from the norm and despite the fact (common to many genealogies) that the quality of the information is uneven, examining this particular genealogy will be useful. The large number of adoptions within a single lineage enables us to analyze the dynamics of adoption within that lineage in some detail.

The entries in the genealogy are sparse: in many cases, nothing is recorded but the man's name and his position in the family tree. Often the dates of his birth and death will be recorded. Less often, the name of his wife will be recorded for posterity. Occasionally her birth and death dates will be recorded, especially if her life was long. An adopted son will frequently be noted as an adopted son. In this particular genealogy, *chi-tzu* is the notation used for a son who has been adopted in and *ch'u-chi* is the notation for a son who had been adopted out. That a son is generally recorded under both his natal and adoptive fathers enables us to trace the relationship between the two men. That the birth date of most men in the genealogy is given enables us to determine the position in sibling order of the man adopted out.

The first question that the information in the genealogy permits us to address is that of the relationship between the natal father and the adoptive father. In 127 cases, the relationship cannot be determined, either because one of the two fathers party to the adoption transaction is not named or because a common ancestor for them cannot be found. Although one must be cautious about drawing conclusions from an absence of information, it seems unlikely that adoptions falling in this category involved brothers or even first cousins. In those cases, the relationship would probably have been clear and traceable. In 151 cases, the relationship between the two fathers is clear. In 89 of these cases, the two men were brothers. In 16 of the cases, they were first cousins. In the remaining 46 cases, they were more distant relatives.[49] Thus there seems to have been a preference for brothers' sons as adoptive sons, although the preference was by no means overwhelming. Adult brothers often lived in a common household, pooling their resources. That there is a sharp drop in preference from brother to cousin as an adoptive son may indicate that cousins were regarded as much more distant relatives than were brothers. Indeed, in this particular genealogy, there were almost as many adoptions of persons of a different surname as there were of first cousins from within the lineage. Shiga Shūzō has pointed out that, popular conceptions of the Chinese extended family notwithstanding, it was extremely rare for adult cousins to share a common household.[50]

The genealogy also enables us to determine the place in the sibling order of sons who were adopted out. As might be expected, eldest sons were rarely given out in adoption. Although primogeniture with regard to the inheritance of property was not widespread in China, there did exist a kind of ritual primogeniture, in which the eldest son assumed a more important position relative to the ancestral cult than did his brothers, hence the reluctance to relinquish such a son. In families with three or more sons, the youngest son was rarely adopted out. Thus it seems that there was a preference for adopting out middle children.[51] The fathers of the sons who were adopted out were typically in their mid-thirties when the child who was to be adopted out was born.[52] The adopting fathers were generally somewhat older.[53] This suggests that a man was often in his forties before he despaired of engendering a child of his own. The expectation that a very young man would not adopt a child was voiced in the Yüan code, where it was specified that a man had to be forty before he would be permitted to adopt a child.[54] Although the Ming code contained no such provision, the data from this genealogy suggest that it was nonetheless customary to defer adoption until the adopting father was in his forties. This calls to mind the provision in the Ming code that a man could not acquire a concubine until he had reached the age of forty with no children. That the natal fathers were somewhat younger also shows a movement of offspring from younger members of a generation to older members of that generation, illustrating the importance of seniority within a generation.

The genealogy, with its bare-bones recitation of names and dates, invites questions that the information in the text itself is inadequate to answer. The explanations of adoption offered by the legal and ritual texts—that it was to get an heir and to perpetuate the ancestral sacrifices—are not adequate to explain all the cases recorded in the Ch'eng genealogy. Men whom we know to have had surviving sons sometimes adopted a son. Ch'eng Hsing-shan (1366–1414), for example, had a son who grew to maturity, but Hsing-shan nonetheless adopted another son.[55] Other men, such as Ch'eng Pieh-ling, adopted more than one son.[56]

Other men might relinquish more than one son in adoption. Ch'eng Huai-te had three sons, two of whom were relinquished in adoption to his brothers.[57] Ch'eng En (b 1430) had five sons, three of whom were adopted out. One was given to his brother, but the other two were given to distant relatives. There are numerous other cases as well.[58] It is likely that a man who surrendered three of his sons for adoption, two of them to distant cousins, was induced to do so by poverty or a position of powerlessness within the lineage. Adoption might function as a leveling mechanism, removing children from poor households where they were a drain on resources and placing them in the households of the better-off.

Perhaps it is the mechanism working within one lineage that we see here. Shiga has suggested that, in fact, this redistribution of human resources was a major function of adoption in traditional China.[59] We shall see some fictional examples of the adoption of sons from humble backgrounds into well-to-do families in chapter 4.

In several of the adoptions in this genealogy, the death of the adoptive father antedates the birth of the adoptive son, sometimes by a year or so, sometimes by several decades. The purpose of these posthumous adoptions, which were not uncommon, was to insure that the spirits of the dead man and his ancestors would receive sacrifices. A widow with no sons was supposed to appoint an heir for her dead husband, in consultation with the lineage elders.[60] Although marriage (and the resulting capacity, even if unfulfilled, to father children and hence become an ancestor) was normally a prerequisite to the appointment of a posthumous heir, certain categories of unmarried men (those who had died in battle, for example, or those whose fiancées chose to live as chaste widows) were also entitled to an heir.

The obligation of a widow to adopt an heir served her own interests as well as those of the spirit of her deceased husband. Indeed, there are cases where a widow adopted a son of her husband's concubine, thus demonstrating the importance of the son to the widow herself. A concubine's son was recognized as a legitimate heir, and in the absence of any other son, was fully qualified to continue the ancestral sacrifices.[61] A widow without children occupied a precarious position in her husband's family. She had severed the ties that bound her to her natal family when she married, yet the ties that bound her to her husband's family might be irrevocably weakened at his death. Children helped to solidify her position.[62]

Occasionally a posthumous adoption would occur long after the death of the adoptive father. Ch'eng Ning (1394–1465) was named heir to his kinsman Erh-wen, who had died in 1372 at the age of five.[63] Ch'eng K'o (1402–1472) was also named heir to Erh-wen.[64] We have no information as to why two men were named heir to Erh-wen. Another case involving a substantial delay was that of a man who died in 1432. The nephew who was appointed his heir was not born until 1458. The child appointed heir had an older brother, who could have been appointed heir to his uncle, but was not.[65] The choice of the second son as heir probably reflects the reluctance to relinquish a first-born son which we discussed earlier. Widows did not unfailingly appoint heirs for their deceased husbands. The widow of Ch'eng Wen-yün (1340–1363) survived him by fifteen years. Yet his heir, the son of a cousin, was not born until 1388, well after her death.[66] Numerous other cases of this sort appear in the genealogy. These posthumous adoptions long after the death of the adopting father clearly indicate the need for an heir to rectify patterns in the world of the spirits. Posthumous adoption has an analogue in spirit marriage, a form of marriage in which a living woman might be married to a dead man or two dead people might be married one to another. Kinship ties are not for this world only.[67]

Most of the sons adopted posthumously were agnatic kin of the proper generation. Occasionally, a man's younger brother or cousin might be adopted, violating the rules of precedence for proper generation.[68] The posthumous adoption of an unrelated child as heir was unusual. When the interests of the spirits were paramount, as they were with posthumous adoptions, ritual correctness was strictly observed.

The Adoption of *Wai-tsu*

As we have seen, however, the interests of the human actors often took precedence over those of the spirits, and in those cases ritual was not always followed. In Chinese ritual, descent was viewed as following through the surname group, that is to say, through the male line. As we saw above, there was a substantial body of opinion that held that biology, like ritual, followed the male line. Relatives through a female line were known as *wai-tsu,* "outside kin." The distance implied by the term itself is reflected in mourning relationships. The mourning relationships between a man and his maternal and affinal relatives were not as close as the mourning relations that bound him to his agnatic relatives. But the importance of agnatic kinship should not blind us to the significance of maternal and affinal networks. In the absence of a male heir, one could use these female kinship networks to obtain one.

The use of female kin networks to get an heir, as well as the use of adoption to create kinship networks, is amply demonstrated by the Ch'eng genealogy. Ch'eng Hung-i (b 1413) had six sons, one of whom was given in adoption to the Ch'ens, the family of his mother.[69] Ch'eng Hsü-wen (1347–1405) had five sons, one of whom was adopted by the Li family from Ch'ien-chai. Hsü-wen himself was married to a woman from the Fang lineage, but other males in his branch of the family were married to Ch'ien-chai Lis.[70]

There are other examples as well. Ch'eng Shao had no heir, so he adopted (*wei tzu*: took as a son) Wen-chi, a son of the T'ung lineage from Hai-chuan. The name Wen-chi is an appropriate generational name for a son of Ch'eng Shao. (Men of the same generation within a family often shared a common character or portion of a character in their given names to indicate their position within the family. Adopted sons might be given the appropriate generational name, indicating that they ranked alongside their siblings and cousins, or they might be given a different name that rendered them distinct.) Numerous men in this branch of the Ch'eng lineage married women from this particular T'ung lineage.[71] Ch'eng Hsiao-hsien had no sons, so he adopted a son of the Shang-lin Fang family as heir. Hsiao-hsien's brother had five sons, but Hsiao-hsien preferred to adopt an outsider.[72] In this case, the marriage relationships with the adoptive family, though extant, do not seem to be close.[73] Ch'eng Yu-jen (1335–1385), one of four sons of I-ch'eng, was adopted out to a family named Shao. A brother of I-ch'eng was married to a woman named Shao, as were several other men in the lineage.[74]

An even more interesting indication of the mechanisms of adoption occurs in the cases of Ch'eng Shao-cheng and Ch'eng Ta-i. They were both sons of Ch'eng Feng-chi, who had eight sons. Shao-cheng was adopted into the P'an family. Ta-i was adopted into the Hu family. Prior to these adoptions there seem to have been no special marriage relationships between the Ch'eng lineage and that of either P'an or Hu. But subsequent to the adoptions, special marriage relationships do emerge. Of thirty-two marriages contracted by the brothers and cousins of the adopted men and their offspring, six were with women surnamed P'an and nine were with women surnamed Hu.[75]

Thus the creation of adoptive ties seems to parallel the creation of affinal ties. There seem to have been certain families with whom the Ch'engs were interested in allying, and they used both adoption and marriage to create the alliances.

But we should not assume that all cross-surname adoptions recorded in the Ch'eng genealogy are with people with whom there also exists a marriage relationship. Ch'eng Hsüeh-wen adopted a boy of the Wang lineage, and there are no recorded marriages of men from his branch of the lineage with women from that family.[76] Ch'eng Wen-t'ung was adopted out to the Chi lineage, with whom his family seems to have had no special marriage relationships.[77]

Although the bulk of the adoptions recorded in the Ch'eng genealogy are between agnatic kinsmen, an intriguing number of them involve people who are related not through the male line, but through a female line *(wai-tsu)*. The late Yüan author Wu Hai, in his criticism of the contemporary prevalence of adoption noted in his preface to the genealogy of a family surnamed P'an: "Today people do not follow the ritual rules; they take a son-in-law, a daughter's son, or other affinal relatives to serve as heir."[78] In setting forth the rules for his own genealogy, Wu felt it necessary to say that people who set up a son-in-law or a daughter's son as heir would not be recorded, and the family would be regarded as extinct *(chüeh)*.[79] Jerry Dennerline has suggested, based on his study of elite families in Chia-ting during the Ming, that adoption among affinal kin was a strategy among newcomers to the elite. Marriage ties might be reinforced and cemented by adoption ties.[80] Let us now turn to an examination of a variety of other sources to see how adoption of *wai-tsu*, of relatives through a female line, is portrayed.[81]

Gazetteer biographies sometimes tell us only that a child was adopted by his maternal relatives, without specifying which of the relatives instigated the adoption or assumed primary responsibility for the child. Ch'en T'ai, who lived during the reign of the Yung-lo emperor (1403–1425), was adopted by his mother's relatives, who were surnamed Ts'ao. He at first assumed their surname, but later resumed use of his father's surname.[82] Liu Tsung-chou, the famous seventeenth-century philosopher, was born several months after the death of his father into a poverty-stricken family. The child Tsung-chou was sent to live with his maternal relatives, who were surnamed Chang. Tsung-chou retained the use of his paternal surname. Later when his paternal grandfather grew old and ill, Tsung-chou returned to care for him, doing chores and preparing medicine.[83] Ni Chang-hou from Sung-chiang was adopted by his maternal grandfather, a man named Chang. Chang looked after the child as if he were his own, and bestowed his surname on him. As far as we know, the use of the name Chang was retained in perpetuity by the descendants of Chang-hou.[84]

Ku Mi, who received his *chin-shih* degree in 1485, was originally raised by maternal relatives named Fu. He took their surname, but later returned to the use of the surname Ku.[85] Wang Te-jen's father, whose original surname was Hsieh, lived with his wife's relatives and assumed the use of their surname. His son continued the use of the surname Wang.[86] Thus gazetteers document adoptions of maternal and affinal kin.

The genealogy of a family named Chou from Chia-ting records the adoption of a boy surnamed Chu by the childless Chou Hsiang-chung. The genealogy further tells us that Hsiang-chung's mother was a Chu and that the boy was a grandson of one of her brothers. But the connection between the two families is more pervasive than that. After Chou Hsiang-chung's childless first wife died, he remarried. His second wife bore him four sons, two of whom married women surnamed Chu.[87] Thus the kinship relation between these two families spans several generations and is reinforced by both marriage and adoption. Jerry Dennerline has shown that the Chia-ting Chous in fact made a practice of cultivating ties with affines by giving them sons in adoption.[88]

Other biographical materials demonstrate that a mother's sister and her husband might adopt a child. Shen Po-kang, from Chang-chou in Su-chou, was originally surnamed Meng. While still a young boy, he was named the heir *(hou)* of his mother's sister's husband, Shen Sheng-wu. Shen Sheng-wu committed a crime and was sentenced to death. Po-kang, who was only seventeen at the time, insisted that he be executed in place of his adopted father. Because of Po-kang's extreme filial piety, Ming T'ai-tsu pardoned Sheng-wu. As far as we know, Po-kang and his offspring maintained the use of the surname Shen in perpetuity.[89] The Hou family of Chia-ting traced their ancestry to a man named Yang, who in the early fifteenth century had become the heir of his mother's brother, a Hou, and assumed the use of their surname.[90]

Biographical data confirm the existence of the practice of adoption by the father's sister and her husband. T'ang P'an, from Wu-hsien in Suchou, was from a family originally surnamed Yüan. His grandfather, Yüan Kuei, had been adopted by a paternal aunt and had assumed her husband's surname, T'ang. Kuei's great-grandson reverted to the use of the surname Yüan.[91] Yao Tsung-jen was adopted as an heir by Ch'in Chang-sheng, his father's sister's husband. He and his offspring are recorded in the Ch'in genealogy, but with generational names that distinguish them from members born in the lineage.[92] Ch'en Ju-lun from T'ai-ts'ang who earned his *chin-shih* in 1533 was originally from a family named Hsü; but since he was raised by the family of his father's sister *(ku)*, surnamed Ch'en, he took their surname.[93] Chu Pang-ch'en's father (a T'ai-ts'ang native who earned his *chü-jen* degree in 1515) married uxorilocally into a family named Wu. Chu was raised by a certain Lu, the husband of his father's sister. Lu educated him, and it was under the surname Lu that he first achieved a degree of prominence. But he ultimately returned to the use of his original surname.[94]

In ten of the adoptions discussed above, the surname of the child was changed to that of the adoptive father. In only four of the cases did the adopted son or his descendants revert to the use of their original surname. The high rate of retention of the surname of the adopted father contrasts with adoptions between unrelated parties where there is, as we shall see, a much higher rate of reversion to the original surname. This seems to indicate that a man was more willing to bear a surname other than that of his father if the name was that of some other relative. Perceptions of kinship extend beyond the narrow categories of the ritual texts. Surname alone does not define kinship.

Shiga has argued that a wife's relatives were preferred over a mother's relatives as adopted sons.[95] The above examples confirm this, but further suggest that a man's sister's sons were preferred to his wife's brother's sons. Mothers' brothers and fathers' sisters (and their husbands) predominate among the adopting parents. A possible reason for the preference of sister's sons over wife's brother's sons is voiced by the commentator to the *Wu-li t'ung-k'ao*. He condemns all adoptions through a female line but concedes: "Your sister's sons have your blood and *ch'i*. But what sort of people are your wife's brother's sons that they may be made your heirs?" He concludes the passage by saying, "They will know their mother but not their father. How depressing!"[96] A man's sister is no longer a member of his lineage (because she has married out), but the commonality of blood and *ch'i* are acknowledged to remain. Thus there are distinctions among various kinds of *wai-tsu*.

There are very few specific data about inheritance in these biographies, though some information can be inferred. The terms used to describe the adoption of Shen Po-kang literally mean "made the heir" *(wei . . . hou),* and so we may assume that Po-kang inherited property. The family of Yüan Kuei called themselves T'ang for three generations; it seems a reasonable assumption that they inherited T'ang property as they passed the surname on to their descendants.

Nor do the biographies discuss the adopted child's participation in the ancestral sacrifices of the adopting family. The inclusion of adopted children in the Chou, Ch'en, and Ch'in genealogies indicates a degree of ritual acceptance of the adoptions. But although Yao Tsung-jen was entered in the Ch'in genealogy, he was given a generational name different from that of his peers, indicating that the ritual acceptance was not complete.

It seems that the adoption of sons related through the female line, be it maternal, affinal, or sororal, occupies a middle ground between agnatic adoptions and the adoption of non-kinsmen.[97] The greater tendency to retain the new surname, the greater evidence of the inheritance of family knowledge and property, and the evidence of ritual acceptance all indicate a higher degree of incorporation into the family unit than we will find in the adoptions of unrelated persons. Relatives through the female line are regarded as kinsmen, and, in times of crisis, may provide heirs. They are not kinsmen of the same quality as those of the patriline, but they are kinsmen nonetheless.

Continuing the Line with Alien Seed: Uxorilocal Marriage

People who call in a son-in-law—what fools!
How do they expect to continue their line with an alien seed?
The old couple will never enjoy filiality or support,

For singlemindedly he'll plot to steal the family fortune.
Anxiety deepens as he acts respectful, yet obstructs uncle and nephew;
Resentment mounts as he joins them, but is jealous of his sister-in-law.
Half a son, an empty name: in vain they suffer indignities.
It would be better to accept fate and have no son.[98]

This poem is cited in a story entitled "Chang T'ing-hsiu t'ao-sheng chiu fu" (Chang T'ing-hsiu Escapes with his Life and Saves his Father) from Feng Meng-lung's *Hsing-shih heng-yen* to give added emphasis to the prose descriptions of a grasping son-in-law. The actions of the son-in-law are detailed clearly in the text of the story (which we shall discuss in detail in chapter 4): the function of the poem is to suggest that the problem is generic. That a uxorilocally married son-in-law is grasping is no more than one might expect. His greed is implied by the nature of the ties that bind him to his in-laws: he is "half a son, an empty name."

Uxorilocal marriage is a form of marriage in which the husband resides with the wife's family. He (or his children) may take the wife's father's surname, though he does not necessarily do so. The property implications of this form of marriage are complex and will be discussed at some length below. Although probably commoner in traditional China than it was at Europe of the same time, the institution was not unheard of in the West. Oliver Cromwell was the descendant of one such English marriage: Cromwell was the name of his great-grandmother's family.[99] The "adopted" husband was common in Japan. For example, in a story by the seventeenth-century author Ihara Saikaku, "Very Sensible Advice on Frugality," it is simply assumed that a third son will marry into another family as an "adopted" husband.[100] The Indian institution of the "appointed daughter"—an heiress who resided with her father's family and whose sons were regarded as sons of her father, not her husband—is a form of uxorilocal marriage.[101]

Uxorilocal Marriage in Law and Ritual

Uxorilocal marriage has been widely described by anthropologists working in Taiwan and Hong Kong.[102] The practice, known as "calling in a son-in-law" *(chao-fu* or *chao-hsü),* has been known in China since antiquity. An instance of uxorilocal marriage is recorded in Ssu-ma Ch'ien's

Shih chi.[103] The first mention of the institution in a legal code seems to have occurred during the Southern Sung. In that code, it is mentioned together with *i-tzu* (a son adopted out of benevolence) and *lien-tzu* (a son adopted by his mother's second husband).[104] Thus law seems to regard uxorilocal marriage as analogous to adoption. Both uxorilocal marriage and adoption involve the transfer of a man from one lineage to another, potentially involving the change of his surname or that of his offspring, and involving a different configuration of property rights than would be the case in a virilocal marriage. A regulation dated 1273 contained in the *T'ung-chih t'iao-ko,* a Yüan dynasty handbook of administrative law, forbids only sons to marry uxorilocally. (The adoption out of an only son was also forbidden.) But there were loopholes. The text adds that if the family was poor or if there was a time limit on the uxorilocal residence, then a single son might be permitted to marry uxorilocally.[105] Poverty partially absolves one of the obligation to order one's family according to strict rules of ritual correctness. And where property is minimal, propriety may be less of an issue. A temporary uxorilocal residence might be permitted because it would not alter ultimate kinship relations. A regulation contained in the *Ta Ming hui-tien* also forbids an only son to marry uxorilocally.[106]

Ming and Ch'ing law required that there be a contract for uxorilocal marriages. According to a regulation of the second year of the Hung-wu reign period (1369), the contract must specify the duration of the uxorilocal residence.[107] Disputes over property arrangements and the naming of the children were too likely to result if the agreement was not fixed. Furthermore, a uxorilocally married son-in-law could leave (with or without his wife) or could be expelled from the family. A formal document outlining his rights and obligations doubtless ameliorated the situation.[108] That this ruling might be necessary is shown in a 1275 ruling in the *T'ung-chih t'iao-ko* which prohibits a uxorilocally married son-in-law from leaving before the contractually stipulated time limit had expired, while noting that such departures were common.[109]

Ming law specified that a man who called in a son-in-law must also adopt a man from his own surname group to carry on the ancestral sacrifices. The son-in-law and the properly appointed heir were to share the property equally.[110] In his manual for magistrates, Huang Liu-hung cautions that even a person with a called-in son-in-law must adopt an heir of the same surname. He goes on to say that any bestowal of property upon the adopted-in son-in-law is an act of charity rather than inheritance.[111] But Shiga has found that in fact it was rare for a man who had called in a son-in-law to adopt another heir.[112] Thus, the called-in son-in-law might serve as a de facto heir to his father-in-law.

Anthropologists working in contemporary Chinese societies have found that uxorilocal marriages are often regarded with distaste.[113] The married-in son-in-law is called a *chui-fu* or *chui-hsü*. The root meaning of *chui* is parasite, implying that the *chui-fu* was himself parasitic. Ming and early Ch'ing fiction corroborates the disfavor in which the institution was held. In P'u Sung-ling's "A-pao," the title character is unwilling to marry uxorilocally, because, as she says, "a son-in-law should not live for long in his father-in-law's house. Since he is poor, he'd be even more despised." This concern with proper forms is heightened by its context. The relationship between A-pao and her groom-to-be began when his spirit left his body and visited her, first in a dream-state and then in the body of a parrot. Love may transcend all bounds, but marriages must be made according to proper forms.[114] In "The Lady Who Was a Beggar," by Feng Meng-lung, an auspiciously begun uxorilocal marriage turns sour. Feng writes that because Mo Chi was a poor orphan and his bride was rich, his friends refrained from commenting on the inferior form of the marriage. Presumably her wealth compensated for any loss in status due to the form of the marriage. But as Mo Chi's prospects improved, he became so ashamed of his wife's background that he attempted to murder her.[115]

In the sixth tale of Ling Meng-ch'u's *Erh-k'e p'ai-an ching-ch'i*, "Li Chiang-chün ts'o jen chiu; Liu shih-nü kuei ts'ung fu" (General Li Wrongly Recognizes her Brother-in-law; The Girl from the Liu Family Lies to Follow her Husband) a proverb disparaging men who marry uxorilocally is cited: "It has always been said: the man who marries into his wife's family brings nothing but a set of testicles."[116] Procreation outside the patriline thus becomes a ribald joke.

But the joke points to a crucial aspect of the institution: a uxorilocally married man produces heirs for another man's (his wife's father's) lineage. This reproductive function is loosely analogous to that of a wife in a virilocal marriage. She produces heirs for her husband's family. Part of the disfavor with which uxorilocal marriage was regarded doubtless stems from this inversion of gender roles. But a uxorilocally married man is not a bride. A description of the ritual to be followed in a uxorilocal marriage contained in the K'ang-hsi period gazetteer for K'uai-chi county is instructive here. The first point of note is that it is necessary to prescribe a special form of ritual. The classical wedding ceremonies, prescribed in great detail in ritual texts, are perceived as not appropriate for uxorilocal marriage. The uxorilocal wedding described in the gazetteer is an example of local customs' attempt to come to terms with and modify ritual according to actual practice. The gazetteer tells us that the wedding ritual should be the same for a uxorilocal marriage as for other marriages, except that the flowered palanquin normally used to carry the bride to her new home should be dispensed with.[117] The bridal sedan chair is not merely a means of transportation. It is crucial to the symbolism of the transfer of the bride from the family of her father to that of her husband. The ritual prescribed in the gazetteer shows the extent and the limitations of the role reversal implied by uxorilocal marriage.

Family instructions indicate displeasure with uxorilocal marriage. The rules of the Hsü family, complied by Hsü Hsiang-ch'ing (1479–1557) forbid uxorilocal marriage.[118] The *Wang Shih-chin tsung-kuei* advised against arranging uxorilocal marriage for a widow.[119]

Motives

The motives for uxorilocal marriage, like those for adoption, were diverse and complex. As the prohibition in the *Wang Shih-chin tsung-kuei* cited above implies, a called-in son-in-law could provide security in one's old age. The *Liu-pu ch'eng-yü*, a work compiled in the early Ch'ing to assist the Manchus in their study of Chinese language and institutions, glosses the phrase "to call in a son-in-law to provide for old age" *(chao-hsü yang-lao)* as follows: "People with no sons who have daughters 'call in a son-in-law' to marry uxorilocally in order to prepare for their old age."[120]

Another motivation for calling in a son-in-law is suggested in an entry in the early Ch'ing encyclopedia, the *Fen-lei tzu-chin*. Under an entry entitled *"ch'u-chui"* (to marry uxorilocally), the encyclopedia quotes from the *Han shu* biography of Chia I (200–168 B.C.):

Therefore, the people of Ch'in, if the household were rich, when the sons grew up, they partitioned the property. If the household were poor, when the sons grew up, they married uxorilocally.

The encyclopedia further quotes Yen Shih-ku:

By saying that he is a *chui-hsü,* one implies that he ought not to go live in his wife's house. He is like a tumor on a person's body, something that ought not to be there. It is also said that *chui* means hostage *(chih);* if the family were poor and does not have the brideprice, then his person serves as a hostage.[121]

Thus the person and labor of the uxorilocal son-in-law substituted for the brideprice. (Marriage in traditional China involved the reciprocal exchange of wealth—the man's family would pay a brideprice to the family of the woman, and the woman's family would provide her with a dowry.) A regulation of 1272 specifies that in the case of a uxorilocal marriage, the brideprice is reduced to half of what it would otherwise have been and stipulates that there must be a matchmaker and a contract.[122] Shiga Shūzō's research has corroborated that in this form of marriage the brideprice paid by the groom's family was generally small or nonexistent.[123] If obtaining the labor of a son-in-law were the aim of the uxorilocal marriage, the marriage contract might specify a time limit for his residence with his wife's family. The limit might be for a set number of years, or it might be specified that the son-in-law would remain until the family had a son who reached maturity.[124]

Another motive for uxorilocal marriage was, of course, obtaining an heir. The son-in-law might himself serve as that heir, or his sons might be adopted into his father-in-law's family. The biography in the T'ai-ts'ang gazetteer of Chou Tsai, who received his *chü-jen* degree during the Hung-chih reign period (1488–1506) tells us that he was married uxorilocally to a daughter of a Wu family. The Wu family had no sons. The biography says that custom demanded he assign half his sons to the Wu lineage. He did, even though popular opinion found the demand excessive.[125]

A man might be induced to marry into a prominent family. Chao Wenhua, originally from Tzu-hsi, moved to Hsiu-shui, then married a woman of the Hsiang family. The Hsiu-shui gazetteer features numerous biographies of both male and female members of the Hsiang clan. Their names appear as well on examination lists as successful candidates. The prominence of this family was doubtless sufficient to make the marriage, even with its required change of residence, attractive to an ambitious young man.[126] The gazetteers are sometimes quite blunt about a man's motives for contracting this form of marriage. Wei Huai-ching, from the area around K'un-shan, married a daughter of the Chung family uxorilocally, because, as his wife's biography tells us, the Chungs were rich.[127]

A man with no family of his own, like Mo Chi in the tale by Feng Meng-lung, might find the prospect of uxorilocal marriage and subsequent incorporation into a family attractive. Fan Yün-lin, for instance, who received his *chin-shih* degree in 1495, originally from Hua-t'ing, was orphaned as a child. He married uxorilocally into the Hsü family from Wu-men (but retained the use of his original surname).[128]

A father might wish to call in as a son-in-law a particularly talented man. The biography of a Miss Ku, from Yü-yao, tells us that her father judged Shih Mao to possess learning *(yu wen hsüeh)* and therefore arranged for him to marry into the Ku family.[129]

Uxorilocal marriages might be contracted for professional reasons. Many branches of knowledge in traditional China, among them medicine, were transmitted from father to son. One of the five categories of physicians described by Li Ch'en (fl 1575–1580) in his *I-hsüeh ju-men* is *shih-i*, physicians practicing in a family tradition. Twenty-six of the 212 medical practitioners described by Li fall into this category.[130] The *I-shuo*, a Sung text reprinted during the Ming, contains an anecdote illustrating how crucial offspring could be to a practitioner in this tradition. Two Sung dynasty doctors, Hsü Lou-t'ai and Sung Ta-lang, treated a wealthy man for an ulcerous back. They demanded an exorbitant fee, which the patient refused to pay. The doctors then administered a drug that aggravated the patient's condition, and he died. Less than a year later, the physician Hsü Lou-t'ai fell ill and died. The tale concludes: "His sons could not marry and thus Hsü's medical knowledge died out."[131] Death is the penultimate penalty; extinction of the line and knowledge was the ultimate penalty.

A doctor with no son might adopt an heir or marry his daughter uxorilocally. We saw earlier how the physician Hsü adopted his sister's son and transmitted medical knowledge to him. The medical community in K'un-shan practiced uxorilocal marriage. Ho Tzu-yün married the daughter of the doctor Liu Kuo-ying and followed his father-in-law's profession (but retained the use of the name Ho for himself and his family).[132] T'ao Huo married the daughter of the doctor Hsü Yüan-fu, as the gazetteer tells us, "in order to continue [Hsü's] medical practice." T'ao's fame as a doctor spread far and wide, exceeding that of his father-in-law.[133]

As remarkable as the family connections among medical practitioners is the presence, in families of renowned male doctors, of female medical practitioners. These gazetteer biographies provided tantalizing clues about the existence of female medical practitioners in the Ming dynasty.[134] The daughter of another family named Hsü was very skilled at reading pulses (one of the chief diagnostic techniques of traditional Chinese medicine) and prescribing medications. She married Wang Yüan-fu, who died after two years of marriage. Their only daughter died before reaching maturity. Madame Hsü then adopted a daughter of the Chao family. After the daughter grew to maturity, Hsü called in a husband for her adopted daughter. The called-in son-in-law also died. Madame Hsü lived to be eighty-six years old, supporting herself through the practice of medicine.[135]

The surname change brought about by uxorilocal marriage might last for several generations. Wang Hsüan was originally from Shanghai. He married uxorilocally into the Kao family of Sung-chiang, moved to Sung-chiang, and assumed the surname Kao. His son, who was appointed to office during the Ch'eng-hua era (1465–1488), is entered in the Sung-chiang gazetteer under the name of Kao.[136] On the other hand, the son of a man married uxorilocally might petition to have the paternal surname restored. The father of Huang Kuan (1362–1402) from Kuei-ch'ih in Anhui married a woman of the Hsü family and took her surname. Kuan petitioned to have the name Huang restored, and the petition was granted.[137]

Conceptions of kinship, notions of how people are related to one another, are also significant in determining the willingness of men to marry their daughters uxorilocally as a means of getting an heir. We saw above that the predominant view of heredity in Ming and early Ch'ing China was that characteristics were passed primarily through the male line. The signifier of kinship was surname. This was the dominant view, but it had no monopoly. Thus we see the Sung Neo-Confucian Ch'en Ch'un writing:

> In the present age, men may take the son of a daughter as heir, thinking that although the family names are different, the kinship in material force (ch'i) is close and that is better than someone with a different family name who is more distant . . . [A]lthough kinship in material force is close, the family names are really different. This theory [adopting a daughter's son] surely does not work.[138]

The tendency to regard a daughter's son as a close relative despite the difference of surname led to the spread of the practice of uxorilocal marriage. Ch'in Hui-t'ien, the compiler of the Ch'ing dynasty *Wu-li t'ung-k'ao*, suggests that popular notions of kinship configuration, which he held to be inappropriate, if not erroneous, might have in fact encouraged uxorilocal marriage as a means of obtaining an heir.

> Nowadays people regard brothers' sons as very distant and daughters and daughters' husbands as very close. Therefore, there are cases where the appropriate person is not adopted, but rather a son-in-law is called in.[139]

Women who married uxorilocally might still have connections to and obligations toward the husband's family. This is illustrated by two cases from the Chia-hsing gazetteer. In both cases, the verb used for "to marry" is *chui,* which quite unambiguously means to marry uxorilocally. Madame Chou married at sixteen. Seven months later, her husband died. She bore him a posthumous child. Her mother-in-law urged her to remarry.[140] Tung Shu-chen, of the same district, was widowed at the age of twenty-four. Despite the fact that her marriage had been uxorilocal, her biography stressed her virtuous attendance on her mother-in-law.[141] Thus uxorilocal marriage is a variant existing in the context of a fundamentally patrilineal society. It is a counterpoint, not an alternative.

As was the case with adoptions, uxorilocal marriages occasionally gave rise to property disputes. A case brought before Chu Hao, the grandfather of the calligrapher Chu Yün-ming, illustrates the problem and one successful solution. A man had no son, so he adopted his son-in-law. The father-in-law's wife subsequently bore a son, who grew up and produced a son of his own. The original couple and their son died, leaving the adopted son-in-law in charge of the property, a thriving business. The worth of the business had under his direction increased considerably. After the grandson reached his majority, he and the son-in-law quarreled over the property. Chu Hao listened to the arguments and ruled that the assets should be divided. He ordered that a list of assets be drawn up preparatory to the division. He then burned incense and invoked the spirits of the ancestors. To these spirits, he reported the conduct of the heirs, outlining the faults and virtues of each party to the dispute. Doubtless moved by the drama of the situation, the son-in-law fell to his knees and admitted that he was partially to blame for the dispute. The grandson, for his part, said that an admission of wrongdoing was all he wanted from his adversary. The two men were reconciled; the lawsuit was dismissed; the business remained intact. To prevent future disputes from arising, Chu Hao recorded the agreement between the two men.[142]

Chu Hao himself, who had only one son, Chu Hsien, of fragile health, married one of his daughters to a young man of the Liu clan from Su-chou. The young man changed his surname to Chu. The daughter died before she produced an heir for her father. Chu Hao, with the consent of the Liu clan, married the young widower to Wang Miao-ching. She gave birth to a son, who took the surname Chu and was regarded as the grandson of Chu Hao. Chu Hsien proved stronger than expected and lived to marry. His wife gave birth to Chu Yün-ming. With the birth of a biological grandson, the necessity for the adoptive one vanished. The adopted son-in-law, Wang Miao-ching, and their son were all allowed to return to the Liu clan and the use of the Liu surname.[143]

As we have seen, genealogies occasionally record uxorilocal marriages among clan members. A particularly creative way of justifying the marriage occurs in the genealogy of the Ch'en clan of Po-hai, Hai-ning.

[Ch'en] Ch'eng was the third son of his father . . . he married a woman of the Chou family who did not give him any male issue. It so happened that the eldest son of Kao Nan-chiang named Liang came to Tungli of Haining to attend school there. Ch'en Ch'eng saw him and was amazed. Then he married his beloved daughter to him. They had a son named Jung who adopted his mother's surname.

The descendants of Ch'en Jung were numerous and illustrious. The extraordinary nature of their ancestor—Kao Liang was of such amazing mien that Ch'en Ch'eng instantly knew he was of the caliber of a son-in-law—perhaps serves to compensate for the inferior form of the marriage.[144] This point is made even more dramatically by an elaboration of the same story by Ch'en Ch'i-yüan, writing in the late Ch'ing.

> My family derived from the Kao family in Po-hai. During the Sung dynasty, the Kao people, related to the Royal house and having rendered meritorious service to the Imperial Court, came southward with emperor Kao-tsung and settled at Lin-an. Our primogenitor named Liang who lived at Huangshan of Jenho in the early days of the Ming period came to Haining and went to school there. One day, overcome with fatigue, he took a nap on the Chao-chia bridge and fell into the water. Ch'en Ch'eng, who ran a bean curd shop at the bridge, was also taking a nap and dreamed of a green dragon coiled under the bridge. He woke up astonished and then saw a man fall into the water. He rushed to his rescue. Having learned about his pedigree, he asked the man to stay with him. Old and without issue, he married his only daughter off to the man and furthermore adopted him as a son. Liang begot a son named Jung who adopted his maternal grandfather's surname, Ch'en, and followed his trade.[145]

The elaborate myth of origins of their branch of the family provides a supernatural justification for an inferior form of marriage. The coiled green dragon asleep under the bridge was an omen auspicious enough to outweigh any considerations of social prejudice. The flourishing of the family after the time of Liang validates the promise of the coiled green dragon.

To sum up, a son-in-law might be called in to provide for the old age of a couple with no son. A household, with or without sons, that needed more labor might arrange for a called-in son-in-law to join them, either for a fixed term or permanently. A son-in-law might be called in to study and transmit his father-in-law's profession. A man with no male heir might call in a son-in-law and name him heir or might simply hope that the union between his daughter and the *chui-fu* son-in-law would produce a son who would bear his name. These motivations, as we have seen, were also motivations for adoption. That Ming and Ch'ing law forbade the naming of a son-in-law as heir, and that the practice nevertheless persisted, has its parallels in the practice of adopting across clan lines.

The chief differences between calling in a son-in-law and adopting a son stem from the greater attachment and sense of duty that the former, as an adult, could be expected to feel toward his natal family. In fourteen of the nineteen actual cases of uxorilocal marriage discussed, the called-in son-in-law did not change his surname to that of the adopting father-in-law. Of the five who did, in three cases the descendants reverted to the use of the original surname. Thus in only two out of nineteen cases was the name change handed down in perpetuity. Further, the contract for a uxorilocal marriage might specify a time limit for the son-in-law's uxorilocal residence and services. These conditions can be juxtaposed with adoption, which, no matter what its limitations, was in theory at least perpetual. Fears that the *chui-fu* son-in-law might abscond (or his fears that he might be expelled) are of course not without parallel in the adoption cases we have discussed. But the position of the *chui-fu* son-in-law is more ambiguous, and the institution correspondingly more fragile, because he joins his new family as an adult. Complete incorporation into the family was out of the question. Uxorilocal marriage, like adoption, was a strategy of heirship. And, like adoption, it was fraught with ambiguity.

Cross-surname Adoptions

We have seen that people violated the prohibition against adopting persons of a different surname when they adopted affinal and maternal relatives. The prohibition was also violated when a man adopted the son of his wife by a prior marriage. In all of these cases, although the child adopted was, according to the categories of traditional Chinese kinship, an outsider, there were connections between the child and his adoptive family, and those connections were of flesh and blood. And these relationships were recognized by contemporary Chinese writers.

But the kin group, whether affinal or agnatic, was not the only support group to which the traditional Chinese family had access. The
neighborhood was an important secondary source of support. Neighbors
pooled their labor when necessary. They assisted one another in financial
matters by forming loan societies, to which each member contributed a
fixed amount of money and from which he was periodically entitled to
withdraw a lump sum. Neighbors also fostered and adopted one another's orphaned and abandoned children. Sometimes, a child would even
be adopted by a complete stranger. Such adoptions often worked well;
other times they did not. The following case studies illustrate both types
of adoption of unrelated persons and both kinds of outcomes.

Chang Hung (1364–1447) was born into the Hou family, who were
tradesmen living in Ch'ang-shu, Su-chou. His mother died five days after
he was born. At the time of his birth, his father was in no position to
make arrangements for the care of his motherless son. A neighbor named
Chang Hui adopted the baby and hired a wet nurse to care for him. Hung
followed the surname of his adoptive father. He showed precocious ability in both reading and writing. His biographies tell us that Ch'ang-shu's
prominence as a center of learning began with Chang Hung.[146]

K'uang I-shih (1346–1418) was orphaned at the age of five during the
disturbances that marked the end of the Yuan dynasty. A neighbor
named Huang adopted the boy and granted him his surname. I-shih's
son, K'uang Chung (1383–1443), the celebrated prefect of Su-chou, was
known as Huang Chung until 1429, when he petitioned for permission
to change his surname. Out of gratitude to the Huang family, he
arranged for one of his brothers to carry on their surname. Even eighty
years after the original adoption, the sense of membership in the natal
family was retained.[147]

Huang Chou-hsing was adopted by a neighbor family named Chou
and assumed the use of their surname. In 1400 he received his *chin-shih*
degree under the name of Chou Hsing. In 1404, he petitioned to have his
original surname restored. The glory of his success accrued to the Huang
ancestors. But as his biographer, Yeh Meng-chu, tells us, he commemo-
rated the Chou family as well, by retaining their surname as part of his
given name.[148]

The biography of Chang T'ai, from T'ai-ts'ang, who received his *chin-*

shih degree in 1463, notes that T'ai was originally from a family surnamed Yao but that his great grandfather had been adopted into a family
named Chang. His descendants continued to use the name Chang.[149]
Although everyday usage placed T'ai with the Changs rather than with
the Yaos, the biography carefully records the other surname. In some
sense, the membership in the original family has not been obliterated.

Tu Wei, a man who lived in Wu-chiang during the reign of the Chia-
ching emperor (1522–1566), was raised in the family of Shen Han. He
assumed the surname Shen and studied together with the other boys of
the Shen family. His biography tells us that he received the benevolence
(en) of the Shen family. But later in life, he reverted to the use of his original surname. The Shen ancestors had no need of him, as there were other
sons to maintain the sacrifices.[150]

These cases demonstrate that the networks a family could rely on
extended beyond the kinship group. The purpose of these adoptions
seems to be more the care of the orphan than the perpetuation of the sacrifices to the ancestors of the adopting father. But Chang Hung's retention of his adoptive father's surname, K'uang Chung's assignment of his
brother to the Huang lineage, and Huang Chou-hsing's incorporation of
the name Chou into his personal name all indicate a sense of ritual incorporation into the new lineage. At the same time, the tendency to revert to
the original surname is further evidence of the strong connections an
adopted-out son felt with his natal family.

The tenuous nature of the adoptive tie is shown by the experience of
the widow of Chou Ts'un-heng. Ts'un-heng was originally a member of
the Wang family but had been adopted into the Chou family *(chi yü
Chou)*. He married a woman of the Yü family. Not long after the marriage and the subsequent birth of a child, Ts'un-heng became seriously
ill. Scheming members of the Chou family, fearing Ts'un-heng's death,
ordered Madame Yü to move her husband back to the Wang household.
They specifically stated that they wanted him to be buried with the
Wangs. After Ts'un-heng's death, Madame Yü and her child did move in
with the Wangs. Through her weaving she supported herself, her child,
and her mother-in-law and was able to provide for the funerals of her
husband and her in-laws.[151] The motive for the adoption had probably
not been to get an heir, for a potential Chou heir was expelled with

Madame Yü. One would assume, had benevolence been the motive for adoption, that the benevolence would have extended to Ts'un-heng's wife and child. The adoption may have been contracted because the Chous had need for extra labor and chose to incorporate that labor into their family. Apparently, it was an arrangement that the Chous desired only for the lifetime of Ts'un-heng himself. The temporary, secular nature of the adoption is further demonstrated by their concern for the purity of the Chou graves. Ts'un-heng was born a Wang and died a Wang, though for much of his productive life he had been a Chou. Another motivation the family might have had in expelling Madame Yü, which the biography does not mention, could have been the desire to prevent her and her child from obtaining the share of the property to which they would have been entitled if they had remained in the Chou household. Another point worthy of note is that contact was maintained between the Chous and Wangs, contacts that were strong enough that the Wang family felt responsibility to the widow and the son of their adopted-out child. True, Madame Yü worked to support her family and was thus an economic asset rather than a liability. Nevertheless, that the Wangs undertook the responsibility for a widow and her small child indicates the persistence of kin bonds beyond adoption.

Another case of the expulsion of an adopted child is that of Wang Tao from K'un-shan. Wang, an impoverished orphan, was adopted as an heir *(wei jen hou)* at the age of nine *sui*. The text is not clear as to whether the adopting family were related or not. If they were kinsmen, it is not likely that they were close relatives. Certain members of the adoptive family plotted to obtain Wang Tao's property. He allowed them to take control of the property, then left the household with his adoptive grandmother and mother, whom he supported.[152]

The 1567 edition of the Yung-chia gazetteer records an anecdote illustrating the difficulties a widow who adopted an unrelated child might face and ways in which she might resolve them. A woman from the Chu family was widowed and had no son. She adopted a child of a different surname, calling him Shou-ming. Her deceased husband's nephew, Shou-ch'eng, coveted the property and planned to expel the adopted son. After the case was taken to litigation, the widow was advised to write out her complaint and burn it to inform the city god. She kowtowed and accused the nephew of scheming to get her property. Five days later, the widow claimed to have seen a spirit *(shen)* descend into the courtyard to inquire about her problem. The gazetteer voices some skepticism about the spirit. But later, there is no skepticism. Several days later, the sky was dark, but there was no thunder. Suddenly there came an earthquake, which killed both the scheming nephew and his father. As if the message were not clear enough, the gazetteer tells us that the earthquake ripped their clothes off them. This convinced the magistrate, who subsequently acquiesed to the wishes of the widow. The legitimacy of the heir of a different surname was upheld.[153] The city god is an analogue to the district magistrate, who adjudicates in this case not according to law, which was of course on the side of the brother and nephew, but according to custom. Blood kinship and legal right were not enough to gain the inheritance. Presumably the greedy and grasping nature of the Chu nephew and his father moved the city god to intercede on the widow's behalf. Justice is not always served by a strict application of the law.

Expulsion was not the only threat to the durability of the adoption. The family of the child's birth might use force to try to get him back. In a case contained in the *Tzu-chih hsin-shu,* a collection of legal cases by the seventeenth-century author Li Yü, a certain Wan Ch'eng, a poor man with five children, was on the point of abandoning the fifth, Shih-lien, when a man named Chou interceded and took the child home. He raised the child as if he were his own, and Shih-lien regarded the Chous as if they were his parents of a second birth *(ch'ung-sheng fu-mu).* Thirty years later, after Wan Ch'eng and his sons had all died, a kinsman tried to force Shih-lien to return to his original family. The magistrate who heard the case, Chou Kung-liang, said that although Shih-lien had not been a family member, he had been nurtured by the Chous. The Chous had cared for him for thirty years: the Wans had abandoned him. Chang ruled that Shih-lien could stay with the Chous, and he punished the Wan kinsman.[154] Here the claim of nurture overrode that of blood.

The case of Yü Ching of K'un-shan, who died during the Hung-wu period (1368–1399), clearly illustrates the problem of dual loyalties. When he was young, Yü Ching lost both his father and mother. He was raised as an adopted son *(yang-tzu)* by a family named Chang and took their surname. While Mr. Chang treated the boy badly, Madame Chang loved and protected him as if she had given birth to him. Ching served her just as if she were his own mother. The most dramatic illustration of this occurred when Madame Chang fell ill. Ching entreated heaven to cure her. Moreover, following an example of a devout son in the *Hsiao ching* (Classic of Filial Piety), he cut off a piece of his own flesh to decoct medicine for his mother. Like the mother in the *Hsiao ching*, Madame Chang was cured. One would think that the sacrifice of Ching's own flesh would be truly symbolic of his incorporation into the Chang family. But although Ching was willing to sacrifice his flesh to Madame Chang, he was not willing to change his surname. In 1425, he petitioned to have his surname restored; the petition was granted. His loyalty was to Madame Chang personally, rather than to the patriline. The biographies of him that appear in both the *K'un-shan jen-wu chih* and the *Su-chou fu-chih* stress his filial piety to both the Chang and Yü lines.[155]

We have very little detailed information about the inheritance arrangements made in these particular cases, but some general inferences may be drawn. Chang Hsü was to have inherited property from landlord Liu, but he chose to relinquish his rights rather than engage in a protracted dispute with the Liu heirs. Wang Tao would have inherited from his adopted family had he not been expelled. Wang Ts'un-heng had a claim on the Chou estate, and that claim was probably a factor in the Chou expulsion of his wife. Thus these cases of non-kin adoption do seem to involve a transfer of property rights, and the transfer of these rights seems to be disputed oftener than was the case with the adoption of relatives, be they agnatic, affinal, maternal, or sororal.

Another striking aspect of these adoptions is the reversion to the original surname, sometimes decades after the original adoption. Indeed, as we saw earlier, reversion to the original surname was the course of action advocated by Chu Hsi and Wu Hai. In three of the cases where there was a change of surname, the adopted son returned to the original surname. In two other cases, the adoptive son was expelled from the adoptive family, and although we do not know for certain that he returned to his original surname, expulsion probably implies such. These reversions suggest that the change in family could not be maintained in perpetuity. Doubtless one motivation for reversion to the original surname was remorse at the neglect of the natal family, as the case of Chang Shih so clearly demonstrates. These cases also indicate that filial piety is not absolute, nor is it necessarily determined by biology. It is true that ritual texts demand absolute and exclusive loyalty to one's father, but Yü Ching and Hsieh Chu are praised for their ability to balance conflicting loyalties. The problem of conflicting loyalties is central to fictional portrayals of adoption, which we shall examine in the next chapter.

4

Fiction

The Ming dynasty was the great era of the flourishing of Chinese vernacular literature. The sixteenth century saw the rise of the novel, and the seventeenth century brought the development of vernacular literature to new heights. Drama too flourished during the period. During this period, the family became a prominent theme in Chinese literature.[1] The domestic is an arena for the exploration of an array of issues that were of vital interest to authors of this period. The question of fate and how it might be manipulated is central to much of late Ming and early Ch'ing fiction. To what degree human beings might be the authors of their own destinies and to what degree destiny is determined by fate are open questions in the late Ming and early Ch'ing. Adoption is portrayed as a mechanism whereby human beings might intervene in the workings of fate.

Adoption occurs frequently in Ming and early Ch'ing fiction. I have located approximately seventy stories or dramas in which adoption is mentioned. These adoptions are generally presented in a straightforward manner, as if the practice of adoption were unremarkable. As Yao K'o-ch'eng observes at the close of the tenth act to Li Yü's play *Ch'iao t'uan-yüan* (The Amazing Reunion): "When a good man has no heirs, he can easily arrange to get one."[2] The merchant Lü Ta in Feng Meng-lung's "Lü Ta-lang huan chin wan ku-jou" (Lü Ta-lang Returns Money and Completes a Family Tie), whose only son had disappeared, explains that he had intended to acquire an adopted son (a *ming-ling-tzu*) to help him with his business, but that he had not gotten around to arranging the adoption.[3] In a story by Ling Meng-ch'u, a prefect asks Madame Wu, who wants her son to be executed, if she has borne or adopted any other sons, implying that the institution of adoption was fairly widespread.[4] Thus the institution was familiar to storytellers and dramatists.

It is of course entirely possible, even likely, that adoptions were more frequent in fiction and drama than they were in real life. Separation and reunion are major themes in literature, so much so that "reunion" (t'uan-yüan) is a technical term in dramatic criticism. Childlessness and adoption are situations rife with fictional possibilities. The melodrama inherent in the situation of the orphan and the childless couple may have made the subject especially attractive to authors of fiction. Plots containing adoption gave authors an opportunity to develop themes of separation and reunion with endless complications. Satirical authors, like the author of the sixteenth-century novel Chin p'ing mei, used improper adoptions to criticize the morality and family management of their characters.[5] Nevertheless, the casual treatment of adoption in fiction indicates that the institution was neither exotic nor obscure and that the storyteller conceived of it as a reasonable solution to the double quandary of the orphan and the childless couple.

Fictional evidence has played an important role in the argument of this book so far. I now want to look at fiction explicitly. First I will look at fictional adoptions in a variety of stories to see how fiction supplements information from other sources. Then I will discuss a group of four stories in which the plot hinges on adoption. It is not my intention to suggest that fiction is to be read as a description of actual behavior. But fiction provides a richly nuanced portrait of an institution we have heretofore seen only in broad outlines.

Blood and Artifice

When the coroner's manual Hsi yüan lu tells us that it has never been the case that a stepson's blood has sunk into a stepmother's bones (see p. 45), it is telling us that there are irreducible barriers to the assimilation of outsiders as kin. In fiction too we find evidence that the adoptive tie is not equivalent to the blood one.

Chu Shih-lao, in Feng Meng-lung's "Mai-yu-lang tu-chan hua-k'uei" (The Oil Peddler and the Courtesan), adopted Ch'in Ch'ung, bestowed his surname on the child, and taught him the trade of oil-seller. During a troubled interlude in a generally satisfactory relationship, Chu exclaims:

"I've treated him like my own son, and yet he has such bad intentions toward me. Since I don't have the blessings of heaven, I might as well give up. After all, he's not my own flesh and blood, and he'll never be on my side. There is nothing I can do except let him go his own way."[6]

Later in the same story, the following poem is cited as evidence that an adopted child cannot expect to be treated in the same manner as a natural child.

Hsiao-chi lost his life because of slander.
Shen-sheng died because of a truckler's words.
If it's like this with a natural son,
What's strange about an adopted son *(ming-ling)* who's falsely accused?[7]

The same ambiguity about adoption, the uneasy sense that fictive ties are not equivalent to those of flesh and blood, occurs repeatedly in Ming and early Ch'ing fiction. Chin-yün, the adopted daughter of the matchmaker Lu in Li Yü's "Ho-ying lou" is angry that her stepfather has permitted her fiance to break her engagement: " 'I am only his adopted daughter. Of course he doesn't care how I feel. If I were his own, I am sure he wouldn't have broken the engagement.' "[8] Lu is in fact a solicitous father, as his concern for Chin-yün during her subsequent illness shows. But Chin-yün nonetheless perceives there to be a dual standard of treatment for "real" and for adopted daughters.

That an adopted child had no necessary claim to parental affection is shown in another of Feng Meng-lung's tales. In "Liang hsien-ling ching-i hun ku-nü" (Two Magistrates Vie to Marry an Orphaned Girl), Chia Ch'ang and his wife buy Shih Yüeh-hsiang. Because they had no children, Mrs. Chia "initially conceived the desire to adopt her as her own daughter *(ming-ling nü-erh)*," but later she mistreats the girl. When Chia Ch'ang reprimands her, she responds by saying " 'That wench comes from another family. What call is there for you to be so fond of her?' "[9]

Chin-yün, Ch'in Ch'ung, and Shih Yüeh-hsiang are all outsiders who have been incorporated into the family. Consciousness of the marginality of their position is something none of them is able to escape. Nor is it something that other members of the family are able to forget. Ties of flesh and blood are primary and irreducible; they are a standard for affection and goodwill. It is a standard, judging from the utterances of Chu Shih-lao, Chin-yün, and Chia Ch'ang's wife, that can be mimicked but never duplicated.

Women in Fiction

The reader may have noted that some of the above examples of unhappy adoptees are not sons, but daughters. Fiction abounds in cases of female adoption. Approximately one-third of the fictional cases I have seen involve women. If we accept the common assumption that the dominant rationale behind adoption was to get a male heir, these adoptions make no sense.[10] If getting a male heir was the goal, why would a family ever adopt a girl? One reason, perhaps, is that an adopted daughter could serve to establish kinship ties between two men. In Li Yü's play *Ch'iao t'uan-yüan,* Yao Tung-shan, who has no sons, does have an adopted daughter. He hopes to acquire a male heir by having her marry uxorilocally.[11]

Or a young girl might be adopted as a future daughter-in-law. This form of adoption, called *t'ung-yang-hsi,* involves the adoption of a girl, often a very young girl, to serve as a future wife for a son. This form of marriage was much less costly than was a wedding between two adults. Furthermore, a girl raised in her mother-in-law's house by her mother-in-law was more likely to be a satisfactory daughter-in-law than a stranger would be. In Taiwan during the early part of the twentieth century, as many as seventy percent of all marriages contracted were of this type.[12] It would be extremely interesting to know the degree to which this practice existed in Ming times. Unfortunately, the sources do not yield satisfactory evidence.

There is some indirect evidence that the custom existed. The family instructions of Hsü Hsiang-ch'ing forbid the adoption in of young brides.[13] The *Yü-li ch'ao-chuan,* a popular religious text, states that persons who sell a girl brought up in their homes to marry their son will be tried in the seventh court of hell.[14] Further evidence is provided by fiction. In the Yüan play *Tou O yüan* (Injustice to Tou O), Tou O is adopted by Mother Ts'ai to serve as a daughter-in-law.[15] Mother Ts'ai promises to treat Tou O as if she were her own daughter.[16] Thus it seems clear that the institution of adopted daughter-in-law was known in Ming China. The Ch'ing evidence is somewhat clearer. The missionary Entrecolles reports in a letter dated 1720 that poor people adopted girls from orphanages to serve as *t'ung-yang-hsi*.[17]

Two stories from the *Ku-chin hsiao-shuo* feature adult women who are adopted to extricate themselves from difficult situations. In "Chin Yü-nu pang-ta po-ch'ing-lang" (Chin Yü-nu Beats an Ingrate), translated as "The Lady Who Was a Beggar," Chin Yü-nu is rescued by the Hsüs after her husband, Mo Chi, tries to drown her because he has been humiliated by the fact that her family is of low social status. They subsequently adopt her and treat her as if she were their real daughter *(chen nü)*; she, in turn, treats them no differently than if they were her real parents. Hsü arranges a marriage between Mo Chi and his "daughter," Yü-nu. After she gives Mo Chi the thrashing that gives the story its title, the marriage resumes, and they live happily ever after. Yü-nu's adoption has transformed her social position. She has been transformed from a hindrance to her husband's ambitions to an asset by a simple shift in status. Chin Yü-nu is mindful of her father's fate: he comes to live with the Hsüs. But it is the death of the Hsüs that she mourns fully, to "repay their benevolence." The story ends by telling the reader that this was the beginning of a long-term relationship between the Hsü family and the Mo family, in which they were "for generations like brothers."[18] Yü-nu's adoption serves her interests in the short run: she is, after all, rescued. But in the long term, her role is to serve as a link between the Hsü and the Mo families.

In another story from the *Ku-chin hsiao-shuo*, "Ch'en Yü-shih ch'iao-k'an chin ch'ai tien" (Ch'en Yü-shih Skillfully Investigates the Gold Hairpin), Madame T'ien leaves her husband upon learning that his intrigues have caused the girl Ku Ah-hsiu to commit suicide. Ah-hsiu's parents then adopt T'ien and marry her uxorilocally to Lu, the fiancé of their deceased daughter. T'ien and Lu produce two sons; one is granted the surname Lu; the other is granted the name Ku. Because the Kus have no son, Lu inherits Ku's property.[19] In both of these cases, a woman seeking refuge from a husband acquires a new set of parents, and in each case, they find her a husband. Yü-nu has what to the modern reader can seem only the grave misfortune of being reunited with the man who tried to kill her; T'ien fares somewhat better. But in both cases, the significant links that are formed are between the new parents and the "new" husband.

Legal texts and clan rules conceptualize the family as patrilineal. As we might infer from the commentaries to the T'ang code (see p. 49), the act of adopting a female child has no serious consequences and hence was to go unpunished. A woman is temporarily and transitorily a member of her father's house; she attains permanent and stable membership in a lineage only upon her marriage. Documents concerned with the management and maintenance of the patriline might well not record female adoptions. The addition or subtraction of a daughter would not change the lineage configuration and hence might go unrecorded. In addition, as the adoption of a daughter would not generally result in her inheriting family property, lawsuits contesting the validity of the adoption were not as likely as they would be for adopted sons. An adoption that does not bear on questions of lineage or is not contested for reasons of property might well be eliminated from genealogies and local gazetteers, as well as from the normative texts dealing with adoption. Thus the silence of the historical record is inconclusive. It seems likely that female adoption was much more widespread than the historical record shows and may even suggest that the wishes of the ancestors were not as compelling a factor in male adoptions as some writers would have us believe.

Incest

If the adoptive relationship were viewed as truly equivalent to the blood relationship, then we might expect to find incest taboos between adoptive relatives. The fictional indications of an incest prohibition created by adoption are ambiguous.

In Feng Meng-lung's "Chao T'ai-tsu ch'ien-li sung Ching-niang" (The Sung Founder Escorts Ching-niang One Thousand *Li*), we find evidence of adoption creating an impediment to marriage. Before setting out on their journey, the Sung founder Chao K'uang-yin and Chao Ching-niang take a vow to be as brother and sister to avoid any semblance of impropriety in their traveling together. As the journey progresses, Ching-niang suggests that she marry her companion to repay him for his kindness. The Sung founder informs her that a marriage between them is not possible: " 'Since we have the same surname, it would be difficult for us to marry. Since we call one another brother and sister, how is it possible that we commit incest?' "[20]

But the moral rectitude of the Sung founder far surpassed that of the ordinary man. In "Nieh Hsiao-ch'ien," a tale by P'u Sung-ling that we discussed briefly in chapter 1, Ning Ts'ai-ch'en reburies the bones of a beautiful ghost, thereby giving her peace. The ghost, Nieh Hsiao-ch'ien, wishes to marry Ning as a secondary wife to reward him for his helping her. Ning's mother objects to a union between her son and a ghost, so the girl suggests an alternate relationship: " 'Since you don't trust a dead person, let me treat him as a brother and serve you as my mother morning and night.' " Ning's mother is amenable to the suggestion. But Hsiao-ch'ien still has designs on the young man and suggests that she spend the night in his room. He urges her to leave, saying: " 'There's no other bed in my study, and besides, as brother and sister, we should avoid suspicion.' "[21] But the suspicion is apparently only the suspicion of an illicit relationship. When Ning's wife dies, his mother, by now thoroughly charmed by Hsiao-ch'ien, no longer objects to the match. Ning and Nieh are married; the marital relationship supersedes the adoptive one.

Other instances of adoption show no concern whatsoever about incest. The creation of fictional kinship ties may in fact facilitate the development of sexual relationships, licit or illicit. In Li Yü's "Ho-ying lou," the resourceful matchmaker Lu has as his task the arrangement of the marriage of children of feuding families. He adopts the son of one of the families and arranges with the girl's father for her marriage to his "adopted son." Lu's own adopted daughter marries the same young man, her adopted brother, as a secondary wife.[22] No concern about incest is shown in the story.

Fictional kinship ties could be used as a ruse to permit lovers to see one another without arousing suspicion. In a story by Ling Meng-ch'u, the widow Wu and her lover swear brotherhood, which allows him to visit her without arousing suspicion.[23] Technically incestuous relationships abound in the novel *Chin p'ing mei.* Hsi-men Ch'ing adopts Wang San-kuan, whose wife and mother he seduces.[24] The singing girl Li Kuei-chieh (Hsi-men Ch'ing's mistress) asks Wu Yüeh-niang (Hsi-men Ch'ing's principal wife) to adopt her. Wu Yüeh-niang is so startled by the request that she does not refuse it. The adoption creates the legal fiction that the mistress is the wife's daughter. Hsi-men Ch'ing's relationship with Li Kuei-chieh, at its inception merely improper, becomes incestuous.[25] Later in the novel, another singing girl, Wu Yin-erh, jealous of the advantages Li Kuei-chieh had obtained through her adoption, arranges to be adopted by another of Hsi-men Ch'ing's wives, Li P'ing-erh. Wu had been the mistress of P'ing-erh's deceased husband.[26] All three of these adoptions were instigated by the adoptee to enhance his or her prestige and social position. As Katherine Carlitz and Paul Martinson have both pointed out, the incestuous nature of the adoptions underscores the perversion of the proper familial relationships, which is a main theme of the novel.[27]

Thus the evidence regarding the seriousness of the incest prohibition within adopted families is inconclusive. There does seem to be the feeling, expressed by Chao K'uang-yin, that sexual relations among those related by adoption are inappropriate. But that feeling could be overcome, as is illustrated by the case of Ning Ts'ai-ch'en and Nieh Hsiao-ch'ien. Sibling incest was more likely to be tolerated than was that between a stepparent and the adopted child. Such relationships, like the ones in the *Chin p'ing mei,* are emblematic of the moral corruption of the parties involved.

The Wondrous Reunion

Let us now turn to a discussion of four stories in which adoptions are central. The first two are from the *Hsing-shih heng-yen,* edited by Feng Meng-lung, the third from Ling Meng-ch'u's *P'ai-an ching-ch'i,* and the final from Li Yü's *Shih-erh lou.* In the pages that follow, we shall see how fictional texts address some of the issues we have already discussed. How does an adopted son juggle the duties not only among various sets of parents, but also among various sets of ancestors? To what degree is human artifice adequate to the task of creating kinship bonds? Concepts such as *ch'ing* (variously translated as passion, emotion, or affection), which are of central importance in late Ming fiction and thought, take on a particular cast in these stories.[28] The stories present, to a greater or lesser degree, a sense of tension between the man-made world and the natural order. They show ways in which the family is a social construct as much as it is a biological one.

Patrick Hanan has argued that a number of the tales in the *Hsing-shih heng-yen,* including the two I will be discussing, were written not by Feng Meng-lung, but rather by a man known by the pseudonym of Lang-hsien. Hanan has noted that filial piety is a more prominent theme in the Lang-hsien stories than in those from Feng's hand.[29] Adoption renders filial piety problematic and hence more interesting to the writer (and reader) of fiction; it is no wonder that Lang-hsien concerns himself with it.

In "Liu Hsiao-kuan tz'u-hsiung hsiung-ti," the tenth story in the *Hsing-shih heng-yen,* translated by Gladys Yang and Yang Hsien-yi as "The Two Brothers," adoption serves as a vehicle for a discussion of themes of disguise and gender identity as well as for a celebration of filial piety.[30]

The introductory story *(ju-hua)* to "The Two Brothers," which is not translated by Yang and Yang, is purportedly a true story, recounted in several Ming miscellanies.[31] (In the Ming vernacular story, the main story is often preceded by an introductory story, the *ju-hua.* The relationship between the *ju-hua* and the main story is complex and variable. In "The Two Brothers" the sordid *ju-hua* serves as a contrast to the tale of virtue in the main story.) The *ju-hua* begins with Sang Mao, a beautiful young man on his way to visit relatives, taking refuge from a storm in a deserted temple. At the temple an old woman seduces him. After the seduction, the young man notices male genitals on the old woman. The old woman confesses that she is in fact a man and that her disguise as a sewing teacher enables her to enter the houses of good families and seduce women. This ruse appeals to Sang Mao, who asks if he may be her disciple. She agrees, binds his feet, and teaches him to sew. After accompanying his teacher for a while, he decides to set out on his own. She gives him parting instructions, cautioning him particularly against spending time in the company of men.

It is in fact the company of men, coupled with his own beauty, that is his undoing. His disguise is so successful that he inflames the passion of a son-in-law in a house where he is posing as a sewing teacher. When the son-in-law attempts to rape him, Mao's gender is revealed. He is then executed by slow slicing.

This story is about perversion and gender inversion. Disguise provides a cover for a man to debauch, indeed, even rape women of good family. The depravity and coarseness of the story serve to set off the delicacy and morality of the main story. As the narrator says in introducing the second story:

> What I have just now told you is a tale of a man disguised as a woman to corrupt public morals. What I am about to tell you is a tale of a woman disguised as a man, a virtuous and pure paragon. [32]

The main story goes as follows: Liu Te, an innkeeper, and his wife are elderly and childless. Liu is scrupulously honest. As he explains:

> "The reason I have no son must be because I did not do enough good in my last life, so in this life I shall be punished by dying without a son to sacrifice to me. How can I go on doing wrong?" [33]

Fang Yung, a weary army officer short on cash, and his son, a "delicate featured lad in small cloth shoes," arrive at the inn. Liu takes them in and feeds them and will not accept payment in return. In the course of exchanging pleasantries, Liu tells Fang that he has no son, and Fang asks why he has not adopted one. Liu replies:

> "Originally my intention was to do exactly that. Then I saw how often adopted sons refuse to look after family affairs, but cause more trouble instead. It is simpler to have none; for if you look for one in a hurry, you won't find a one to suit you. That is why we gave up on the idea. If we found one as good as your son, that would be fine, but how is that possible?" [34]

Fang becomes ill and dies, and Liu Te sees to the burial. Fang's son offers to become an adopted son of the Lius. Liu and his wife are delighted at the suggestion.

"If you are willing to do this, then it means Heaven is granting me a son. How can I treat you like a servant? From now on, let us treat one another like father and son."

"Since you consent," said the boy, "let me kowtow to you now."

He set two chairs in the middle of the hall and asked Liu and his wife to be seated, and then paid his respects to them as a son and changed his surname to Liu. But Liu, not wanting him to give up his former surname completely, made Fang his personal name, and henceforth he was called Liu Fang.[35]

The arrangement works very well. A poem commemorates it:

> Liu Fang, without parents, found parents;
> Liu Te, without a son, found a son.
> The boy served the dead and served the living;
> The army officer, though dead, not dead.[36]

Not only have Liu Fang and Liu Te found one another, but "the army officer," Fang Yung, has also been taken care of. Fang Yung is "not dead" because his son maintains the sacrifices to him. The acquisition of another set of parents does not obviate the need to care for the first set.

Several years later, Liu Te takes in another destitute and injured traveler, an orphan named Liu Ch'i. As Liu Te is taking Liu Ch'i home, bystanders comment on his virtue. They conclude, "What a pity he has no son. It's certainly true that Heaven has no discrimination." Another bystander points out that Liu Fang is "better than a real son" and is "Heaven's way of rewarding him."[37] Liu Fang and Liu Ch'i, about the same age, become fast friends. They take a vow of brotherhood. After a while, Liu Ch'i goes home to attend to the burial of his parents' bones. But he returns shortly, because he has been unable to buy a plot of suitable land.

"I have nowhere to stay in my old home," he said, "so I have brought the bones back to beg for a plot of ground to bury them. Then I would like to be your son and remain here to serve you every day. Would you agree?"

"There is plenty of vacant land. Choose what you like. As for becoming my son, that would be doing me too much honor."

"If you will not take me as your son, it means you do not agree to my request."

He asked Old Liu and his wife to take the seats of honor and kowtowed to them; then he buried his parents' bones behind the house. After that the two brothers worked together, going so diligently about their tasks that the tavern prospered more and more. They also served their parents well as befitted true sons. Everyone in town rejoiced that old Liu, though childless, had sons as a recompense for his acts of private virtue *(yin te)*.[38]

As time goes on, Liu Te dies. On his deathbed, he summons his two adopted sons and says:

"We were childless in our old age, and thought that at our death we would become ghosts with no one to sacrifice to us. Little did we know that Heaven would take pity on us and give us both of you to be our sons. Though in name *(ming)* you are adopted, in actuality *(ch'ing)* you are better than blood heirs. I can die now without regret. If after my death you will go on working together and keep up this small property, I shall close my eyes in peace in the Nine Springs."[39]

The name *(ming)* and the actual situation *(ch'ing)* are contrasted. *Ch'ing* also means emotion, and the line could be rendered "The emotion I feel for you exceeds what I would feel for blood heirs." The word in this context doubtless carries both connotations.

After Liu dies, the two sons mourn him. Liu Ch'i is anxious that the two of them find wives. Liu Fang unaccountably refuses to marry. There is a good bit of humorous interchange as pressure on Liu Fang to marry mounts. Finally Liu Fang sends Liu Ch'i a poem:

> Nesting swallows fly in pairs
> Heaven ordained their coupling long ago
> The female has her mate and is content
> But why does the male not recognize the female?[40]

When Liu Ch'i reads the poem, he exclaims, " 'So my brother is in fact a woman!' " The male disguise had been adopted, it turns out, when Fang was traveling with her father, as a simple manner of convenience. Liu Ch'i and Liu Fang marry, and a final poem celebrates the whole episode:

> Without love, brothers are as feuding kingdoms
> With altruism, strangers become as relatives.[41]

The phrase I have translated as "with altruism" *(yu i)* is contrasted with *wu ch'ing,* "without love." There is a pun intended here—an adopted son is an *i-tzu,* so the last line could also read that "with adoption, strangers become close relatives."

All three sets of parents are buried together. The sacrifices to all three are collectively maintained. The happy ending necessitates that no one be abandoned. Indeed, when Liu Ch'i initially proposes his adoption, he offers to serve Liu Te in exchange for a place to bury his parents. Far from being an abandonment of duties to his natal parents, Liu Ch'i's adoption enables him better to fulfill his duties to them.

Liu Te, whose virtue the narrator takes great pains to describe, had been wary of adopting a son because adopted sons are so frequently unsatisfactory. Liu has resolved not to adopt a child, and good sons literally stumble his way. Even adopted sons are granted by heaven. The relationship between virtue and offspring we saw above (pp. 14–19) is maintained.

The story also suggests, especially in the final poem, the power of sentiment *(ch'ing)* to create ties. Affection supplants blood ties, and, as the final poem tells us, without affection, brothers are like "feuding kingdoms." A family is a moral unit as well as a biological one.

A very different tale of adoption is contained in the same collection. "Chang T'ing-hsiu t'ao-sheng chiu-fu" (Chang T'ing-hsiu Escapes with his Life and Saves his Father)—at nearly fifty pages, the longest in the *Hsing-shih heng-yen*—revolves around the attempts of Chang T'ing-hsiu and his brother Wen-hsiu to avenge the wrong done their father. The two brothers are involved in three adoptions, but avenging the wrong done their father is the unifying motif of the story.[42]

The story has no prose *ju-hua.* Rather, it opens with a poem that affirms the central role of heaven in human affairs:

> All affairs come from heaven; no one can force them.
> So what good is it to exert yourself to make plans?[43]

Chang Ch'üan is a carpenter who has two talented sons, T'ing-hsiu and Wen-hsiu. A rich man named Wang Hsien commissions Chang to do some carpentry for him. Although Wang has no sons, he has two daughters. The eldest is named Jui-chieh, and she is married uxorilocally to a scoundrel named Chao Ang. Chao, who is the son-in-law described in the poem on pp. 99–100, is the orphaned son of Wang's oldest friend. But he has no redeeming qualities of his own, as we shall soon see. Wang is pleased by the carpentry, but seems downcast. His wife, the Lady Hsü, asks why. In the course of a long speech, he responds:

"Just think—I've worked half a century and accumulated this small property. But we've not been able to have a son to inherit it and to continue the ancestral sacrifices. Although we have these two daughters, even if we nurture them for more than a hundred years, they'll end up as someone else's daughters-in-law, and won't concern themselves with us."[44]

She responds by suggesting that he adopt one of Chang's sons. Wang is delighted by the idea and (after first ascertaining that the boy can read) asks Chang if he would be willing to give T'ing-hsiu up in adoption. Chang at first demurs, saying that as an artisan he has no aspirations to a status as high as that of Wang. But when Wang persists, Chang assents. Wang selects an auspicious day for the adoption and has new clothes made for T'ing-hsiu. In the new clothes, T'ing-hsiu "didn't seem at all like the son of a poor family."[45] His new role in life can be donned as easily as a new set of clothes, or so it seems. As he is leaving the family of his birth, his mother gives him instructions to be filial to his new family. She sees herself as an ally of his new mother, not as a rival.

The adoption is formalized at a banquet, during which the key ritual is the "four bows and eight prostrations" T'ing-hsiu performs to his new parents. He bows to all of his new relatives and receives the name of Wang T'ing-hsiu. Only the son-in-law Chao Ang is unhappy at the installation of a rival heir. Wang sends T'ing-hsiu and his brother to school and is so pleased with their progress that he proposes that T'ing-hsiu marry his second daughter, Yü-chieh.

Chao Ang can no longer conceal his jealousy and tells his father-in-law that the adoption of T'ing-hsiu "had not been a hundred percent correct."[46] Chao warns Wang that if Wang marries his daughter to this son of a carpenter the family will be subject to ridicule. Wang dismisses his son-in-law's criticisms, and the two families exchange betrothal gifts.

Chao Ang is an evil and angry man, but he is not clever enough to

scheme revenge on his own. His wife tells him how to trump up a charge
of robbery against Chang Ch'üan. As Chao later says, one might tolerate
the son of a carpenter as a son-in-law, but never the son of a thief. The
scenes that follow show Chinese officialdom as venal and corrupt.
Indeed, the narrative quotes a proverb, "An official who sees money is
like a fly who sees blood."[47] The charges are rather easily manufactured
up, and Chang is arrested.

When Wang Hsien, who had been away on business, returns, he initially doubts the truth of the charges, but the force of local gossip
(financed by Chao Ang) convinces him of its truth. Chao Ang urges
Wang to expel T'ing-hsiu and to find an appropriate husband for Yü-
chieh. Wang does expel T'ing-hsiu. T'ing-hsiu protests his innocence,
sobbing, saying that even if Wang beats him to death he will not leave.
But leave he does.

When the Lady Hsü hears the crying, she assumes it is simply her husband beating one of the servants, and so pays no particular attention. But
when she discovers that T'ing-hsiu has been expelled, she is distraught,
as is her daughter Yü-chieh. T'ing-hsiu goes to the jail and tells his father
what has happened. Chung I, in jail for committing murder to right an
unspecified wrong, figures out that the villain must be Chao Ang. The
two brothers plan to file a complaint against Chao Ang. But Chang
Ch'üan and Chung I are not circumspect about their discussions, and a
jailer who reports to Chao Ang gets wind of the plans. It is a world where
murderers are on the side of righteousness (indeed, Chung I's given name
means righteousness) and jailers are corrupt. Chao Ang hires thugs to
pose as boatmen who are to take the brothers to the prison. The brothers
are thrown into the water.

But we are only halfway through the story, and the brothers are rescued. Wen-hsiu is rescued by a man named Ch'u Wei, who is more than
sixty, has no children, and is a good man. Almost immediately upon res-
cuing Wen-hsiu, Ch'u proposes that he adopt the boy. He also offers to
help Wen-hsiu avenge the wrongs done him, his brother, and his father.
"Although Wen-hsiu yearned for his parents, at this point he had no
alternative, so he assented. He bowed *(pai)* to Ch'u Wei as a father and
changed his name to Ch'u Ssu-mao."[48]

T'ing-hsiu is saved by an acting troupe. Impressed by his good looks, they want him to become an actor. He is reluctant, at least in part because actors are held in such low esteem, but finally agrees. Young, handsome, and talented, he makes a fine actor. He stays with the troupe for nearly a year, until he catches the eye of a wealthy patron, Shao Ch'eng-en. Shao has a daughter, but no son. He wants to adopt T'ing-hsiu. T'ing-hsiu, who had been held a near-prisoner by the actors, is more than willing. He says that the adoption would be the "benevolence of rebirth." The ritual is accomplished by a simple bowing.

Shao wants to marry his daughter to T'ing-hsiu, but he fears that since he first adopted him as a son, there might be gossip. The point is moot, for T'ing-hsiu himself has reservations. He does not want to marry before he has avenged his father. And he does not know whether Wang Yü-chieh is still waiting for him or not. (She is indeed waiting. She attempted suicide when her father began to make preparations for her to marry someone else, but was rescued.) Shao lets the matter rest.

Wen-hsiu leaves the Ch'u household to go home and encounters T'ing-hsiu on the road. The two of them do not initially recognize one another, but they do feel a kind of kinship, as if they are the same "bones and flesh," and they eventually recognize one another. Shortly thereafter, they pass the civil service examinations. Wen-hsiu and Shao Ch'eng-en meet, and the boy declares himself to be the nephew of his elder brother's adoptive father. Shao, still looking for a match for his daughter, suggests that Wen-hsiu marry her. Wen-hsiu, though interested, responds that he can't do so without permission from his parents.

The two brothers go home. An acting troupe is at the Wang household, and T'ing-hsiu joins them in presenting a scene from the *Ching ch'ai chi* (The Golden Hairpin) in which the heroine, Ch'ien Yü-lien, tries to commit suicide rather than marry a man other than her absent fiancé. The narrator tells us that T'ing-hsiu is expressing his hopes that Yü-chieh too had resisted marriage. The Wangs are outraged that their erstwhile adopted son and son-in-law is plying an actor's trade, but eventually a reconciliation is effected. The happy ending is predictable: Chao Ang and his two thugs are executed. Chao's wife Jui-chieh commits suicide. Wang is reunited with his adopted son. Chang Ch'üan is released from prison, as is Chung I. T'ing-hsiu marries Yü-chieh. Wen-hsiu marries Shao's daughter. After their adoptive fathers die, each son mourns the adoptive father for the requisite three years and then changes his surname back to Chang. And Chang Ch'üan lives to be ninety, in good health. He is, finally, properly avenged. T'ing-hsiu has three sons—the second son is an heir to the Wang family, and the third is an heir to the Shao family. Wen-hsiu has two sons, and the second becomes an heir to the Ch'u family. The sons and grandsons all prosper and attain high office. It is a happy ending with a resounding sense of closure.

The grasping and evil nature of Chao Ang is a compelling critique of the institution of uxorilocal marriage. The uncertainty we saw above as to whether adoption creates an impediment to marriage is repeated here: Shao worries that marrying his daughter to his adoptive son might cause gossip, but Wang apparently does not.

The first adoptive father, Wang Hsien, is a stock figure in Ming and early Ch'ing fiction: an essentially good man who does not quite understand the world around him and who is hence easily manipulated. His wife, the Lady Hsü, by contrast, does not fall prey to Chao Ang's lies, but she is powerless to convince her husband. Wang's failures are failures of moral insight. He is made a fool of, and that is punishment enough.

The other two adoptive fathers, Shao and Ch'u, are given scant attention in the story. We know that they are moral men of high social status. But none of the adoptive fathers has nearly the significance, either to the narrative or to the sons, as does Chang Ch'üan. Although the ending is meticulous in its distribution of heirs—everyone gets at least one—and its care for the sensibilities of Shao and Ch'u—their adoptive sons mourn them fully and wait until the end of the mourning period to change their surnames back—there is no doubt where the ultimate loyalties of T'ing-hsiu and Wen-hsiu lie. Shao and Ch'u are not rivals to Chang Ch'üan: indeed, they assist the Chang brothers in their quest for revenge. Ritual duties are shared, but emotional loyalty returns to the family of birth.

The third story, "Chang Yüan-wai i-fu ming-ling-tzu; Pao Lung-t'u chih-chuan ho-t'ung-wen" (Chang Yüan-wai Adopts a Son; Pao Lung-t'u Figures Out a Tally Document), from Ling Meng-ch'u's *P'ai-an ching-ch'i,* also features the struggle between a uxorilocal son-in-law and another adopted heir, but this time the villain is the mother-in-law.[49]

The *ju-hua* concerns a struggle over property between a married-in son-in-law and a young heir. The *ju-hua* ends with a poem with clear views about inheritance: "How can someone of a different surname obtain a large fortune? / It should go to one's own son—of that there can be no doubt."[50]

The main story begins by telling a tale set in the Sung dynasty. There are two brothers, Liu T'ien-jui and Liu T'ien-hsiang. T'ien-hsiang had no children, but his wife, Madame Yang, had a daughter from a previous marriage. T'ien-jui was married to a woman named Chang and had a son named An-chu.

> Now Madame Yang was neither virtuous nor wise, and privately plotted that when her daughter grew up she would call in a son-in-law, and grant the bulk of the estate to him. Because of this the sisters-in-law occasionally had words.[51]

Drought caused a sudden shift in economic fortunes, and it was decided that T'ien-jui and his family would leave and seek their living elsewhere. The family drew up a document detailing property arrangements, anticipating the eventual return of T'ien-jui and his family.

T'ien-jui and his family went to a village called Hsia-ma in Shansi province, where they encountered a wealthy, childless, and virtuous old man named Chang. Chang decided that he wanted to adopt the three-year-old An-chu, and the child's parents consented. When the child's parents became ill, his adoptive parents "looked after them as if they were bone and flesh" and provided them with medical care. But it was to no avail, and the young couple died.

Fifteen years passed, Ling tells us, as if in a moment, and when An-chu is eighteen, Chang tells him the story of his origins. Chang had been scrupulous about seeing to it that An-chu attended to the sacrificial needs of his parents, albeit unwittingly. At the Ch'ing-ming festival every year, Chang had An-chu worship at unidentified graves, which of course were those of his natural parents. After An-chu learns the truth, he decides to take the bones of his parents back to the ancestral home and rebury them. Chang has no objections, indeed, encourages him and gives him the contract that the two brothers had drawn up so that he can prove his identity to his uncle. But before An-chu meets his uncle, he meets his aunt, Madame Yang. Not only does she take the contract and later deny ever having seen it or him, she also beats him. A neighbor who had been witness to the contract (and to whose daughter An-chu had been betrothed) takes An-chu to Judge Pao, whom we've seen above (p. 15). The judge asks Madame Yang if An-chu is a relative or not. She replies that he is not. A jailer thereupon falsely reports that An-chu has died of his injuries and Pao tells Madame Yang:

> "If he had been a relative, since you are senior and he is junior, your beating him to death would be no more serious than 'mistakenly killing a son or grandson,' and you would not have to pay with your life—a fine of a couple of coins would do."[52]

He goes on to explain that the penalty for killing a stranger is much more serious—she might be executed. She immediately claims that he is her nephew and produces the document as proof. An-chu is then revealed to be alive. The reunion with his rather crass and unwelcoming relatives is the happy ending. Madame Yang is merely fined; her victim was her relative after all. Liu is not punished, because he was unaware of his wife's activities. Like Wang Hsien in the earlier story, he is a good man who simply does not understand the world around him. An-chu returns to his original surname and is heir to both the Chang and the Liu families. The uxorilocal son-in-law is expelled.

A poem ends the story:

> Even an adopted son and a stepfather show virtue;
> But flesh and bone natural relatives are disloyal.
> Only time will tell your predetermined fate,
> So what point is there in hatching schemes?[53]

Again we see that uxorilocal heirs are scheming (or their mothers-in-law scheme on their behalf). Adoption may mimic blood ties, but it is clear that the blood ties are paramount. But, as this story makes clear, blood ties alone do not make a happy family. Adopted sons may show virtue, and that virtue may transcend the ties between blood relatives.

The relationship between virtue, fate, and nature is taken to a final conclusion in a short story and a play on the same theme by the early Ch'ing author Li Yü. Keith McMahon has written of the "satirical viewpoint" of early Ch'ing fiction, and Patrick Hanan has written of Li Yü's fondness for social paradox. Adoption plays a central role in his story "Sheng wo lou" (The House Where I Was Born) and the play following the same general plot, *Ch'iao t'uan-yüan* (The Amazing Reunion).[54] The story was first published in 1658, the play ten years later. The play is much longer than the story; Eric Henry has described the differences.[55]

Li Yü is interested in ingenuity and in artifice, and using adoption as a central theme gives full play to his sense of ingenuousness. The plot of the story is roughly as follows: Yin Hou is childless and very rich. After years of childlessness, Yin built a new house in the hopes that by altering the geomantic configurations of his residence he could have a son. His wife did give birth to a son. The pleasure of the birth of the son was diminished only by the fact that the child had only one testicle. When the child was three or four, he vanished. Tigers had been troubling the area, and it was assumed that the child had been killed by a tiger. Twenty years went by, and no second child was born. Friends suggested that Yin take a concubine, but he refused. When they further suggested that he adopt a son, he responded in a way that echoes the concerns of Liu Te in the *Hsing-shih heng-yen* story:

"To adopt a son is not a frivolous matter; you need to find the right person. It seems to me that before my eyes now there's no such deserving person. Furthermore, if I were to take my 10,000 *chin* estate and give it to someone, it would be the case that, in ordinary times, he'd have some affectionate intentions *(ch'ing-i)* toward me. No matter how much I loved him, it wouldn't be too much. So I would give him my estate to return his kindness and repay his virtue. If I died tomorrow, I'd have no regrets under the Nine Springs. But if I did not consider whether or not he was affectionate *(yu ch'ing)* or whether or not he was reliable *(k'e-t'uo)*, but merely saw a child and wanted to adopt him, then as long as I'm alive he'll feign reverence because he wants my property. But his ceaselessly calling us mother and father is mouthing mere words. As soon as I am dead, I am I and he is he, and what connection can there be?

"If the heir is established before the stepfather has died, then 'as soon as he wields power, all his orders must be followed.' He tyrannizes his father and mother, and taunts them for having no son and daughter. If he doesn't get his way, he'll hound them until they die a day earlier, so he might become master of the house a day sooner. This in fact frequently happens in families who have adopted an heir. This property of mine was earned by my blood and sweat, and I can't bear simply to give it away to just anyone; I want to wait for an affectionate *(yu ch'ing)* and dutiful *(yu i)* son. Before I adopt him I want to experience his kindness, and that will put my mind at ease. Then I'll bestow kindness on him. Other people invest capital to gain interest. I want him to invest interest to gain capital."

One day Yin said to his wife, "Everyone around here knows we're rich, and which one doesn't dream of becoming our heir? Having heard my arguments, there will always be someone coming with a baited hook, to lure me with feigned affection and false intentions. It would be best if I left home, and travelled around to different regions, meeting strangers and testing their affection and intentions. Should I happen to find this kind of deserving man, willing to serve me with a true heart, I'll bring him back and establish him as an heir. How would that be?" She responded, "That's exactly what you should do."[56]

Yin Hou does go search for a son. He ties a piece of straw to his hat to indicate that he is for sale, and wears a placard with the following verse inscribed on it:

> Old and without a son
> I sell myself as someone's father.
> I ask for only ten ounces of silver.
> If interested, cash on delivery and
> No further regrets.[57]

Everywhere he goes, the old man in his beggar disguise is mocked. One day a young man defends him, and the assembled ruffians ask why he doesn't buy the old man. The young man, a fine fellow named Yao Chi, does. Thus the central act of the story is motivated by a taunt. Yao had been looking for a father for a long time, but he had been hindered in his search by the fear that people would suspect that he was motivated by the search for material gain. In what is surely an extraordinary reversal of normal procedure, the adoption transaction is completed before the two men have even exchanged surnames. Because normal channels for getting an heir are tarnished by greed, extraordinary measures must be taken. Yin behaves in as obstreperous a manner as possible, even feigning illness, to test the devotion of Yao. Yao passes the test. But a shade of suspicion remains—Yin does not tell Yao his true surname or place of residence. When Yin tells Yao that they come from the same district, Yao comments: " 'The old proverb is apt: Even though we're not related, we're from the same place. Meeting you today must be because of an affinity *(yüan-fa)* from a former life.' "[58] The destiny of Yao and Yin has several more twists in it before it finally resolves itself.

Yao leaves Yin to search for Miss Ts'ao, his fiancée, who has been kidnapped by bandits. Yin realizes too late that Yao knows neither Yin's correct name nor place of residence.

Meanwhile, the bandits are selling the kidnapped women, who have been concealed in large sacks. Yao buys a woman, hoping to locate Miss Ts'ao. The woman he has purchased is old enough to be his mother; and Yao, a resourceful young man, makes the best of the situation. He tells the old woman: " 'I had planned to buy a wife but got you instead. A lady of your age is old enough to be my mother. Since I don't have one, why don't you become my adopted mother?' " She is grateful for his kindness, but rather perplexed by it, asking why he is proposing such a thing when there is no prior connection between them *(mei yüan mei ku)*.[59] Yao's adoptive mother tells him that among the captive women there had been an exceptionally beautiful and refined young woman, who would make a good wife for him. She tells him that the young woman can be identifed by the jade ruler she carries on her person, a talisman that can be felt through the sack. Yao had given just such a memento to Miss Ts'ao, and sure enough, the young woman the old lady has in mind for him to marry is none other than his fiancée. The old woman leads Yao and his bride back to her home. The old woman is, it turns out, none other than Mrs. Yin. Yin is overjoyed at the double reunion with his wife and adopted son. Yao is astonished to discover that the Yin home is identical to a home he had dreamed of as a child. He tells the astonished assembly of the dream. Yin tells him that he had a son who wandered off at the age of four. Yao responds, " 'I was born twenty years ago and never heard anyone say I had any parents other than the Yao family.' "[60] His fiancée breaks into laughter and says:

"Such nonsense! Are you still dreaming? In my neighborhood, who didn't know your story? It was just that no one wanted to talk about it to your face. When you asked to marry me, my father and my mother were very taken with you, and would have liked to have you as a son-in-law. It was

just that other people said you weren't the bone and flesh of the Yao family
—that you were a wild seed brought in from elsewhere. So they weren't willing to permit the marriage. Someone as smart as you, how can you know so
little of your own origins?"[61]

It was Yao's search for Ts'ao that separated the two men; it is information she provides that makes the reunion possible. She is the agent of
their separation and the agent of their reunion.

Meanwhile, Yin verifies that Yao has only one testicle and takes it as
proof that he is the missing child. The reunion is carried to its ultimate
conclusion—adoptive parents are identical to real parents and all tensions dissolve. The happy ending carries itself generation after generation
as the family prospers.

The play is replete with detail that the much shorter story lacks. The
narrative of the short story tells us that Yin Hou is afraid that scheming
friends and relatives will offer sons in adoption. The play shows the
scene. As soon as Yin announces to his wife his intention of leaving home
to search for a worthy son, a cousin of his wife's arrives, bearing a gift of
wine and, more to the point, of a son to offer Yin in adoption. He sings
of his plans to install his son as heir to Yin's fortune, and concludes tri-
umphantly: " 'I'll never again wear a cotton coat; I'll never again wear a
cotton coat.' "[62] Once he enters Yin's presence, he is scarcely more circumspect. When Yin asks why he has come, the cousin responds: " 'I've
come for only one reason. Because you have no son, you should adopt
your nephew. So I've chosen an auspicious day and brought the child
over to you, as a ready-made son and heir. Will you accept him or
not?' "[63] As Yin demurs, saying that the adoption of an heir is a complex
issue, requiring further consideration, a neighbor enters, announcing his
plans to offer his son to Yin in adoption, after which he sings, " 'I'll never
again have to mind the store; I'll never again have to mind the store.' "
His presentation to Yin precisely echoes that of the cousin.[64]

The two men, neighbor and cousin, get into a fight, complete with
hair-pulling, over whose offer is more appropriate. A good deal of the
humor derives from the fact that neither son is appropriate. The neighbor argues, using an elaborate graphic pun, that the surnames of the two
men, I and Yin, can with a simple change be made interchangeable.[65]

The cousin, outraged at this logic, mocks the neighbor. But the neighbor proceeds to use his "rich schemes," as the cousin calls them, to discredit the cousin's claim. This too depends on a pun. The cousin is a cousin of Yin's wife, a *piao-hsiung*. The neighbor says that as a *piao* (cousin) is a *piao* (prostitute), Yin might as well adopt a child of a prostitute as the child of his wife's cousin.

The humor in the scene derives from expectations of what is proper and contravention of those expectations using verbal cleverness. Normal sources of adopted sons are no good—because normal concerns for money obstruct sincerity. As Eric Henry has written, in the world of Li Yü, "The only actions that can be proven to be totally sincere are those which are totally gratuitous."[66] But there is a difference here with the greed of Chao Ang in the *Hsing-shih heng-yen* story and Madame Yang in the *P'ai-an ching-ch'i* story. Their greed is violent and cruel. The greed in Li Yü's play is humorous because Yin Hou can see through it. Greed is merely a distraction.

The adoption of Yao in the play is couched in extravagant language that recalls the mimicry of birth we have already seen in the *hsüeh-pao* ritual above (p. 88), where the adoptive mother mimics giving birth. Yao swears to Yin that this is no ordinary adoption, using language clearly indicating that adoption mimics birth, even to the point of metaphorical labor pains.

> "From this time on, I'm not an orphan,
> And you, father, won't be alone in your old age.
> Don't say I'm an adopted child
> I'll make you my natural father in the end;
> We are like bone and flesh from two once-dead but newly-revived families.
> This is not a case of tumbleweed tracks meeting in the road;
> Clearly it is an instance of bearing another child, re-experiencing labor pains."[67]

The irony is, of course, that Yin is Yao's natural father, in the beginning as well as in the end. The metaphor of male labor pains suggests that. Adoption is a social rebirth, which, rather than distancing itself from original birth, seeks metaphorically to reenact it. Giving birth has become metaphorically possible for a man. The play ends, as does the story, with a resounding reunion.

Li Yü is explicitly interested in fate and in coincidence. Patrick Hanan calls "Sheng wo lou" Li Yü's "finest extravaganza,"[68] and it is both fine and extravagant. Li Yü does not let the coincidences go unremarked. When it is revealed that the two parents that Yao Chi has purchased independently are in fact husband and wife (but before it is revealed that Yao is their long-lost son), the narrator comments: "As it turns out, the Creator's ingenuity *(tsao-wu chih ch'iao)* is a hundred times that of man. It is just as if he were deliberately arranging events so that someone could turn them into a play or a story."[69]

Li's characters do in fact take action. Yin Hou, worried that any son who wants to be adopted will be greedy and grasping, does not give up on the idea, as had Liu Te in the *Hsing-shih heng-yen* story. He goes in search of an adopted son who will not know of the wealth of the Yin family. The artificial ignorance is necessary because the motives of someone who knew of Yin's wealth would automatically be suspect.

Li Yü's characters take action. But of course the actions they are taking are not the actions they think they are taking. As Eric Henry says: "Again and again in his work, regardless of whether the tone in the passage in question be serious or gay, teasing or straightforward, one comes across the idea that human and supernatural agencies are equally and harmoniously responsible for the accidents of our existence."[70]

Yin Hou thinks he is adopting a stranger; he is adopting his own son. Yao Chi thinks he is establishing a fictive relationship with a woman old enough to be his mother, and she turns out to be his mother. By taking action to remedy their situations, they induce heaven to intervene. The human actors are functioning on one plane and the actions of heaven are on another plane. The happy ending results when the two planes intersect. Heaven and man have been laboring for the same ends. The irony in *Ch'iao t'uan-yüan* is that heaven has arranged it, after all. As the characters sing at the end of the play:

> When people are separated, heaven makes them meet again.
> When heaven is rent, people will mend it.
> Neither heaven nor human can be discounted.[71]

There are other tales in which an adopted child is revealed to be a long-lost blood relation. In "Chang Ch'eng" by P'u Sung-ling, for example, the child Chang Ch'eng is wounded by a tiger. A certain Mr. Chang finds him and nurses him back to health. As Mr. Chang has no sons, he adopts the foundling. Some time later, Chang Na, Ch'eng's older brother, finds the lost boy. Mr. Chang and Na, in the course of exchanging pleasantries, discover that they are from the same native place and that their fathers bear the same surname. Indeed, their fathers are the same man. Thus, Mr. Chang, Chang Na, and Chang Ch'eng are brothers. Old Mrs. Chang, the first wife of the father of Na and Ch'eng, had been carried off into slavery along with her son, thus dividing the family. Mrs. Chang dryly comments to her son: " 'Adopting your own brother, you'll get demerits for that one!' "[72]

In another story, virtuous conduct on the part of the parent propels fate to intercede and effect a reunion. In "Lü Ta-lang huan chin wan kujou," Lü Ta-lang finds some money:

> He thought to himself, "When the ancients saw money, they didn't take it, but returned it. I'm now more than thirty years old and have no son. Of what use would this ill-gotten wealth be to me?"[73]

He returns the money to its original owner, a man named Ch'en. Ch'en, out of gratitude, offers his daughter in marriage to Lü's son. But Lü has no son. Lü's only son Hsi-erh had wandered off into a crowd at a religious festival when he was six years old, and Lü's efforts to find him have been of no avail. Ch'en has a young boy he had purchased when the child was about six. The child seems of good character and clever. Ch'en offers to give the child to Lü as an adopted son so that the two of them may be bound by the marriage of their offspring. Lü is greatly startled when Ch'en calls the child Hsi-erh, and upon questioning the child concludes that his newly adopted son is in fact his long-lost one.[74]

In her study of the legends of Yao, Shun, and Yü, *The Heir and the Sage,* Sarah Allan identifies the conflict between virtue and heredity, community and kinship as one of the central tensions in Chinese society. She sees the legends of dynastic founding as myths that mediate those tensions.[75] Adoption serves as a mediator of the values of virtue and those of heredity. One may transform a man of virtue, a sage, into an heir. But adoption gives rise to its own set of tensions, which might be conceptualized as a variant of that between heredity and virtue. It is a tension between those obligations incurred by biology and those incurred by artifice. In these stories, both sets of needs are met. The values of virtue and heredity, community and kinship are all upheld. The revelation that the biological parents (the values of heredity) and the adoptive ones (those of virtue) are one is more than an amusing plot device: it illuminates and resolves a central tension in Chinese society. The sage is revealed to be the heir, after all.

Conclusions

Let us return to the image with which this work opened: that autumn day in 1524 when the Forbidden City was beseiged with officials protesting the Shih-tsung emperor's refusal to permit himself to be named the adopted son of the Hsiao-tsung emperor. The political crisis was resolved by the arrest and the flogging of the offending officials. The emperor had his way, although at great cost. The reign of Shih-tsung was undistinguished, even by the lax standards of the mid-Ming, and it has been suggested that the enervating experience of the succession struggle was at least partly to blame.

But the moral issues raised were not easily laid to rest. How might a man serve two fathers? Under what conditions might one abandon the parents who gave one birth and offer allegiance and filial piety to others? How far might human artifice go to remedy natural deficiency? The answers to these questions, as I have tried to show in the preceding pages, are fraught with ambiguity. Indeed, the ambiguity is a central part of the story. There is no single answer to the questions posed by the Shih-tsung emperor. One does not flog one's ministers over issues about which there is broad cultural consensus.

If we were to reduce the argument of the preceding pages to a simple scheme, it would run as follows: Law and other normative texts, viewing the family as a patrilineal and patriarchal institution with a primary obligation to continue ancestral sacrifices, prohibited adoption across surname lines. The distinction between insider and outsider, though perhaps not absolute, was sharply drawn. But adoption across surname lines was nonetheless relatively prevalent. And furthermore, the practice was accompanied by an ideological structure that described and justified adoption across surname lines. This competing ideology, encapsulated in the term *ming-ling tzu,* suggests that the lines dividing outsider from insider, stranger from kinsman could in fact be crossed.

Yet, and this is another kind of paradox, if we examine cases of adopted children of a different surname, we find that they are frequently not unrelated to the adopting family, but might well be *wai-tsu*, relatives through a female line. As we have seen, explicit kinship ideology (as well as much medical theory) states that kinship resides chiefly in the male line and is signified by a common surname. Yet adoption behavior indicates that significant kinship ties are not restricted to relations among persons of the same surname. *Wai-tsu* are significant kin after all.

Thus the practice of kinship, at least in regard to adoption, is frequently at odds with portions of its articulated ideology. In a sense, the argument is circular. The people of traditional China say they disapprove of adoptions of persons of a different surname: in fact their reluctance is to adopt people with whom there is no tie of kinship or other affinity. The kin group continues to protect the interests of that group and to regulate recruitment into the group: it is merely exercising that protection and regulation on grounds rather different from those it says it is. In a sense, one could perhaps argue that the explicit articulation of ideology may be seen as metaphor for an underlying ideology. Explicit kinship ideology is concerned with exclusivity, with order, and with ritual. The underlying ideology is less exclusive, to be sure. But it is far from all-encompassing. It does not recommend, for example, the adoption of orphans from orphanages. The exclusivity it does harbor is defined on grounds other than that of the explicit ideology. Surname is not necessarily seen as the sole determinant of kinship. When Ch'in Hui-t'ien argues that a daughter is possessed of the same *ch'i*, the same material substance, as her father, he is arguing that a daughter's son might be a more suitable heir than would be the son of a wife's brother. He is explicitly mounting an argument for exclusivity, an argument based on the continuity of *ch'i* rather than on surname. To both groups, those arguing for and those arguing against adoption across surname lines, the continuation of the family line is important, perhaps the most important aspect of family strategy. But definitions of what the line is and how it may be continued differ. Propriety may be as much to the point as kinship.

Despite the disagreement about adoption in the Ming sources, there are certain common themes derived from the conception of the family as portrayed in these sources. No one writing on adoption in Ming China suggests that the ancestral sacrifices do not matter; no one suggests that the capacity of the person adopted to be incorporated into the lineage is not important. The disagreements are over whether the potential for transformation from one surname group to another exists. Those who advocated adoption did not assert that the values of ancestors and lineage do not count: they simply insisted that one need not be dogmatic in defining or honoring those values, and they suggested that other values may count as well.

Most of the sources we have examined reflect a certain degree of tension and ambiguity about adoption. The ambiguity exists on several levels, which may be clearly seen even in those texts that seem to make most strongly the argument against adoption. The law itself contains loopholes. Commentaries to legal codes concede that a person could be adopted as a *yang-tzu* provided he did not change his surname, did not inherit, and did not participate in ancestral sacrifices. The code itself permitted an abandoned child under the age of three to change his surname (although his status as an heir was vague). And the law itself was seldom enforced. Genealogies that rail against the practice yet contain notations of persons adopted both in and out reinforce the picture of ambiguity. Disapproval was not sufficient to stamp out the practice, nor was it strong enough to obliterate records of those who engaged in it.

The ambiguity is not undifferentiated, however. Fiction is frequently casual in its mention of adoption and concerns itself neither with chaos within the lineage nor with unappeased ghosts. But late Ming and early Ch'ing fiction is peopled with kinsmen made treacherous by greed. Property is the symbol of the integrity of the kin group. And in fiction we see clearly both the pathos of the adopted child and the triumph of moral will over biological inadequacy. The central problem facing an adopted child in fiction is reconciling conflicting duties to two sets of parents. In a work like Li Yü's *Ch'iao t'uan-yüan,* where adoptive parents are revealed to be biological parents, the problem of filial piety owed to two sets of parents is neatly addressed. That is one answer to the question of how a person might serve two fathers.

Neither law nor ritual provides fully satisfactory answers to these questions. Mourning texts indicate that a legally adopted child is fully incorporated into his adopted family, but he has not left his old family.

And penal law does not regard adopted sons to be the full equivalent of a natal son. An adopted son is punished more severely for committing a crime against his adoptive father than a natal son would be. Adoption is a compact; transgressions violate that compact.

The example of adoption demonstrates ways in which Chinese family law is conservative. It serves as one more caution against reading law as a description of social practice. Indeed, a certain amount of the central paradox of this work can be explained in terms of the conservatism of the law. But the core of the law is conservative rather than changeless. T'ang adoption law, for example, reflects a greater concern with status than does Ming or Ch'ing law. Ming law represents a liberalization of earlier law, a series of concessions to actual practice. The details may change, but the core of the law—that one may not adopt someone of a different surname—is derived from ritual and a ritualistic conception of what the family is.

The distinction between law as written and law as enforced, between positive law and custom, is quite starkly drawn. Adoption is not the only issue where practice seems to have run counter to legal prescription. Concubines were not permitted in the Ming dynasty for men under forty or for men who had sons; persons of the same surname were not permitted to marry; adult brothers were not permitted to live separately. We know that adult brothers routinely divided households, that young fathers took concubines, and that persons of the same surname married. None of these laws seems to have been rigorously enforced. Reformers do not advocate using the law to bring about change in a practice they abhor. Adoption is a moral and social issue, not a legal one. The issues are larger than can be encompassed by a tidy legal fiction. Unappeased ghosts find no comfort in judicial sleight of hand.

The biological world is fragile; yet the family is not constituted by mere biology. The Chinese family is a moral construct as well as a biological one. Filial piety resides in the mind of the son, not in the bones of the parents. We have seen a number of moral and emotional attitudes that serve to mediate between the rules of biological succession and the actual conditions people found themselves in. For Chu Hsi, one such crucial attitude was sincerity. An equivalent role is ascribed to affection (ch'ing) and duty (i) in late Ming and early Ch'ing fiction. Legal artifice might not be adequate to establish kinship ties, but moral will might suffice.

Notes

Introduction

1. For the Great Ritual Controversy, see *Ming shih* (Peking: Chung-hua shu-chü, 1974), *chüan* 17, pp. 215–222; *Ming Shih-tsung shih-lu* (Taipei: Academia Sinica, 1966–1968), 41/8a–26a and passim. See also Carney T. Fischer, "The Great Ritual Controversy in the Age of Ming Shih-tsung," *Bulletin: Society for the Study of Chinese Religions,* no.7 (Fall 1979): 71–87; idem, "The Great Ritual Controversy in Ming China" (Ph.D. dissertation, University of Michigan, 1977); Rudolf Herzer, "Der Streit über das Grosse Rituel: Ein Hofkontroverse der frühen Chia-ching Zeit," *Oriens Extremis* 19:2 (Dec. 1972): 65–83.

2. *Shih-tsung shih-lu,* 1/2a, p. 3.

3. Cited in Fischer, "The Ritual Controversy in Ming China," p. 109.

4. *Shih-tsung shih-lu,* 39/9a, p. 1001.

5. *Ming shih,* 196, p. 5186.

6. Cited in Fischer, "The Ritual Controversy in Ming China," p. 225.

7. Ibid.

8. *Shih-tsung shih-lu,* 39/9a, p. 1001.

9. See the discussion of the P'u-i controversy in Fischer, "The Ritual Controversy in Ming China," chap. 3, pp. 52–92.

10. Sarah Allan, *The Heir and the Sage* (San Francisco: Chinese Materials Center, 1981), esp. pp. 141–142.

11. Howard Wechsler, *Offerings of Jade and Silk: Ritual and Symbol in the Legitimation of the T'ang Dynasty* (New Haven, Conn.: Yale University Press, 1985).

12. Li Yü, *Ch'iao t'uan-yüan,* in *Li Yü Ch'üan-chi,* ed. Helmut Martin (Taipei: Ch'eng-wen, 1970), vol. 11, *shang* 30a, p. 4653.

13. A listing of all anthropological accounts that report adoption would be prohibitively long. Maurice Freedman, in "The Family in China, Past and Present," in his *The Study of Chinese Society* (Stanford, Calif.: Stanford University Press, 1979), p. 244, notes that in upper-class families in traditional China "adoption was easy." In addition to the works that explicitly address the issue of adoption listed in notes below, see Stevan Harrell, *Ploughshare Village: Culture and Context in Taiwan* (Seattle: University of Washington Press, 1982). Plough-share village in northern Taiwan seems to be distinguished from nearby villages

(like those studied by Ahern and the Wolfs) by its weak lineage organization. See also Emily Martin Ahern, *The Cult of the Dead in a Chinese Village* (Stanford, Calif.: Stanford University Press, 1973). Myron L. Cohen, *House United, House Divided: The Chinese Family in Taiwan* (New York: Columbia University Press, 1976), p. 27, notes that during the period for which he studied Yen-liao (1920–1964), there was a decline in the importance of adoption, which he attributes to the decline in infant and child mortality.

14. Arthur Wolf and Chieh-shan Huang, *Marriage and Adoption in China, 1845–1945* (Stanford, Calif.: Stanford University Press, 1980), p. 57.

15. Ibid., p. 204.

16. Ibid., pp. 214–215.

17. James L. Watson, "Agnates and Outsiders: Adoption in a Chinese Lineage," *Man* 10:2 (June 1975): 298–299.

18. See, for example, H. P. Chiu, "The Origin and Purpose of Adoption," *China Law Review*, no. 3 (Feb. 1930): 79–88; idem, "Questions Concerning the Adoption of Children," *Chinese Law and Government*, Spring 1961, pp. 60–63 (reprinted from *Kung-jen jih-pao*, April 11, 1957).

19. Jack Goody, *The Development of the Family and Marriage in Europe* (Cambridge: Cambridge University Press, 1983), p. 40. Goody notes that while Salvien condemned adoption, Bede did not.

20. Cited in Paul Gonnet, *L'adoption Lyonnaise des orphelins légitimes (1536–1797)* (Paris: Librarie Générale de Droit et de Jurisprudence, 1935), p. 15.

21. Goody, *The Family and Marriage*, p. 73.

22. Ibid.

23. See Stephen B. Presser, "The Historical Background of the American Law of Adoption," *Journal of Family Law* 11 (1971), esp. pp. 453–456 for an elaboration of this view.

24. *Black's Law Dictionary* (4th ed., 1968), p. 70. Cited by Presser, p. 8.

25. Jack Goody, "Adoption in Cross-cultural Perspective," in *Production and Reproduction: A Comparative Study of the Domestic Domain* (Cambridge: Cambridge University Press, 1976), p. 69; Wolf and Huang, *Marriage and Adoption*, pp. 112–113.

26. The notion of "transactions in parenthood" is developed by Ward Goodenough in "Epilogue: Transactions in Parenthood" in Vern Carroll, *Adoption in Eastern Oceania* (Honolulu: University of Hawaii Press, 1970), pp. 391–410.

27. See the essays collected in Carroll, ed., *Adoption in Eastern Oceania*, and in Ivan Brady, *Transactions in Kinship: Adoption and Fosterage in Oceania* (Honolulu: University of Hawaii Press, 1976). Elizabeth Mandeville, who has done work among the Kamano of the Eastern Highlands district of Papua New Guinea, has identified six types of transactions in parenthood. See her "Kamano Adoption," *Ethnology* 20:3 (July 1981): 231–234.

28. J. A. Crook, *Law and Life of Rome* (Ithaca, N.Y.: Cornell University Press, 1967), p. 111.

29. Ibid., esp. chap. 4, "Family and Succession" (pp. 98–138); R. Monier, *Manuel elementaire de droit romain,* 6th ed. (Paris: Editions Domet Montchrestien, 1947), 1:263–270; Marcel Henri Prévost, *Les adoptions politiques à Rome sous la Republique et le Principat* (Paris: Recueil Sirey, 1949). See also Goody, "Adoption in Cross-cultural Perspective," pp. 69–71. John Eastburn Boswell, in his *"Exposito* and *Oblatio:* The Abandonment of Children and the Ancient and Medieval Family," *American Historical Review* 89:1 (Feb. 1984): 10–33, discusses informal adoption arrangements in antiquity.

30. John Dawson Mayne, *Treatise on Hindu Law and Usage* (London: Stevens and Haynes, 1898), p. 123. Max Müller has identified the texts as dating from approximately 600–200 B.C. (Mayne, p. 14).

31. Ibid., p. 109.

32. Ibid., p. 111.

33. S. J. Tambiah, "Dowry and Bridewealth and the Property Rights of Women in South Asia" in Jack Goody and S. J. Tambiah, eds., *Bridewealth and Dowry* (Cambridge: Cambridge University Press, 1974), p. 81.

34. See Vern Carroll, "Introduction: What Does 'Adoption' Mean?" in Carroll, *Adoption,* p. 5. See also Howard et al., "Traditional and Modern Adoption Patterns in Hawaii," p. 32; Anthony Hopper, "Adoption in the Society Islands," p. 52; and Paul Ottino, "Adoption on Rangiroa Atoll, Tuatamoto Archipelago," p. 92, all in Carroll, *Adoption.* See also the essays in Brady, *Transactions in Kinship.* See also Philip L. Ritter, "Adoption on Kosrae Island: Solidarity and Sterility," *Ethnology* 20:1 (Jan. 1981): 49, where he says that 25 percent of all adoptions were to distant or non-kin.

35. Howard et al., "Adoption Patterns," in Carroll, *Adoption,* p. 32.

36. Ritter, "Kosrae Island," p. 46, describes a clear distinction between adoption and fostering.

37. I. J. McMullen, "Non-Agnatic Adoption: A Confucian Controversy in Seventeenth and Eighteenth Century Japan," *Harvard Journal of Asiatic Studies* 35 (1975): 130–189. The reference to Muro Kyūsō is on p. 165. See also Harumi Befu, "Corporate Emphasis and Patterns of Descent in the Japanese Family," in R. J. Smith and R. K. Beardsley, *Japanese Culture: Its Development and Characteristics* (London: Methuen, 1963), p. 34; John C. Pelzel, "Japanese Kinship: A Comparison," in Maurice Freedman, *Family and Kinship in Chinese Society* (Stanford, Calif.: Stanford University Press, 1970); Chie Nakane, *Japanese Society* (London: Weidenfield and Nicholson, 1970), chap. 1; R. A. Moore, "Adoption and Samurai Mobility in Tokugawa Japan," *Journal of Asian Studies* 29:3 (May 1970): 617–632; Kozo Yamamura, *A Study of Samurai Income and Entrepreneurship* (Cambridge, Mass.: Harvard University Press, 1974), pp. 79–83 and passim; and Tsugaru Fusamaro, *Die Lehre von der Japanischer Adoption*

(Berlin: Mayer and Miller, 1907). For more recent Japanese practices, see Joy Larsen, "Family Law Reform in Postwar Japan: Succession and Adoption" (Ph.D. dissertation, University of Colorado at Boulder, 1983).

Chapter 1

1. See, for example, the discussions in Wolfram Eberhard, *Social Mobility in Traditional China* (Leiden: E. J. Brill, 1962), p. 155.

2. *Meng-tzu chu-shu, SPPY,* vol. 178, 7*hsia*/6b. Translated in James Legge, *The Chinese Classics* (Oxford: Oxford University Press, 1935) (hereafter, Legge), vol. 2, p. 313. Citations are too numerous to mention. But in "Nan Meng-mu chiao-ho san-ch'ien," the sixth tale in Li Yü's *Wu sheng hsi* (Taipei: Chin-hsüeh shu-chü, 1969), the homosexual Hsü Wei marries, because "of the three unfilial acts, to have no descendants is the worst" (p. 359). The *Fu-jen liang-fang* (Good Prescriptions for Women) (Taipei: Shang-wu yin-shu-kuan, 1977), a medical text compiled during the Sung dynasty by Ch'en Tzu-ming, cites the injunction in its section on infertility (8/1a).

3. Li Yü, "Ho-ying lou," in *Shih-erh lou* (Taipei: Chang-ko, 1975), p. 14. Translated by Nathan Mao as "The Reflections in the Water" in *Li Yü's Twelve Towers* (Hong Kong: Chinese University Press, 1975), p. 8. The phrase Mao has rendered "rambling ghosts" reads "be Ao-jo's ghost," an allusion to a passage in the *Tso chuan.* For the relevant passage, see *Ch'un-ch'iu Tso-shih chuan Tu-shih chi-chieh, SPPY,* vol. 39, 10/10a–10b, see the translation in Legge, vol. 5, pp. 295–297. The specific lines alluded to are: "If the ghosts must be seeking for food, will not those of our Jo-ao clan be famished?" Li Yü has transposed the characters of the clan's name.

4. Ling Meng-ch'u, "Li K'o-jang ching ta k'ung-han; Liu Yüan-p'u shuang sheng kuei-tzu," *P'ai-an ching-ch'i* (Taipei: Shih-chieh shu-chü, 1975) (hereafter, PACC), 20, p. 410. My translation is modified somewhat from Dell R. Hales, "The *P'ai-an Ching-ch'i:* A Literary Criticism" (Ph.D. dissertation, Indiana University, 1969), p. 202.

5. "Chieh-hsing shih-lieh," *Huang-ming chih-shu,* p. 288. *Le-ling hsien-chih* (1792), 3/47. Cited in Leif Littrup, *Sub-bureaucratic Government in China in Ming Times: A Study of Shandong Province in the Sixteenth Century* (Oslo: Universitetsvorlaget, 1981), pp. 39–40.

6. See, for example, *Pu-chiang hsien-chih* (1580), 9/2b–3a.

7. P'u Sung-ling, "T'u ou," in *Liao-chai,* vol. 2, *chüan* 5, p. 661. Translated by Herbert A. Giles as "The Clay Image" in *Strange Stories from a Chinese Studio* (Hong Kong: Kelly and Walsh, 1936), p. 432.

8. Li Yü, "Feng-hsien lou," in *Shih-erh lou,* p. 294. Mao translation as "The Male Heir" in *Twelve Towers,* p. 109.

9. *Lung-t'u kung-an,* 2/47b.

10. P'u Sung-ling, "Nieh Hsiao-ch'ien," in *Liao-chai,* vol. 1, *chüan* 2, p. 167. Translated by Timothy A. Ross as "The Ghost Wife" in Y. W. Ma and Joseph S. M. Lau, eds., *Traditional Chinese Stories: Themes and Variations* (New York: Columbia University Press, 1978), p. 408. Also translated by Giles as "The Magic Sword" in *Strange Stories,* p. 83.

11. *Pei-yu chi,* in *Ssu-yu chi* (Shanghai: Ku-tien wen-hsüeh ch'u-pan-she, 1956), p. 204. See the translation and discussion in Gary Seaman, *Journey to the North: An Ethnohistorical Analysis and Annotated Translation of the Chinese Folk Novel* Pei-yu chi (Berkeley and Los Angeles: University of California Press, 1987), p. 163.

12. Ch'en Tzu-ming, *Fu-jen liang-fang,* 9/3a. *Feng-shui* posits the belief that the physical forces of the earth have the power to affect the quality of human life. Hence it is of the utmost importance that cities and houses, as well as graves, be sited in accordance with proper principles of *feng-shui.*

13. Ibid., 9/11b.

14. *Chi-ssu chen-pao,* 1a–2a. Printed in the *She-sheng tsung-yao* compiled by Hung Chi (1638). Translated and discussed by Wolfram Eberhard in *Guilt and Sin in Traditional China* (Berkeley and Los Angeles: University of California Press, 1967), p. 79.

15. Ch'ü Yu, "Fu-kuei fa-chi ssu-chih," in *Chien-teng hsin-hua* (Shanghai: Ku-tien wen-hsüeh ch'u-pan-she, 1957), *chüan* 3, pp. 63–65. Translated by Herbert Franke and Wolfgang Bauer, retranslated by Christopher Levenson in *The Golden Casket: Chinese Novellas of Two Millennia* (London: Penguin Books, 1966) as "The Donors of Riches and Honor," p. 265.

16. *Hsi-yu chi* (Peking: Jen-min wen-hsüeh ch'u-pan-she, 1972 ed.), ch. 47, p. 660. Translated by Anthony Yu as *Journey to the West* (Chicago: University of Chicago Press, 1978), vol. 2, p. 364. Also translated by Arthur Waley as *Monkey* (New York: Grove Press, 1958), p. 254.

17. Feng Meng-lung, "Chiang Hsing-ko ch'ung-hui chen-chu shan," *Ku-chin hsiao-shuo* (Peking: Jen-min wen-hsüeh ch'u-pan-she, 1979), *chüan* 1, p. 34. Translated by Jeanne Kelley as "The Pearl Shirt Reencountered" in Ma and Lau, *Traditional Chinese Stories,* p. 292. See also the translation by Cyril Birch, "The Pearl Sewn Shirt," in his *Stories from a Ming Collection* (Bloomington: Indiana University Press, 1958), p. 96.

18. Feng Meng-lung, "Sung Hsiao-kuan t'uan-yüan p'o chan-li," *Ching-shih t'ung-yen* (Hong Kong: Chung-hua shu-chü, 1978), *chüan* 22. The first quotation comes from p. 308; the second from p. 312. Translated by Gladys Yang and Yang Hsien-yi as "The Tattered Felt Hat" in *The Courtesan's Jewel Box* (Peking: Foreign Languages Press, 1957), p. 223. My translation is modified from that of Yang and Yang.

19. P'u Sung-ling, "Lei ts'ao," in *Liao-chai,* vol. 1, *chüan* 3, p. 419. Translated

by Giles as "The Thunder God," in *Strange Stories,* p. 256. The Shao-wei (Minor Subtlety) star governs the behavior of *shih tai-fu,* major and minor officials. My translation is modified from that of Giles.

20. Cynthia Brokaw, "Yüan Huang (1533–1606) and the Ledgers of Merit and Demerit," *Harvard Journal of Asiatic Studies* 47:1 (June 1987): 137–195; and Sakai Tadao, "Confucianism and Popular Educational Works," in *Self and Society in Ming Thought,* ed. William Theodore de Bary (New York: Columbia University Press, 1970), pp. 331–366.

21. Yüan Huang, *Hsün-tzu yen, TSCCCP,* vol. 168, p. 6. On p. 5 of the same text, Yüan Huang lists an "excess of transgressions" as a cause for infertility.

22. Brokaw, "Yüan Huang," p. 162.

23. T'ao Tsung-i, *Ch'o-keng-lu, TSCCCP,* vol. 44, *chüan* 28, p. 432. Cited in Robert van Gulik, *Sexual Life in Ancient China* (Leiden: E. J. Brill, 1974), p. 204. The phrase *t'ien-yen* is a popular equivalent for *t'ien-huan,* which appears in the *Ling-shu ching,* annotated by Wang Ping (c 762), for men who do not develop secondary sexual characteristics. See the *Huang-ti nei-ching ling-shu, chüan* 5, section "Wu yin wu wei," p. 65, contained in Chang Yü, *Erh-shih-erh tzu* (Chiang-su shu-chü, 1874–1877), vol. 61.

24. For an anthropologist's description of twentieth-century Chinese fertility cults, see Francis L. K. Hsu, *Under the Ancestors' Shadows,* rev. ed. (Stanford, Calif.: Stanford University Press, 1971), pp. 76–78. For a detailed description of the nine childbirth-related goddesses at a Peking temple in the early part of this century, see Anne Swann Goodrich, *The Peking Temple of the Eastern Peak* (Nagoya: Monumenta Serica, 1964), pp. 53–76.

25. *Ching-shih t'ung-yen, chüan* 22, p. 309. My translation is modified from that of Yang and Yang, "Tattered Felt Hat." I have seen no other references to Ch'en-chou Niang-niang, but it is obvious from this context that she is a childbirth deity.

26. "Kuan-shih-yin p'u-sa p'u-men-p'in," chapter 25 in *Ta-sheng Miao-fa lien-hua ching* (Hong Kong: Fo-ching liu-t'ung ch'u, 1988), 7/445.

27. Cited and discussed in Herbert Franke, "Zu einem apokryphen Dharani-sutra aus China," *Zeitung der Deutschen Morganlandischen Gessellschaft* 134:2 (1984): 318–336.

28. See, for example, the ivory Kuan-yin with a child in *The Arts of the Ming Dynasty: An Exhibition Organized by the Arts Council of Great Britain and the Oriental Ceramic Society* (London: Charles F. Ince and Sons, 1958), pl. 99, illus. 367. For a popular woodcut of uncertain date, see *The Graphic Art of Chinese Folklore* (Taipei: National Museum of History, Republic of China, 1977), p. 7.

29. Herbert Franke, "Chih-hsü," in *Dictionary of Ming Biography,* ed. L. Carrington Goodrich and Chaoyang Fang (New York: Columbia University Press, 1976), p. 244.

30. *Hsi-yu chi,* ch. 9, p. 110. Yu, *Journey,* vol. 1, p. 203.

31. Hsieh Chao-che, *Wu tsa-tsu* (Peking: Chung-hua shu-chü, 1959), *chüan* 1, p. 22.

32. Clarence Burton Day, *Chinese Peasant Cults* (Taipei: Chung-wen Publishing Company, 1974), p. 93. Chang Hsien is a popular subject for woodcuts. See, for example, the example reproduced in Paul Serruys, "Les cérémonies du mariage," *Folklore Studies* 3:1 (1944): 146.

33. Hu Ying-lin, cited in Serruys, "Mariage," pp. 142–143. For a discussion of the Kao-mei, an ancient Chinese fertility divinity, see Chow Tse-tsung, "The Childbirth Myth and Ancient Chinese Medicine: A Study of Aspects of the *wu* Tradition," in *Ancient China: Studies in Early Civilization,* ed. David T. Roy and Ts'uen-hsuin Tsien (Hong Kong: The Chinese University Press, 1978), p. 58 ff. For a discussion of early aspects of the cult, see Tetsui Yoshinori, "Kobai no kigen ni tsuite no ichi shiron," *Tōhō shukyō* 30 (Oct. 1967): 20–34.

34. *P'ai-an ching-ch'i, chüan* 6, p. 110; Hales, p. 112. Translated by Tsung-tung Chang as "Die Rache des Bakkalaureus Kia," in *Chinesischer Liebesgarten* (Kunzelsau: Horst Erdmann Verlag, 1964), p. 242. For another deity who grants offspring, see Julia K. Murray's discussion of Hariti in "Representations of Hariti, the Mother of Demons, and the Theme of 'Raising the Alms-Bowl' in Chinese Painting," *Artibus Asiae* 43:4 (1981–82): 253–268. See also the discussion of Hariti in Glen Dudbridge, *The Hsi-yu chi: A Study of Antecedents to the Sixteenth-Century Novel* (Cambridge: Cambridge University Press, 1970), pp. 16–18 and passim, and Noel Peri, "Hariti la mère de demons," *Bulletin de l'Ecole Française d'Extrême Orient* 17:3 (1917): 1–103.

The White-robed Kuan-yin Scriptures *(Pai-i Kuan-yin ching)* are also recited by Shih Chi in *Ching-shih t'ung-yen, chüan* 25, p. 378. He is more than forty years old and has no children. He also promises 300 taels of silver to restore a Buddhist temple on the day of his son's birth. A son is indeed born to him.

35. *Hsing-shih heng-yen, chüan* 39, pp. 841–851.

36. *Chin p'ing mei* (Hong Kong: Kuang-chih shu-chü, 1955). In chapter 40, Nun Wang tells Wu Yüeh-niang of the potion. See the translations by Franz Kuhn, *Kin P'ing Meh, oder die abenteuerliche Geschichte von Hsi Men und seinen sechs Frauen* (Leipzig: Insel Verlag, 1930), p. 394, and E. Clement Egerton, *The Golden Lotus* (London: Routledge, 1939), vol. 2, pp. 182–183.

37. *Chin p'ing mei,* ch. 68. Egerton, vol. 2, p. 231.

38. For example, Ch'en Tzu-ming, *Fu-jen liang-fang, chüan* 8; *Chang-shih i-t'ung, chüan* 15. See also the section "Tzu ssu lun" in the *Ch'an-pao pai-wen* and the section "Lun tzu" in the *Nü-k'o pai-wen.* The two latter essays are substantially the same. For a discussion of fertility in Ming and early Ch'ing medical texts, see Angela Leung, "Autour de la naissance: La mère et l'enfant en Chine aux XVIe et XVIIe siècles," *Cahiers internationaux de sociologie* 76 (1984): 52–58.

39. *Ming-tai lü-li hui-pien,* vol. 2, p. 501; *Ta Ming lü chi-chieh fu-li,* vol. 2, 6/9a, p. 654.

40. *Tu-li ts'un-i,* vol. 2, *chüan* 11, p. 294.

41. Cheng T'ai-ho, *Cheng-shih kuei-fan, TSCCCP,* vol. 167, p. 10. On the Cheng communal family, see John Dardess, "The Cheng Communal Family: Social Organization and Neo-Confucianism in Yuan and Early Ming China," *Harvard Journal of Asiatic Studies* 34 (1974): 7–52.

42. *Ching-shih t'ung-yen, chüan* 25.

43. See, for example, *P'ai-an ching-ch'i, chüan* 20, p. 432.

44. *Yüan-shih shih-fan, Chih-pu-tsu chai ts'ung shu,* vol. 130, 3/7a–7b. Patricia Buckley Ebrey, *Family and Property in Sung China: Yuan Ts'ai's Precepts for Social Life* (Princeton, N.J.: Princeton University Press, 1984), p. 287.

45. Hsieh Chao-che, *Wu tsa-tsu, chüan* 4, p. 214.

46. P'u Sung-ling, "Heng-niang," in *Liao-chai,* vol. 3, *chüan* 10, pp. 1431–1435. Translated in Levenson, *The Golden Casket,* pp. 375–380.

47. *Liao-chai,* vol. 3, *chüan* 11, p. 1523.

48. *Ta Ming lü chi-chieh fu-li,* vol. 2, 6/2a, p. 641.

49. For Western language discussion of the precise meaning of the various terms, see: *kuo-fang:* Pierre Hoang, *Le mariage chinois au point de vue légal* (Shanghai: Imprimerie de la Mission Catholique Orphelinat de t'ou se wei, 1898), pp. 11 and 22. *hou:* Tch'en Si-tan, *L'adoption en droit chinois* (Shanghai: Imprimerie de l'orphelinat de t'ou se wei, 1924), p. 8. *chi-tzu:* Guy Boulais, *Manuel de code chinois* (Shanghai: Imprimerie de la Mission Catholique, 1924), p. 187. *ssu:* Boulais, p. 187. *ch'i-yang:* Hoang, *Mariage,* p. 22. *i-tzu:* Boulais, p. 187. *pao-yang:* Hoang, *Mariage,* p. 22. See also the discussion in I. R. Burns, "Private Law in Traditional China (Sung Dynasty): Using as a Main Source of Information the Work *Ming-kung shu-p'an Ch'ing-ming chi*" (Ph.D. dissertation, Oxford, 1973).

50. *P'ai-an ching-ch'i, chüan* 21, pp. 402–404.

51. See, for example, *Hsing-shih heng-yen, chüan* 10, pp. 205, 211; Li Yü, "Ho-ying lou," in *Shih erh lou,* p. 19, translated by Mao as "The Reflections in the Water" in *Twelve Towers,* p. 11.

52. See Ann Waltner, "Adoption of Children in Ming and Early Ch'ing China" (Ph.D. dissertation, University of California at Berkeley, 1981), chapter 9.

53. Ibid.

54. See the discussion in Marjorie Topley, "Cosmic Antagonisms: A Mother-Child Syndrome" in *Religion and Ritual in Chinese Society,* edited by Arthur Wolf (Stanford, Calif.: Stanford University Press, 1974), pp. 233–250.

55. See the discussion in chapter 3.

56. See the discussion in Jack Goody, "Adoption in Cross-cultural Perspective," in his *Production and Reproduction: A Comparative Study of the Domestic Domain* (Cambridge: Cambridge University Press, 1976), p. 68.

57. Hung Mai, *Jung-chai sui-pi, SPTK, hsü pien,* vol. 331, 8/7a–7b. The relevant section is entitled "Jen wu i i wei ming" (Persons and things that are called *i*). Among the examples given is "false hair." Current usage for false teeth is *i-ch'ih.* These latter two examples reinforce the sense of the word *i* as meaning that which has been appropriated from outside. I am grateful to William Boltz for his comments on this subject. See the debate between Mencius and Kao-tzu, where Kao-tzu defines *i* as "external, not internal" in contradistinction to *jen,* which is "internal, not external." *Meng-tzu chu-shu, SPPY,* vol. 178, 11 *shang*/2b (Legge, *Chinese Classics,* vol. 2, p. 397). See also the discussion of *i* in Tu Wei-ming, *Centrality and Commonality: An Essay on the* Chung-yung (Honolulu: University of Hawaii Press, 1976), pp. 74–75 and passim.

58. *T'ung-su pien, chüan* 15, p. 171.

59. The five relationships are detailed in *Mencius, Meng-tzu chu-shu, SPPY,* vol. 177, 5 *hsia*/2a. (Legge, *Chinese Classics,* vol. 2, pp. 251–252.)

60. Chang Tsai, *Chang-tzu ch'üan-shu, SPPY,* 1/1a. Translated in Wing-tsit Chan, *A Sourcebook in Chinese Philosophy* (Princeton: Princeton University Press, 1963), p. 497. On Chang Tsai, see Ira Kasoff, *The Thought of Chang Tsai (1020–1077)* (New York: Cambridge University Press, 1984).

61. See, for example, the discussion in David M. Schneider, *A Critique of the Study of Kinship* (Ann Arbor: University of Michigan Press, 1984).

62. For a discussion of the impact of English attitudes toward blood on the virtual absence of adoption in common law, see Stephen B. Presser, "The Historical Background of the American Law of Adoption," *Journal of Family Law* 11 (1971): 448–456. The American jurist William Whitmore suggested in his *Law of Adoption* that "considering the fact that the subjects of adoption are largely taken from the waifs of society, foundlings or children whose parents are depraved or worthless; considering also the growing belief that many traits of the mind are hereditary and almost irradicable," adoption be temporary throughout a child's minority, with the option of ratifying the arrangement once it was clear how the child had turned out. Cited and discussed in Presser, pp. 467–468. See also David M. Schneider, *American Kinship* (New York: Prentice Hall, 1968). Schneider discusses flesh and blood as the central symbol of American kinship: "The symbols of American kinship consist of the unity of flesh and blood, in the fact that the child looks like a parent or takes after a grandparent, and in the affirmation that blood is thicker than water" (p. 49).

63. *Ch'iao t'uan-yüan,* act 3, *Li Yü ch'üan-chi,* vol. 11, *shang*/8a, p. 4609. For a summary of the play, see Eric P. Henry, *Chinese Amusement: The Lively Plays of Li Yü* (Hamden, Conn.: Archon Books, 1980), pp. 186–202.

64. A. H. Sturtevant, *A History of Genetics* (New York: Harper & Row, 1965), p. 2.

65. Ibid., p. 17.

66. Ibid., pp. 121–122.

67. See, for example, *Fu-jen liang-fang*, 9/5b.

68. N. J. Girardot, *Myth and Meaning in Early Taoism: The Theme of Chaos (hun-tun)* (Berkeley and Los Angeles: University of California Press, 1983), p. 137.

69. Wei Hsi, *Wei Shu-tzu jih-lu*, in *Hsün-su i-kuei*, in *Wu-chung i-kuei, SPPY,* vol. 1549, 3/30b. I have followed the translation of Shiga Shūzō, "Family Property and the Law of Inheritance in Traditional China," in *Chinese Family Law and Social Change*, ed. David Buxbaum (Seattle: University of Washington Press, 1978), p. 123.

70. See Charlotte Furth, "Concepts of Pregnancy, Childbirth and Infancy in Ch'ing Dynasty China," *Journal of Asian Studies* 46:1 (February 1987): 7–35; and idem, "Blood, Body and Gender: Medical Images of the Female Condition in China, 1600–1850," *Chinese Science* 7 (1986): 43–66.

71. *Wang Chung-shu ch'üan-hsiao ko*, in *Hsün-su i-kuei*, in *Wu-chung i-kuei, SPPY,* vol. 1549, 3/20a.

72. Cited by Maurice Freedman, "The Chinese Domestic Family," in his *The Study of Chinese Society* (Stanford, Calif.: Stanford University Press, 1979), p. 237. The translation of the sacred edict comes from Frederic W. Baller, *The Sacred Edict with a Translation of the Colloquial Rendering* (Shanghai: American Presbyterian Mission Press, 1898), p. 9. On the sacred edict, see Victor Mair, "Language and Ideology in the Written Popularization of the *Sacred Edict*" in *Popular Culture in Late Imperial China*, ed. David Johnson, Andrew J. Nathan, and Evelyn Rawski (Berkeley and Los Angeles: University of California Press, 1985), pp. 325–359.

73. Feng Meng-lung, *Shan-ko* (Shanghai: Chung-hua shu-chü, 1962), 1/2a. See also Cornelia Topelmann, *Shan-ko von Feng Meng-lung: Eine Volkslieder-sammlung aus der Ming-Zeit* (Wiesbaden: Franz Steiner, 1973), p. 139.

74. Ch'in Hui-t'ien, *Wu-li t'ung-k'ao* (Taipei: Hsin-hsing shu-chü, 1971), 147/13a.

75. Li Yü, "Tuo-chin lou," in *Shih-erh lou*, p. 32. Translated by Nathan Mao as "The Jackpot" in his *Twelve Towers*, p. 14.

76. P'u Sung-ling, "Chiao-no," in *Liao-chai*, vol. 1, *chüan* 1, p. 63. Translated by Giles as "Miss Chiao-no" in *Strange Stories*, p. 28.

77. P'u Sung-ling, "T'u ou," in *Liao-chai*, vol. 2, *chüan* 5, p. 662. Translated by Giles as "The Clay Image" in *Strange Stories*, p. 424.

78. P'u Sung-ling, "Yeh-ch'a kuo," in *Liao-chai*, vol. 1, *chüan* 3, p. 348. Translated by Giles as "Country of Cannibals" in *Strange Stories*, p. 247.

79. P'u Sung-ling, "T'u ou," in *Liao-chai*, vol. 2, *chüan* 5, p. 662.

80. *Hsi-yu chi*, ch. 9; Yu, *Journey*, vol. 1, p. 206.

81. *Hsi-yu chi*, ch. 9; Yu, *Journey*, vol. 1, p. 209.

82. Liu Hsiang, *Lieh nü chuan pu-chu* (Ch'ang-sha: Shang-wu yin-shu kuan, 1938), 3/4. Translated by Albert O'Hara, *The Position of Women in Early China* (Taipei: Mei Ya Publications, 1971), p. 80.

83. Yüan Ts'ai, *Yüan-shih shih-fan*, 3/6b. Ebrey, *Family and Property*, p. 286.

84. Ebrey, *Family and Property*, p. 111.

85. Yüan Ts'ai, *Yüan-shih shih-fan*, 1/22a–22b. I have followed the translation in Ebrey, *Family and Property*, pp. 215–216.

86. On the issue of merit and heredity and the ways in which the myth of Yao and Shun serves to mediate this tension, see Sarah Allan, *The Heir and the Sage* (San Francisco: Chinese Materials Center, 1981).

87. *Lun-yü chu-shu, SPPY,* vol. 173, 6/2a. (Legge, *Chinese Classics,* vol. 1, p. 186.)

88. See, for example, Clair Hayden Bell, "The Call of the Blood in the Medieval German Epic," *Modern Language Notes* 37:1 (1922): 17–26.

89. Ibid., p. 18.

90. Arthur Dickson, *Valentine and Orson: A Study in Late Medieval Romance* (New York: Columbia University Press, 1929).

91. Michel de Montaigne, *Essays,* trans. J. M. Cohen (Harmondsworth, Middlesex; Baltimore: Penguin Books, 1958), p. 155.

92. P'u Sung-ling, "Wang Kuei-an," in *Liao-chai,* vol. 3, *chüan* 12, pp. 1635–1636. Translated by Giles as "The Boat Girl Bride" in *Strange Stories,* p. 358.

93. P'u Sung-ling, "Wang Shih-hsiu," in *Liao-chai,* vol. 1, *chüan* 3, p. 371. Translated by Giles as "Football on the Tung-t'ing Lake" in *Strange Stories,* p. 252.

94. *Feng-su t'ung-i* (Peking: Centre Franco-Chinoise D'etudes Sinologiques, 1943) 3/108; *I-lin, SPPY,* vol. 1418, 4/3b–48. On the history of the textual transmission of the *Feng-su t'ung-i,* see Michael Nylan, "Ying Shao's *Feng-su t'ung-yi:* An Exploration of Problems in Han Dynasty Political, Philosophical and Social Unity" (Ph.D. dissertation, Princeton, 1982), pp. 339–353. The case is also included in the *Che-yü kuei-chien, TSCCCP,* vol. 134, *chüan* 6, p. 89. The commentary gives a number of similar cases. For example, two families claim a cow, and each is asked to harm it. The family who refuses to harm the cow is perceived to be its rightful owner. See also *T'ang-yin pi-shih, SPTK, hsü pien,* vol. 321, 1/4b. Translated by Robert van Gulik, *Parallel Cases from under the Pear Tree* (Leiden: E. J. Brill, 1956), pp. 80–81.

95. H. T. Francis and E. J. Thomas, *Jataka Tales* (Cambridge: Cambridge University Press, 1916), pp. 464–465.

96. Li Hsing-tao, *Pao Tai-chih chih chuan hui-lan chi tsa-chü,* in *Yüan ch'ü hsüan,* compiled by Tsang Mao-hsün (Peking: Wen-hsüeh ku-chi k'an-hsing she, 1955), p. 14a. Translated and discussed in Ching-hsi Perng, *Double Jeopardy: A Critique of Seven Yüan Courtroom Dramas* (Ann Arbor: Michigan Papers in Chinese Studies, 1975), p. 66 ff. A similar story is contained in the *T'ang-yin pishih,* translated by van Gulik in *Parallel Cases from under the Pear Tree,* pp. 79–80. The ultimate source of the story is the *Wei shu* (Wei dynastic history), 66/

3b–4. Van Gulik has read the name "Kou" as "Hsün." Kou T'ai's three-year-old son was kidnapped. Several years later the child was discovered in the home of a man named Chao Feng-po. Each man claimed that the child was his own and had neighbors who supported his claim. The governor-general of Yangchow ordered the two men incarcerated in separate prisons and sent word to each of them that the child had died. Kou wailed bitterly; Chao merely sighed. Thus the governor-general recognized Kou as the true father. In this case, the ties of sentiment are what distinguished real kinship from false claims.

97. Franke, "Dharani-sutra," pp. 330–331. The woman drowns the child who has caused her such suffering. She becomes pregnant again, and again the child causes her much suffering and she drowns it. When the process repeats itself for a third time, and the child has already been put in the drowning basin, Kuan-yin appears to the woman and explains that the child is the victim from a former life and that only her piety in this life has saved her. The victim/child decided, on the advice of the Bodhisattva, to stop his attempts at revenge. Kuan-yin tells the woman to sell her possessions so she can afford to commission the copying of the sutra a thousand times, presumably in expiation of her twice-successful infanticide as well as out of gratitude to Kuan-yin for saving her. Such is her piety that she lives to be ninety-seven, and when she is reborn, it is as a man, in China. Testimonials such as this are conventional appendices to religious texts. One still sees them in temple literature.

98. "Yüan-shih t'ien-tsun chi-tu hsüeh-hu chen-ching" (HY 72), in "Tung chen pu," "Pen wen lei," section "Su chiu," *Cheng-t'ung Tao-tsang* (Taipei: I-wen, 1962).

99. *Chin p'ing mei*, ch. 59, Kuhn, *Kin ping yeh*, p. 492. Egerton, *Golden Lotus*, vol. 3, p. 87.

100. "Hua-teng chiao Lien-nü ch'eng fo chi," in *Yü ch'uang chi*, included in *Ch'ing-p'ing shan-t'ang hua-pen*, issued about 1550 (Shanghai: Ku-tien wen-hsüeh ch'u-pan-she, 1957), pp. 193–206. Cited by Jaroslav Prusek, "The Narrators of Buddhist Scriptures and Religious Tales in the Sung Period," in his *Chinese History and Literature* (Prague: Czechoslovak Academy of Sciences, 1970), p. 224. For examples of earlier tales, see Kuen-wei Lu Sundarajan, "Chinese Stories of Karma and Transmigration" (Ph.D. dissertation, Harvard, 1979).

101. See Sundarajan, p. 188.

102. Li Yü, "San-yü lou," in *Shih-erh lou*, p. 51 ff. Translated by Mao as "Buried Treasure" in *Twelve Towers*, p. 22. Ch'en Hsi-i, *Ch'en Hsi-i hsin-hsiang pien*, in *Hsün-su i-kuei, Wu-chung i-kuei*, SPPY, vol. 1548, 1/17b.

103. Ch'en Hsi-i, in Ch'en Hung-mou, *Wu-chung i-kuei*, SPPY, vol. 1548, 1/17b.

104. Ch'en Tzu-ming, *Fu-jen liang-fang*, 9/3a. For a discussion of other, similar texts, see Eberhard, *Guilt and Sin in Traditional China*, pp. 78–79. Eberhard writes that in later time periods, the taboos regarding auspicious times for inter-

course were so complicated that lists of auspicious days were printed and sold on the streets. P'an Kuang-t'an calculated that only 100 days a year were auspicious for sexual relations (ibid., p. 35, n. 79). See also Hsu, *Under the Ancestors' Shadow*, pp. 151–154. Hsu calculates the number of taboo days in the twentieth century to number about twenty per year.

105. *Ch'an-ching*. Translated by van Gulik in *Sexual Life*, p. 147.

106. Lu Ts'an, *Keng ssu pien* (Shanghai: Commercial Press, 1937), 6/120.

107. Liu Hsiang, *Lieh nü chuan*, 1/6. Translated by O'Hara, in *Position of Women*, pp. 23–24. T'ai Jen is the mother of Wen Wang, one of the sage kings of antiquity. Many of these injunctions about the behavior of a pregnant woman may be found elsewhere in the classical tradition, where they apply not to the behavior of a pregnant woman, but to the behavior of a *chün-tzu*, of a superior man. See, for example, *Lun-yü chu-shu*, SPPY, vol. 174, 10/5a (Legge, *Chinese Classics*, vol. 1, p. 232): "He did not eat what was discolored, or what was of bad flavor, nor anything which was ill-cooked, or not in season." *Lun-yü chu-shu*, SPPY, vol. 174, 10/5a (Legge, *Chinese Classics*, vol. 1, p. 232): "He did not eat meat which was not cut properly, nor what was served without its proper sauce." *Lun-yü chu-shu*, SPPY, vol. 174, 10/5b (Legge, *Chinese Classics*, vol. 1, p. 233): "If his mat was not straight, he did not sit on it." *Li chi Cheng-chu*, SPPY, vol. 27, 1/8b (Legge, *Li Chi: Book of Rites*, [New Hyde Park, N.Y., University Books, 1967], vol. 1, p. 76): "Do not saunter about with a haughty gait nor stand with one foot raised." I have not yet found other classical references for the injunctions against lying on one's side or sitting sidewise. Presumably these attitudes are both *pu cheng*, not upright, which has, as does its English equivalent, both moral and spatial connotations.

108. Both passages are cited in the *Yin-shan cheng-yao*, compiled in 1330 by Hu Ssu-hui. The passage is cited and translated in Paul Unschuld, *Medicine in China: A History of Pharmaceutics* (Berkeley and Los Angeles: University of California Press, 1986), pp. 216–217. Unschuld says that the section "Food to be Avoided During Pregnancy" in the *Yin-shan cheng-yao* is copied from Sun Ssu-miao's *Ch'ien-chin yao-fang*. The substance of the two paragraphs is similar, but the order of presentation of the foods differs somewhat. On Sun and the *Ch'ien-chin yao-fang*, see Catherine Despeux, *Prescriptions d'acuponcture valant mille onces d'or: Traite d'acuponcture de Sun Simiao du VIIe siecle* (Paris: Guy Tredaniel, 1987), pp. 9–37.

109. van Gulik, *Sexual Life*, p. 132. The text of the *Tung-hsüan-tzu* was reconstructed at the beginning of this century by Yeh Te-hui. See his *Shuang-mei ching-an ts'ung-shu*, vol. 1, p. 5b.

110. *Yen-shih chia-hsün*, TSCCCP, vol. 167, p. 3.

111. *I-shuo*, compiled by Chang Kao (Taipei: Hsin-wen feng ch'u-pan kung-ssu, 1983), 9/27a.

112. "Ch'an-pao tsa-lu," appended to *Nü-k'o pai-wen*, compiled by Ch'i

Chung-fu (Chü-chin t'ang, 1795), 7a. The appendix is not included in the edition published in Shanghai in 1983 by the Shanghai ku-chi shu-tien. The texts with *pai-wen* (hundred questions) in the title all seem to be related to one another.

113. *Fu-jen liang-fang,* 10/1a. Furth ("Pregnancy," p. 7) notes that by the eighteenth century these traditional prescriptions had fallen into disuse.

114. Wang K'en-t'ang, *Nü-k'o chun-sheng* (Taipei: Hsin-wen-feng ch'u-pan kung-ssu, 1974), 4/12a.

115. Paul Unschuld, *Medicine in China: A History of Ideas* (Berkeley: University of California Press, 1985), p. 197.

116. Furth, "Pregnancy," p. 8.

117. Wang K'en-t'ang, *Nü-k'o chun-sheng,* 4/12a–15a.

118. Ibid., 4/12b.

119. *Chang-shih i-t'ung* (Shanghai: K'e hsüeh chi-shu ch'u-pan she, 1963), p. 526.

120. Chang Lu, *Sun Chen-jen pei-chi Ch'ien-chin fang* (Shanghai: Chung-yüan shu-chü, 1930), 2/4b.

121. *Nü-k'o pai-wen,* p. 5a. *Wan-shih yu-ying chia-mi,* by Wan Ch'üan, in *Ku-chin t'u-shu chi-ch'eng* (Shanghai: Chung-hua shu-chü, 1934), vol. 456, 421/29b.

122. *Nü-k'o pai-wen* (1983), p. 5a. *I-shuo,* 9/27a.

123. *Nü-k'o pai-wen* (1983), p. 5a.

124. Ibid.

125. *Wan-shih yu-ying chia-mi,* in *Ku-chin t'u-shu chi-ch'eng,* vol. 456, 421/29b. *Fu-jen liang-fang,* 10/15b; *Nü-k'o pai-wen,* hsia/46a.

126. *Chang-shih i-t'ung,* p. 525.

127. *Fu-jen liang-fang,* 10/15b.

128. Chang Lu, *Sun Chen-jen pei-chi Ch'ien-chin fang,* 2/4b.

129. *Chin p'ing mei,* chap. 75. Summarized and discussed by Katherine Carlitz, "The Role of Drama in the *Chin P'ing Mei:* The Relationship between Fiction and Drama as a Guide to the Viewpoint of a Sixteenth-Century Chinese Novel" (Ph.D. dissertation, University of Chicago, 1979), p. 34, and idem, *The Rhetoric of Chin p'ing mei* (Bloomington: Indiana University Press, 1986), pp. 62–63.

130. Li Yü, "Feng-hsien lou," in *Shih-erh lou,* p. 287.

131. Li Yü, *Wu sheng hsi,* pp. 545–593.

132. Cited in Ch'in Hui-t'ien, *Wu-li t'ung-k'ao,* 147/30b.

133. Hsü Ch'un-fu (fl 1556), *Ku-chin i-t'ung ta-ch'üan,* 88/15b (1570 edition held at University of California, Berkeley).

134. Li Shih-chen, *Pen-ts'ao kang-mu* (Peking: Jen-min wei-sheng ch'u-pan-she, 1975), 4:2950. Cited and translated by Furth, "Blood, Body and Gender," p. 4. On wet nurses, see Victoria Cass, "Female Healers in the Ming and the Lodge of Ritual and Ceremony," *Journal of the American Oriental Society* 106:1 (Jan.–

Mar. 1986), pp. 233–240; Leung, "Autour de la naissance," pp. 63–65; Furth, "Pregnancy," pp. 22–23.

135. On concerns about wet nurses, see the passage in the *Ku-chin t'u-shu chi-ch'eng,* vol. 324, 45/1a–3b.

136. Li Yü, "Ho-ying lou," in *Shih-erh lou,* pp. 3–4, translated by Mao as "The Reflections in the Water," *Twelve Towers,* p. 2. The lines cited by Li Yü read: *ming-ling yu tzu/ shih ku ssu chih.* The reference to the Book of Odes is to Mao no. 197, *Mao-shih chiang-i, SKCS,* vol. 236, 6/1a (Legge, *Chinese Classics,* vol. 4, p. 334). Legge translates the lines as: "The mulberry insect has young ones/And the sphex carries them away/Teach and train your young ones/And they will become as good as you are." Legge reads *ku* (grain) as *shan* (good). If we do not accept this emendation, then the last line would read something like: "And they will resemble the grain (they eat)." Allusions to this passage following Li Yü's interpretation of it are fairly common. That wet nurses have an influence on the children they nurse is asserted in the T'ang encyclopedia *T'ung-tien.* There, as in Li Yü, the assertion is supported by saying "*kuo-luo* resemble the grain they eat" (cited in *Wu-li t'ung-k'ao,* 147/30b). The commentary to the *Wu-li t'ung-k'ao,* in an argument regarding a particular case of adoption in which the adopted child has not been named an heir, says: "It is not a case of the reciprocity of a *kuo-luo* resembling the grain it eats" (147/29b). Similar beliefs are evidenced in early modern Europe. See, for example, William Buchan, who in his *Medicine Domestique* (1775) writes: "One is sometimes surprised to see the children of upright and virtuous parents display, from their earliest years, a fundamental baseness and malice. We can be certain that it is from their nurses that these children derive all their vices. They would have been decent had their mothers nursed them." Cited in Jacques Donzelot, *The Policing of Families* (New York: Pantheon, 1979), p. 11. Laurent Joubert, in his *Erreurs populaires et propos vulgaires touchant la médicine et la regime de santé* (Bordeaux: S. Millanges, 1579), book 2, p. 157, explains that a mother's milk is her menstrual blood, transformed and whitened. Thomas Becon, the chaplain to Archbishop Cranmer, wrote: "For children, by drinking in strange milk also drink in strange manners and a strange nature" (cited in Goody, *The Development of the Family and Marriage in Europe* (Cambridge: Cambridge University Press, 1983), p. 70. See also Caroline Walker Bynum, *Holy Feast and Holy Fast: The Religious Significance of Food to Medieval Women* (Berkeley and Los Angeles: University of California Press, 1987), pp. 270–271.

137. *Hung lou meng,* chap. 19 (Taipei: Kuang-wen shu-chü, 1977). David Hawkes, trans., *The Story of the Stone* (Bloomington: Indiana University Press, 1979–1987), vol. 1, p. 384.

138. Sung Tz'u (fl 1226–1264), *Hsi yüan lu hsiang-i* (Shan-tung shu-chü, 1886). See the translation by Brian McKnight, *The Washing Away of Wrongs* (Ann Arbor: University of Michigan Press, 1981). The passage about the blood

test is contained in an appendix which McKnight has not translated. For the significance of this work, which was frequently recommended in magistrates' handbooks and was the only work of its kind to be officially recognized during the Ch'ing dynasty, see Alison Wayne Conner, "The Law of Evidence during the Ch'ing Dynasty" (Ph.D. dissertation, Cornell University, 1979), p. 9 and passim. This method of ascertaining the identity of a corpse was cited in magistrates' manuals such as the *Fu-hui ch'üan-shu*. See, for example, Huang Liu-hung, *A Complete Book Concerning Happiness and Benevolence: A Manual for Local Magistrates in Seventeenth-Century China*, trans. Djang Chu (Tucson: University of Arizona Press, 1984), p. 375 (*chüan* 16).

139. Sung Tz'u, *Hsi yüan lu hsiang-i*, 1/97b–98a.

140. "Meng-chiang-nü pien-wen," in *Tun-huang pien-wen chi*, ed. Wang Chung-min (Taipei: Jen-min wen-hsüeh ch'u-pan-she, 1957), vol. 1, *chüan* 1, p. 33. My translation is slightly modified from that of Arthur Waley, *Ballads and Stories from Tun-huang* (London: George Allen and Unwin, 1960), p. 147.

141. Sung Tz'u, *Hsi yüan lu*, p. 69a.

142. Sung Tz'u, *Hsi yüan lu hsiang-i*, 1/97b.

143. P'u Sung-ling, "T'u ou," in *Liao-chai*, vol. 1, *chüan* 5, pp. 621–622. Neither will the son of a very old man cast a shadow. See van Gulik, *Pear Tree*, p. 79, case 3A. See also *Che-yü kuei-chien*, 3/1. That a child does not cast a shadow is here too used as a test of paternity. An eighty-year-old man had a daughter, but no sons. He remarried, and his young wife bore him a son. After his death, his daughter challenged the paternity of the boy. The judge Peng Chi (d 55 B.C.) said: "I have heard that a son by an aged father cannot bear cold and that in the sun his body will cast no shadow." Using this test, he was able to establish the legitimacy of the young heir. The commentary to the *Che-yü kuei-chien* (3/16) says that there are some people who doubt the validity of the test and gives further examples. The *Fa-yüan chu-lin*, a seventh-century text, also gives examples of a deceased husband returning and having sexual relations with his wife. See Sundarajan, p. 158.

144. Yen Chih-t'ui, *Yen-shih chia-hsün*, p. 4. This citation is not to be found in the *Lün-yü*. But the Han dynasty author Chia I (220–168 B.C.) cites Confucius as having said it. See the *Chia I hsin-shu*, SPPY, vol. 1422, 5/3b. It can also be found in Chia I's biography in the *Han shu*, 48/19. For another explicit discussion of the importance of childhood education, see *Chin p'ing mei*, chap. 35.

145. Cited in Ch'in Hui-t'ien, *Wu-li t'ung-k'ao*, 147/30b.

146. Cited in R. Génestal, *Histoire de la légitimation des enfants naturels en droit canonique* (Paris: Bibliothèque de l'École des Hautes Études, Sciences Religeuses, 1905), p. 26 ff.

Chapter 2

1. For a discussion of Chinese law as a codification of *li*, see Ch'u T'ung-tsu, *Law and Society in Traditional China* (Paris: École Pratique des Hautes Études, 1961), esp. pp. 9, 283. For a discussion of family law as reinforcing *li*, see David Buxbaum, "A Case Study of the Dynamics of Family Law and Social Change in Rural China," in David Buxbaum, ed., *Chinese Family Law and Social Change* (Seattle: University of Washington Press, 1978), p. 223.

2. *I-li Cheng-chu, SPPY,* vol. 23, 11/3a.

3. Shiga Shūzō, *Chugoku kazoku hō no genri* (Tokyo: Sobunsha, 1968), pp. 313, 584.

4. *T'ang-lü shu-i* (Shanghai: Commercial Press, 1934), 2/108; Niida Noboru, *Tōrei shūi* (Tokyo: Tōhō bunka gakuin Tokyo kenkyujo, 1933), p. 233.

5. *T'ang-lü shu-i*, 2/109. Wallace Johnson translates *tsa-hu* as "general bondsman." See his *The T'ang Code* (Princeton, N.J.: Princeton University Press, 1979), p. 297.

6. *Sung hsing-t'ung* (Peking: Kuo-wu-yüan fa-shih chü, 1918), 12/9b.

7. Ibid., 12/9a.

8. Ibid., 12/8a.

9. *Ta Ming lü chi-chieh fu-li*, 5 vols., ed. Kao Chü (Taipei: Tai-wan hsüeh-sheng shu-chü, 1970), vol. 2, 4/9a, p. 558. *Ta Ming lü*, in *Huang Ming chih-shu*, 13/98a.

10. *Tu-li ts'un-i ch'ung-k'an pen*, ed. Hsüeh Yün-sheng (Taipei: Cheng-wen ch'u-pan-she, 1970), vol. 2, *chüan* 9, p. 249. On the banner organization, see Jonathan Spence, *Ts'ao Yin and the K'ang-hsi Emperor, Bondservant and Master* (New Haven, Conn.: Yale University Press, 1966), pp. 1–7.

11. *Ming-tai lü-li hui-pien*, comp. Huang Chang-chien (Taipei: Academia Sinica, 1979), vol. 2, pp. 462, 464.

12. *Ta Ming lü chi-chieh fu-li*, vol. 2, 4/11b, p. 558.

13. *Ming-tai lü-li hui-pien*, vol. 2, pp. 463, 464.

14. *Ta Ming lü chi-chieh fu-li*, vol. 2, 4/10b–11a, p. 556–557. *Ta Ch'ing lü-li hui-t'ung hsin-ts'uan* (Taipei: Wen-hai ch'u-pan-she, 1964), *ts'e* 2, 7/1a–b, 21b–22a. Guy Boulais, *Manuel du code chinois* (Shanghai: Imprimerie de la Mission Catholique, 1924), p. 188.

15. See, for example, *Ta Ch'ing lü-li*, *ts'e* 2, 7/1a–b, 21b–22a.

16. Shiga, *Hō no genri*, p. 314.

17. *Yüan-shih shih-fan*, in *Chih-pu-tsu chai ts'ung-shu*, vol. 130, 1/22a.

18. Niida Noboru, " 'Seimei shū kokon mon' no kenkyū," *Tōhō gakuhō* 4 (1933): 153–154.

19. *Ming-tai lü-li hui-pien*, vol. 2, p. 464.

20. Ch'in Hui-t'ien, *Wu-li t'ung-k'ao* (Taipei: Hsin-hsing shu-chü, 1971), 147/6b–7a.

21. Shiga, *Hō no genri*, p. 349.

22. *Sung hsing-t'ung*, 12/8a.

23. Shiga, *Hō no genri*, pp. 313, 340; Niida, "Seimei shū," p. 156; *Tu-li ts'un-i*, vol. 2, *chüan* 9, p. 246.

24. Huang Liu-hung, *Fu-hui ch'üan-shu*, 20/12b. Djang Chu, trans., *A Complete Book Concerning Happiness and Benevolence: A Manual for Local Magistrates in Seventeenth-Century China* (Tucson: University of Arizona Press, 1984), p. 453.

25. See the discussion in I. R. Burns, "Private Law in Traditional China (Sung Dynasty): Using as a Main Source of Information the Work *Ming-kung shu-p'an Ch'ing-ming chi*" (Ph.D. dissertation, Oxford, 1973), passim.

26. *Ta Ming lü chi-chieh fu-li*, vol. 2, 4/10b, p. 556.

27. Su Mao-hsiang, *Hsin-k'e ta Ming lü-li lin-min pao-ching* (1632), 4/9a.

28. *Ta Ch'ing lü-li, ts'e* 2, 7/21b.

29. Huang Liu-hung, *Fu-hui ch'üan-shu, chüan* 20. Chu translation, p. 453.

30. Ch'in Hui-t'ien, *Wu-li t'ung-k'ao*, 147/12a.

31. Su Mao-hsiang, *Hsin-k'e ta Ming lü-li*, 4/9a. *Ta Ming lü chi-chieh fu-li*, vol. 2, 4/9a, p. 553. *Ta Ch'ing lü-li, ts'e* 2, 7/21a ff. Boulais, *Manuel du code chinois*, pp. 188–190. Patricia Ebrey says that in the Sung dynasty, children so adopted could inherit. See her "Conceptions of the Family in the Sung Dynasty," *Journal of Asian Studies* 43 (Feb. 1984): 234.

32. Su Mao-hsiang, *Hsin-k'e ta Ming lü-li*, 4/9a. See also Ch'in Hui-t'ien, *Wu-li t'ung-k'ao*, 147/18b.

33. Shiga, *Hō no genri*, p. 314; The edition of the *Ch'ing ming chi* I have used is *Meikō shohan seimei shū* (Tokyo: Koten Kenkyūkai, 1964), "Hu-chüeh," pp. 87–91. See also the discussion in Burns, "Private Law," p. 202.

34. Su Mao-hsiang, *Hsin-k'e ta Ming lü-li*, 4/9a. The *yin* is a hereditary privilege granting rights to office.

35. *Ta Ming lü chi-chieh fu-li*, vol. 2, 4/10b, p. 556.

36. *Tu-li ts'un-i*, vol. 2, *chüan* 9, p. 247.

37. *Ch'ing shih, chüan* 121, p. 1443.

38. Huang Liu-hung, *Fu-hui ch'üan-shu*, 20/12a. Chu translation, p. 453.

39. *Ta Ming lü chi-chieh fu-li*, vol. 2, 4/10b, p. 556; *Tu-li ts'un-i*, vol. 2, *chüan* 9, p. 250.

40. Shiga, *Hō no genri*, p. 584. Niida Noboru, *Shina mibun hōshi* (Tokyo: Zayu baikan kokai, 1943), p. 775.

41. *I-li Cheng-chu*, SPPY, vol. 23, 11/3a. Translated by John Steele, *The I-li or Book of Etiquette and Ceremonial* (Taipei: Ch'eng-wen, 1966), vol. 2, p. 12.

42. *I-li Cheng-chu*, SPPY, vol. 23, 11/3a. Steele, *The* I-li, vol. 2, p. 11.

43. *I-li Cheng-chu*, SPPY, vol. 23, 11/8a for parents; 11/15a for brothers.

44. Ibid., 11/15a.

45. Ibid.

46. The text lists the following terms: *ti*, your father's principal wife; *chi*, a wife your father married after he was married to your mother; *tz'u*, a concubine with no children of her own who "adopts" you; and *yang*, a woman who has adopted you.

47. *Tu-li ts'un-i*, vol. 4, *chüan* 37, p. 947. *Ta Ming lü chi-chieh fu-li*, vol. 4, 20/38b, p. 1618.

48. *Tu-li ts'un-i*, vol. 4, *chüan* 37, p. 951.

49. *Ta Ming lü chi-chieh fu-li*, vol. 2, 6/37b, p. 712; *Tu-li ts'un-i*, vol. 2, *chüan* 12, p. 312. For a discussion in English on *i-chüeh*, see Ch'u, *Law and Society*, pp. 122–123.

50. *T'ung-tien, Ssu-k'u shan-pen ts'ung-shu ch'u-pien*, vol. 256, 96/9b. The prescriptions originate in the *I-li*. An adopted son diminishes the mourning for his natal parents (*I-li Cheng-chu*, SPPY, 11/8a) and that a daughter who has married diminishes the mourning for her natal parents (*I-li Cheng-chu*, SPPY, 11/8b).

51. Cited in *Ming-tai lü-li hui-pien*, vol. 2, p. 801.

52. Ibid., vol. 2, p. 840.

53. Ibid., vol. 2, p. 844. A child is counted as one *sui* at birth. At each passage of the lunar new year, he is counted one year older. Thus by Western reckoning a person who is 16 *sui* is between 14 and 15 years old.

54. Ibid., vol. 2, p. 843.

55. Ibid., vol. 2, p. 836.

56. Ibid., vol. 2, p. 843.

57. Ernest Alabaster, *Notes and Commentaries on Chinese Law* (London: Luzac, 1899), p. 168.

58. Ibid., p. 170.

59. *Ming-tai lü-li hui-pien*, vol. 2, p. 499. *Ta Ming-lü chi-chieh fu-li*, vol. 2, 6/1a–6a, pp. 639–649. The Ch'ing proscription is contained in *Tu-li ts'un-i*, vol. 2, *chüan* 11, p. 291.

60. *Hsiung Mien-an Pao-shan t'ang pu-fei-ch'ien kung-te-li*, compiled by Hsiung Hung-pei. Contained in *Hsün-su i-kuei*, in Ch'en Hung-mou, *Wu-chung i-kuei*, SPPY, vol. 1549, 4/50b.

61. See Hui-chen Wang Liu, *The Traditional Chinese Clan Rules* (Locust Valley, N.Y.: J. J. Augustin, 1959), p. 62 ff. See also Joanna M. Meskill, "The Chinese Genealogy as a Research Source," in Maurice Freedman, ed., *Family and Kinship in Chinese Society* (Stanford, Calif.: Stanford University Press, 1970), p. 150; Hugh Baker, *Chinese Family and Kinship* (New York: Columbia University Press, 1979), pp. 60, 82; idem, *A Chinese Lineage Village: Sheung Shui* (Stanford, Calif.: Stanford University Press, 1968), p. 49. For a discussion of somewhat more liberal clan rules, see Hu Hsien-chin, *The Common Descent Group in China and Its Functions* (New York: Viking Fund Publications in Anthropology, 1948), p. 44. See also the prefaces to genealogies by the late Yüan author Wu Hai in *chüan* 1 of *Wu Ch'ao-tsung hsien-sheng wen-kuo-chai chi*, TSCCCP, vol. 475.

62. *K'uai-chi Ch'in-shih tsu-p'u,* "Fan-li," item 10, n.p.

63. See, for example, the *Chia-ting Chou-shih chia-p'u* and the *Hsin-an Ch'eng-shih t'ung-tsung shih-pu.* See chap. 3 for more details.

64. Yao Shun-mu, *Yao yen, TSCCCP,* vol. 168, p. 3.

65. Hu, *Common Descent Group,* pp. 139, 145.

66. See, for example, the "Yü Kung" section of the *Shang shu K'ung chuan, SPPY,* vol. 4, 3/7b, where it says "He distributed land and surnames." There is some disagreement as to whether the referent to the pronoun is Yao or Yü, but for the purposes of my argument, either sage king is adequate. See also Ku Yen-wu, "Hsing," in *Jih chih lu chi-shih, SPPY,* vol. 1628, 23/1a–1b.

67. Chang Shih, "I-le-t'ang chi," quoted in Asami Keisai, "Yoshi bensho," *Nihon Jurin susho,* ed. Seiki Gichiro (Tokyo: Toyo kenkokai, 1927–1929), p. 3. Translated by I. J. McMullen, "Non-Agnatic Adoption: A Confucian Controversy in Seventeenth and Eighteenth Century Japan," *Harvard Journal of Asiatic Studies* 35 (1975): 142.

68. Shih Chiung (Ch'ing) compiler, *Shang-yü Shih-shih chia-p'u* manuscript copy, National Central Library of Taiwan, no. 3024, p. 11a.

69. *Lü-shih ch'un-ch'iu chiao-shih* (Taipei: Chung-hua ts'ung-shu wei-yüan hui, 1958), *chüan* 8, p. 101; *Shang-chün-shu chien-cheng* (Taipei: Kuang-wen shu-chü, 1975), 2/10a. See J. J. L. Duyvendak, trans., *The Book of Lord Shang* (London: Arthur Probsthain, 1928), p. 225.

70. *I-li Cheng-chu,* 11/8a.

71. *Kuo yü, SPPY,* vol. 1114, 10/8a.

72. *Ch'un-ch'iu Tso-shih chuan Tu-shih chi-chieh, SPPY,* vol. 40, 12/16b. (James Legge, *The Chinese Classics* [Oxford: Oxford University Press, 1935], vol. 5, p. 355.)

73. Wing-tsit Chan, *Neo-Confucian Terms Explained (The* Pei-hsi tzu-i) (New York: Columbia University Press, 1986), p. 152.

74. Wilt Idema and Stephen H. West, *Chinese Theater 1100–1450: A Sourcebook* (Wiesbaden: Franz Steiner Verlag, 1982), p. 386.

75. Ku Yen-wu, *Jih chih lu chi-shih, SPPY,* vol. 1628, 23/18b.

76. *Ta Ming lü chi-chieh fu-li,* vol. 5, 25/1a, p. 1835.

77. Niida, *Tōrei shūi,* p. 263.

78. Shen Kua, *Meng-hsi pi-t'an, TSCCCP,* vol. 56, pp. 160–161.

79. *Li-chi Cheng-chu, SPPY,* vol. 27, 1/9b.

80. *Ch'un ch'iu Tso-shih chuan Tu-shih chi-chieh, SPPY,* vol. 43, 20/13b. (Legge, *Chinese Classics,* vol. 5, pp. 573, 580.)

81. Ibid., *SPPY,* vol. 38, 6/13b. (Legge, *Chinese Classics,* vol. 5, pp. 185, 187.) Other citations in the *Tso chuan* indicate that same surname marriage existed, although it was not approved of. See, for example, 18/24b.

82. *Kuo yü, SPPY,* vol. 1114, 10/8a–b.

83. *T'ang-lü shu-i*, 14/1a; *Ta Ming lü chi-chieh fu-li*, vol. 2, 6/16a–b, pp. 669–670.

84. *Ta Ming lü chi-chieh fu-li*, vol. 2, 6/16a–b, pp. 669–670. See the discussion in Ch'u, *Law and Society*, pp. 94–96.

85. Ku Yen-wu, "Ch'ü-ch'i pu ch'ü t'ung-hsing," in *Jih chih lu chi-shih, SPPY,* vol. 1623, 6/1b–3a; see also T'ien I-heng, "Hsing," in *Liu-ching jih-cha* (Taipei: Kuang-wen shu-chü, 1969), 2/7b–8b, pp. 88–90.

86. Ku Yen-wu, "Ch'ü-ch'i pu ch'ü t'ung-hsing," in *Jih chih lu chi-shih, SPPY,* vol. 1623, 6/1b–3a.

87. Ch'u, *Law and Society,* p. 93. The case dates from 1790.

88. Shiga, *Hō no genri,* p. 590.

89. Ibid., pp. 586–589.

90. Su Mao-hsiang, *Hsin-k'e ta Ming lü-li lin-min pao-ching,* 4/8b. *Ta Ch'ing lü-li, ts'e* 2, 7/21a.

91. Su Mao-hsiang, *Hsin-k'e ta Ming lü-li lin-min pao-ching,* 4/9a.

92. Hsü San-chung, *Hsü San-chung chia-tse,* in *Ku-chin t'u-shu chi-ch'eng* (Shanghai: Chung-hua shu-chü, 1934), vol. 325, *chüan* 52, p. 11.

93. Herbert A. Giles, trans., *Yü-li ch'ao-chuan,* appended to his *Strange Stories from a Chinese Studio* (Hong Kong: Kelly and Walsh, 1936), p. 475.

94. G. W. Clarke, trans., "The *Yü-li* or Precious Records," *Journal of the Royal Asiatic Society, North China Branch* 28:2 (1894): 293. The text translated by Clarke dates from 1857, but it purports to be a copy of a Sung dynasty text.

95. Li Yü, *Tzu-chih hsin-shu* (Shanghai: T'u-shu chi-ch'eng yin-shu-chü, 1894), part 1, 13/11a.

96. *Tung-ming pao-chi,* cited in Wolfram Eberhard, *Guilt and Sin in Traditional China* (Berkeley and Los Angeles: University of California Press, 1967), p. 33. The particular text Eberhard is citing is contemporary, but the Yü-li tradition itself dates back to the eleventh century.

97. *Yü-li ch'ao-chuan,* translated by Giles in *Strange Stories,* p. 472.

98. *Sung hsing-t'ung,* 12/8a.

99. Chu Hsi, *Chu-tzu ta-ch'üan, SPPY,* vol. 1483, 46/17a, translated by McMullen in "Non-Agnatic Adoption," p. 141.

100. Cited in McMullen, "Non-Agnatic Adoption," p. 142.

101. Wu Hai, *Wu Ch'ao-tsung hsien-sheng wen-kuo-chai chi,* 1/13–14; see the discussion in Patricia Buckley Ebrey, "The Early Stages of Descent Group Organization," in *Kinship Organization in Late Imperial China,* ed. Patricia Buckley Ebrey and James L. Watson (Berkeley and Los Angeles: University of California Press, 1986), p. 49.

102. Wu Hai, *Wu Ch'ao-tsung hsien-sheng wen-kuo-chai chi,* 1/24.

103. *Ch'un-ch'in Tso-shih chuan Tu-shih chi-chieh, SPPY,* vol. 37, 5/19a. (Legge, *Chinese Classics,* vol. 5, pp. 156–157.)

104. *Lun-yü chu-shu,* SPPY, vol. 173, 2/6a. (Legge, *Chinese Classics,* vol. 1, p. 154.)

105. *Li chi Cheng-chu,* SPPY, vol. 27, 1/28a. (James Legge, *Li Chi: Book of Rites* [New Hyde Park, N.Y.: University Books, 1967], vol. 1, p. 116.)

106. *Ch'un-ch'iu Ku-liang chuan Fan-shih chi-chieh,* SPPY, vol. 55, 15/5b. (Legge, *Chinese Classics,* vol. 5, pp. 428–429.) Legge himself dismisses this interpretation as unlikely. Commentaries cited in the *Ku-chin t'u-shu chi-ch'eng,* vol. 325, *chüan* 52, p. 11, also in Ch'in Hui-t'ien, *Wu-li t'ung-k'ao,* 147/9a–10a. The Ch'un-ch'iu passage and its Ku-liang commentary are cited by the Sung author Ch'en Ch'un (cited in Chan, *Neo-Confucian Terms Explained,* p. 151) and by the late Yüan author Wu Hai (*Wu Ch'ao-tsung hsien-sheng wen-kuo-chai chi,* 1/24) in their discussions of contemporary adoption practices.

107. *Ch'un-ch'iu Ku-liang chuan Fan-shih chi-chieh,* SPPY, vol. 55, 15/6a.

108. Ibid., 15/5b.

109. *Ch'un-ch'iu Kung-yang chuan Ho-shih chieh-ku,* SPPY, vol. 51, 19/5a.

110. Cited in Ch'in Hui-t'ien, *Wu-li t'ung-k'ao,* 147/9b.

111. Ibid., 147/9a–10a.

112. *Feng-su t'ung-i* (Peking: Centre Franco-chinois d' études sinologiques, 1943), *chüan* 3, p. 105. Reconstructed from *I-lin,* SPPY, vol. 1417, 4/36–48, and from *T'ai-p'ing yü-lan* (Shanghai: Shang-wu yin-shu-kuan, 1935), *chüan* 361 *(Jen shih pu),* p. 6b, and *chüan* 883 *(Shen kuei pu),* p. 6b. See the discussion in Ch'u, *Law and Society,* p. 19.

113. Ch'en Ch'un (1153–1217), *Pei-hsi tzu-i,* TSCCCP, vol. 112, *chüan hsia,* pp. 59–60. Translated in Chan, *Neo-Confucian Terms Explained,* pp. 150–151. Ch'en Ch'un cites the source of the anecdote as the *Ch'un-ch'iu fan-lu,* but as Wing-tsit Chan points out, it is not contained in the present version of that work.

114. William Theodore de Bary, *Sources of Chinese Tradition,* 2 vols. (New York: Columbia University Press, 1960), vol. 1, pp. 488–489, citing *Chu-tzu ch'üan-shu,* 51/2a–20a.

115. For a discussion of *ch'i,* see Tu Wei-ming, "The Idea of the Human in Mencian Thought: An Approach to Chinese Aesthetics," in *Theories of the Arts in China,* ed. Susan Bush and Christian Murck (Princeton: Princeton University Press, 1981), p. 68. Tu defines *ch'i* as the "psycho-physiological power associated with breathing and the circulation of the blood" and cites translations of *ch'i* as "material force" (Wing-tsit Chan), "matter-energy" (Homer Dubs), and "vital spirit" (Frederic Mote).

116. Wu Hai, *Wu Ch'ao-tsung hsien-sheng wen-kuo-chai chi,* 1/20–21; Ebrey, "Early Stages of Descent Group Organization," p. 49.

117. *Yung-chia hsien-chih* (1566), 1/256.

118. *T'ai-ts'ang chou-chih* (1804), p. 1619a.

119. *Ta Ming hui-tien,* 5 vols. (Taipei: Tung-nan shu-pao-she, 1963), vol. 2, 34/9b, p. 621. Translated in Ray Huang, *Taxation and Government Finance in*

Sixteenth-Century Ming China (Cambridge: Cambridge University Press, 1975), p. 202. My translation is modified somewhat from that of Huang.
    120. *Wu-li t'ung-k'ao,* 148/17a.
    121. *Shang shu K'ung chuan, SPPY,* vol. 4, 4/9b. (Legge, *Chinese Classics,* vol. 3, pp. 209-210.)
    122. *Chu-tzu ta-ch'üan, SPPY,* vol. 1491, 58/31a-b. The final segment of the passage is quoted by McMullen, "Non-Agnatic Adoption," p. 141.
    123. *Chuang-tzu,* 1/1. Translated by Burton Watson, *Chuang-tzu: Basic Writings* (New York: Columbia University Press, 1965), p. 24.
    124. *Mao shih chiang-i, SKCS,* vol. 236, 6/1a. (Legge, *Chinese Classics,* vol. 4, p. 334.) Some sources identify the *ming-ling* as *chilo simplex,* others as *helio simplex,* others as *heliothus armigera.*
    125. Cited in Li Shan's commentary to Liu Ling's "Chiu te sung" in *Wen hsüan, SPPY,* vol. 2307, 47/5b; *Fa-yen, SPPY,* vol. 1419, 1/1b.
    126. *Fa-yen, SPPY,* vol. 1419, 1/1b.
    127. *T'ai-p'ing yü-lan,* 946/7a-b. The various commentaries are assembled in the *Ku-chin t'u-shu chi-ch'eng,* vol. 325, *chüan* 52, p. 16.
    128. The story is based on a misunderstanding of the actual behavior of the two creatures. The wasp, which in fact is not sterile, stings the caterpillar and lays her eggs in its stunned body. Thus the larvae that spring from the caterpillar's body are indeed wasps, not creatures "transformed" into wasps.
    129. *Lun-yü chu-shu, SPPY,* vol. 174, 12/4a. (Legge, *Chinese Classics,* p. 256.) Arthur Waley, *The Analects of Confucius* (New York: Random House, 1938), p. 166. My translation varies slightly from both Legge's and Waley's.
    130. *Ch'un-ch'iu Kung-yang chuan Ho-shih chieh-ku, SPPY,* vol. 50, 18/3a.
    131. *Han shu, SPPY,* vol. 462, 68/6b. Translated in Burton Watson, *Courtier and Commoner in Ancient China: Selections from the History of the Former Han* (New York: Columbia University Press, 1974), p. 133.
    132. *Hou Han shu, SPPY,* vol. 491, 88/14a.
    133. Quoted in *Sung-shih chi-shih pen-mo* (Peking: Chung-hua shu-chü, 1978), p. 312. The adage is also repeatedly cited in the discussion of the proper ordering of the ancestral temple in the Sung dynastic history (*Sung shih* [Peking: Chung-hua shu-chü, 1977], *chüan* 106, p. 2567 ff.). The P'u-i controversy centered on Sung Ying-tsung (1032-1067). He had been adopted by his predecessor, Jen-tsung. The key issue in the controversy was the manner in which Ying-tsung should treat his natural father.
    134. Carney T. Fischer, "The Great Ritual Controversy in the Age of Ming Shih-tsung," *Bulletin: Society for the Study of Chinese Religions,* no. 7 (Fall 1979), pp. 3-74. The phrase was much bandied about during the Ritual Controversy. Chang Ts'ung cited it only to refute its applicability to the Ming situation. Lou Tzu-k'uang, *Min-su ts'ung-shu.* Supplement 4, *Chia fan p'ien,* no. 13, *Ch'u-chi yang-tzu* (Taipei: Chung-kuo min-su hsüeh-hui, 1979), p. 267.

135. This connection has been noted by anthropologists working on contemporary Taiwan. It has been made with great force by Emily Martin Ahern, who demonstrates that people offered sacrifices only to those ancestors from whom they inherited property (*The Cult of the Dead in a Chinese Village* [Stanford, Calif.: Stanford University Press, 1973], p. 155). Stevan Harrell's *Ploughshare Village* offers an important qualification to this, though it is not a qualification that substantially refutes Ahern's assertion. In Ploughshare village, most ancestors had no property to bequeath to posterity. According to Harrell, "They cannot be blamed for the lack. We might say more accurately then that Taiwanese make tablets for the ancestors if the ancestors have given them their due. What exactly their due is depends on what the ancestors had to give" (*Ploughshare Village: Culture and Context in Taiwan* [Seattle: University of Washington Press, 1982], p. 202). Rubie Watson notes the connection between property and sacrifices in the New Territories of Hong Kong in *Inequality among Brothers* (New York: Cambridge University Press, 1985), pp. 44–54.

136. Sarah Allan, *The Heir and the Sage* (San Francisco: Chinese Materials Center, 1981).

137. *Shang shu K'ung chuan*, SPPY, vol. 4, 1/3. (Legge, *Chinese Classics,* vol. 3, p. 23.) My translation is modified somewhat from Legge's.

138. See, for example, the discussion in Tu Wei-ming, *Centrality and Commonality: An Essay on the Chung-yung* (Honolulu: University of Hawaii Press, 1976), pp. 58, 63, 79. Tu writes (p. 58) "To be filial is not merely to continue a family line. It is true that, following a statement in the *Book of Mencius,* it has been a strong folk belief in China that the failure to produce male progeny is among the most serious kinds of unfilial behavior. This may give the impression that filial piety, as reverence for parents, entails the primary obligation of continuing the biological line of the family. Whether the word 'posterity' *(hou)* in the injunction of Mencius refers to a specific pattern of lineal continuity, its main concern is the ethicoreligious obligation of the son to his father."

139. Ku Ying-t'ai, *Ming-shih chi-shih pen-mo* (Taipei: San-min shu-chü, 1963), *chüan* 51, p. 532.

140. James L. Watson, "Agnates and Outsiders: Adoption in a Chinese Lineage," *Man* 10 (1976): 293–306.

141. *Hsin-an Ch'eng-shih t'ung-tsung shih-p'u*, 17/13a. Manuscript in National Central Library, Taiwan.

142. Yüan Ts'ai, *Yüan-shih shih-fan*, 1/17a; Patricia Buckley Ebrey, *Family and Property in Sung China: Yuan Ts'ai's Precepts for Social Life* (Princeton, N.J.: Princeton University Press, 1984), p. 206.

143. Yüan Huang, "Kung-kuo-ke," in his *Hsün-tzu yen*, TSCCCP, vol. 168, p. 13.

144. Cited in Sakai Tadao, "Confucianism and Popular Educational Works,"

in *Self and Society in Ming Thought,* ed. William Theodore de Bary (New York: Columbia University Press, 1970), p. 358.

145. *Sung-chiang fu chih,* 55/14b.

146. *T'ai-ts'ang chou chih* (1804), 34/4a.

147. *T'ai-ts'ang chou chih* (1644), 13/83b.

148. *Jen-ch'iu Pien-shih tsu-p'u* (1772), 18/9. Charlotte Furth brought this reference to my attention.

149. *Wu-li t'ung-k'ao,* 147/22b–24a.

150. *Yüan-shih shih-fan,* 1/17a; Ebrey, *Family and Property,* p. 206.

151. *Wu Chiao-tsung hsien-sheng wen-kuo-chai chi,* 1/12; Ebrey, "Early Stages of Descent Group Organization," p. 49. My translation is modified from Ebrey's.

152. See Margery Wolf, *Women and the Family in Rural Taiwan* (Stanford, Calif.: Stanford University Press, 1973), esp. pp. 32–41.

153. *K'un-shan hsien-chih* (Ch'ien-lung ed.), *chüan* 15.

154. Li Yü, "Tuo-chin lou," in *Shih-erh lou.* Translated by Mao as "The Jackpot" in *Twelve Towers.* Feng Meng-lung, *Ku-chin hsiao-shuo* (Peking: Jen-min wen-hsüeh ch'u-pan-she, 1979), *chüan* 10; translated by Susan Arnold Zonana and the editors in *Traditional Chinese Stories: Themes and Variations,* ed. Y. W. Ma and Joseph S. M. Lau (New York: Columbia University Press, 1978), as "Magistrate T'eng and the Case of Inheritance," p. 500. See also Feng Meng-lung, *Hsing-shih heng-yen* (Hong Kong: Ku-tien wen hsüeh ch'u-pan-she, n.d.), *chüan* 35; translated by Susan Arnold Zonana and the editors in Ma and Lau as "Old Servant Hsü," p. 26.

155. John Dardess, *Confucianism and Autocracy: Professional Elites in the Founding of the Ming Dynasty* (Berkeley and Los Angeles: University of California Press, 1983), p. 55. See also the discussion of Wu Hai in Ebrey, "Early Stages of Descent Group Organization," p. 49 ff.

156. Derk Bodde and Clarence Morris, *Law in Imperial China* (Philadelphia: University of Pennsylvania Press, 1973), p. 59.

157. Boulais, *Manuel du code chinois,* pp. 197–198. *Tu-li ts'un-i,* vol. 2, *chüan* 9, p. 259; *Ta Ming lü-li chi-chüeh fu-li,* 4/25b–26b (vol. 2, pp. 586–588).

158. Ku Yen-wu, *Jih chih lu,* chi-shu, SPPY, vol. 1625, 13/39a.

159. *Huang Ming yung-hua lei-pien* (Taipei, Kuo-feng ch'u-pan she, 1965), vol. 6, 100/1a.

160. Tai Yen-hui, *Chung-kuo shen-fen-fa shih* (Taipei: Ssu-fa hsing-cheng-pu, 1959), pp. 89–90. Liu Ch'ing-po, *Yang-nü ch'ung-hun t'ung-chien chih yen-chiu* (Taipei: Shang-wu yin-shu-kuan, 1969), p. 6. Hsüeh Yin-sheng, cited in Derk Bodde and Clarence Morris, *Law in Imperial China* (Cambridge, Mass.: Harvard University Press, 1968), p. 64.

161. Hsü Hsüeh-mo, *Kuei yu-yüan ch'en-t'an,* TSCCCP, vol. 72, pp. 7–8.

162. Ch'en Chi-ju, *Chen-chu ch'uan,* TSCCCP, vol. 134, *chüan* 3, p. 43.

Chapter 3

1. *Ming-tai lü-li hui-pien,* comp. Huang Chang-chien (Taipei: Academia Sinica, 1979), vol. 2, pp. 462, 464.

2. Nor was the practice new with the Ming. For references to the sale of children during the Six Dynasties, see Wang Yi-t'ung, "Slaves and Other Comparable Social Groupings during the Northern Dynasties (386–618)," *Harvard Journal of Asiatic Studies,* p. 313, which enumerates references to the practice from the *Wei shu.* See also Nancy Lee Swann, *Food and Money in Ancient China* (New York: Octagon Books, 1974), pp. 149, 164. See also Homer Dubs, *History of the Former Han Dynasty,* vol. 3 (Baltimore: Waverly Press, 1938–1944), p. 523.

3. *Ta Yuan T'ung-chih t'iao-ko* (Peking: Kuo-li Pei-p'ing t'u-shu kuan, 1930), 4/17b.

4. Romeyn Taylor, *Basic Annals of Ming T'ai-tsu* (San Francisco: Chinese Materials and Research Aids Center, 1976), p. 98.

5. Hai Jui, *Hai Jui chi* (Peking: Chung-hua shu-chü, 1962), p. 165. See also Michel Cartier, *Une réforme locale en Chine au XVIe siècle: Hai Jui à Chun'an* (Paris: Mouton, 1973), p. 88.

6. Feng Ying-ching, *Ching-shih shih-yung pien hsü-chi* (Ming ed.), 17 (*li chi* 3), 23ab. Cited in Albert Chan, *The Glory and Fall of the Ming Dynasty* (Norman: University of Oklahoma Press, 1982), pp. 88–89.

7. James B. Parsons, *Peasant Rebellions of the Late Ming Dynasty* (Tucson: University of Arizona Press, 1970), p. 4.

8. J. J. M. de Groot, *Sectarianism and Religious Persecution in China* (Amsterdam: Johannes Muller, 1903–1904), p. 114.

9. Richard C. Temple, ed., *The Travels of Peter Mundy in Europe and Asia 1608–1667* (London: Haklyut Society, 1919), vol. 3, p. 263. Cited in Robert B. Marks, *Rural Revolution in South China: Peasants and the Making of History in Haifeng County, 1570–1930* (Madison: University of Wisconsin Press, 1984), p. 7.

10. Helen Dunstan, "The Late Ming Epidemics: A Preliminary Survey," *Ch'ing-shih wen-t'i* 3:3 (Nov. 1975), p. 12. Citing *T'ung-hsiang hsien-chih,* 20/8a–10b.

11. Ku Yen-wu, *T'ien-hsia chün-kuo li-ping shu* (T'u-shu chi-ch'eng chü, 1901), 2/2b.

12. Ku Yen-wu, "Su Sung erh fu t'ien-fu chih chung," *Jih chih lu chi-shih,* SPPY, vol. 1624, 10/8b.

13. Mark Elvin, *The Pattern of the Chinese Past* (Stanford, Calif.: Stanford University Press, 1973), p. 256. Citing Hosono Kōji, "Minmatsu Shinsho no okeru doboku kankei," *Tōyō Gakuho,* 50:3 (Dec. 1976), p. 26.

14. *Yüan-shih shih-fan,* in *Chih-pu-tsu chai ts'ung-shu,* vol. 130, 3/44, 45. Patricia Buckley Ebrey, *Family and Property in Sung China: Yüan Ts'ai's Precepts*

for Social Life (Princeton, N.J.: Princeton University Press, 1984), pp. 197, 299–300.

15. Arthur Wolf and Chieh-shan Huang, Marriage and Adoption in China 1845–1945 (Stanford, Calif.: Stanford University Press, 1980), p. 205; James L. Watson "Agnates and Outsiders: Adoption in a Chinese Lineage," Man 10:2 (1975): 305 n. 8.

16. Kwan-wai So, Japanese Piracy in Ming China during the Sixteenth Century (East Lansing: Michigan State University Press, 1975), p. 10.

17. Yü-li ch'ao-chuan, translated by Herbert A. Giles in Strange Stories from a Chinese Studio (Hong Kong: Kelly and Walsh, 1936), p. 478.

18. Ernest Alabaster, Notes and Commentaries on Chinese Law (London: Luzac, 1899), p. 381. Tu-li ts'un-i, vol. 2, chüan 9, p. 250; Ta Ming lü-li chi-chüeh fu-li, vol. 2, 4/12b–15a, pp. 558–564.

19. Guy Boulais, Manuel du code chinois (Shanghai: Imprimerie de la Mission Catholique, 1924), pp. 177–178. Tu-li ts'un-i, vol. 2, chüan 9, p. 250.

20. Min-shang-shih hsi-kuan tiao-ch'a pao-kao-lu (Taipei: Chin-hsüeh shu-chü, 1969), p. 1595. Cited in Wolf and Huang, Marriage and Adoption, p. 109.

21. Giles, Strange Stories, p. 114, note.

22. V. R. Burckhardt, Chinese Creeds and Customs (Hong Kong: South China Morning Post, 1954), p. 107.

23. Niida, Shina mibun hōshi, pp.775, 779–781.

24. Ta Ming lü chi-chieh fu-li, 4/9b, 11a. Translated and discussed in Mi Chu Wiens, "The Origins of Modern Chinese Landlordism," in Festschrift in Honor of the Eightieth Birthday of Professor Shen Kang-po (Taipei: Lien Ching 1976), p. 293.

25. See, for example, Hsiao Yung, Ch'ih-shan hui-yüeh, TSCCCP, vol. 127, p. 14. See also Chang Lü-hsiang, Yang-yüan hsien-sheng ch'üan-chi (Taipei, 1968), 32/10b. Cited in Oyama Masaaki, "Large Landownership in the Jiangnan Delta Region during the Late Ming–Early Qing Period," in State and Society in China: Japanese Perspectives on Ming-Qing Social and Economic History, ed. Linda Grove and Christian Daniels (Tokyo: University of Tokyo Press, 1984), p. 11. Wang Meng-chi cited in Elvin, Chinese Past, p. 240. Chou Ch'en (1381–1453) cited by Fu I-ling in Ming Ch'ing nung-ts'un she-hui ching-chi (Hong Kong: Shih-yung shu-chü, 1972), p. 80.

26. Cited by Oyama, "Large Landownership," p. 112.

27. Feng Meng-lung, Shan-ko (Shanghai: Chung-hua shu-chü, 1962), 4/29a.

28. Wiens, "Chinese Landlordism," pp. 302–303, 307.

29. Chang Lü-hsiang, Yang-yüan hsien-sheng ch'üan-chi, 48/13b. Cited in Wiens, "Chinese Landlordism," p. 307.

30. Wang Meng-chi, Chia-hsün yü-hsia p'ien. Cited in Hosono Kōji, "Doboku kankei," p. 26. Also cited in Wiens, "Chinese Landlordism," p. 305.

31. Oyama, "Large Landownership," esp. pp. 114–115.

32. Shih T'ien-chi, in T'ang Piao, ed. *Jen-sheng pi tu-shu,* 8/12b. Cited in Oyama, "Large Landownership," p. 112.

33. Nelson Wu, "Tung Ch'i-ch'ang," in Arthur F. Wright and Denis Twitchett, *Confucian Personalities* (Stanford, Calif.: Stanford University Press, 1962), pp. 286–289.

34. Cited in Oyama, "Large Landownership," p. 113.

35. Hsiao Yung, "Hsü hsia," in *Ch'ih-shan hui-yüeh, TSCCCP,* vol. 127, p. 14.

36. Cited in Fu I-ling, *Nung-ts'un she-hui,* p. 79.

37. "Hsing-ke t'iao-li," in *Hai Jui chi,* p. 72. I consulted the French translation of Cartier in *Une réforme locale en Chine au XVIe siècle,* p. 126.

38. Elvin, *Chinese Past,* p. 240. Hosono Kōji, "Doboku kankei," p. 28. Ch'in Hui-t'ien, *Wu-li t'ung-k'ao,* 14/16a. Wiens, "Chinese Landlordism," pp. 302–303; Oyama, "Large Landownership," p. 156, n. 72.

39. *Ch'ing-pai lei-ch'ao,* comp. Hsü K'o (Taipei: Shang-wu yin-shu-kuan, 1967), 16/6.

40. Hugh Baker, *A Chinese Lineage Village: Sheung Shui* (Stanford, Calif.: Stanford University Press, 1968), pp. 47–49. See also Justus Doolittle, *Social Life of the Chinese* (New York: Harpers, 1865), vol. 2, p. 226, which describes an adoption banquet.

41. *Chin p'ing mei* (Hong Kong: Kuang-chih shu-chü, 1955), chap. 69. In that chapter Hsi-men Ch'ing adopted Wang San-kuan.

42. "Chieh-i" in *Lung-t'u kung-an, chüan* 5, 9b–12a. Translated by Leon Comber as "The Net of Heaven," in *The Strange Cases of Magistrate Pao* (Rutland, Vt.: Charles Tuttle, 1964), pp. 66–67.

43. *Hao ch'iu chuan,* translated by Franz Kuhn, *Eisherz und Edeljaspis, oder die Geschichte einer glucklichen Gattenwahl* (Leipzig: Inselverlag, 1947), pp. 171–178.

44. *Ju-lin wai-shih* (Peking: Tsuo-chia ch'u-pan-she, 1956), chap. 25, p. 249.

45. Cited in Wolf and Huang, *Marriage and Adoption,* p. 109.

46. See Marjorie Topley, "Cosmic Antagonisms: A Mother-Child Syndrome," in *Religion and Ritual in Chinese Society,* ed. Arthur Wolf (Stanford, Calif.: Stanford University Press, 1974), for a description of the similarities between bonding and marriage. For an amplification of this view, see James Pierce McGough, "Marriage and Adoption in Chinese Society with Special Reference to Customary Law" (Ph.D. dissertation, Michigan State University, 1976).

47. See the studies in Patricia Ebrey and James L. Watson, *Kinship Organization in Late Imperial China 1000–1940* (Berkeley and Los Angeles: University of California Press, 1988). See also Ted Telford, "Survey of Social Demographic Data in Chinese Genealogies," *Late Imperial China* 7:2 (Dec. 1986): 118–148; Stevan Harrell, "The Rich Get Children: Segmentation, Stratification and Population in Three Chekiang Lineages, 1550–1850," in Susan Hanley and Arthur

Wolf, *Family and Population in East Asian History* (Stanford, Calif.: Stanford University Press, 1985), pp. 81–109.

48. For a discussion of Hui-chou (Hsin-an) see Keith Duane Hazelton, "Lineages and Local Elites in Hui-chou, 1500–1800" (Ph.D. dissertation, Princeton, 1984). See also Harriet Zurndorfer, "The *Hsin-an ta-tsu chih* and the Development of Chinese Gentry Society," *T'oung Pao* 67:3–5 (1981): 154–215. For a discussion of Hsin-an, see Hilary Beattie, *Land and Lineage in China: A Study of T'ung-ch'eng County, Anhwei, in the Ming and Ch'ing Dynasties* (Cambridge: Cambridge University Press, 1979), pp. 10–11.

49. *Hsin-an Ch'eng-shih t'ung-tsung shih-p'u* in 14 *chüan, 5 t'se*. Compiled by Ch'eng Hui-min.

50. Shiga Shūzō, "Family Property and the Law of Inheritance in Traditional China," in *Chinese Family Law and Social Change,* ed. David Buxbaum (Seattle: University of Washington Press, 1978), p. 116.

51. *Hsin-an Ch'eng-shih t'ung-tsung shih-p'u.*

52. Ibid.

53. Ibid.

54. Cited in Tai Yen-hui, *Chung-kuo shen-fen fa-shih* (Taipei: Ssu-fa hsing-cheng-pu, 1959), p. 90.

55. *Hsin-an Ch'eng-shih t'ung-tsung shih-p'u,* 15 *hsia*/6b–7a.

56. Ibid., 15 *hsia*/5a. For other examples, see 15 *hsia*/3a, where Yüeh-wen, who has a natal son, adopts Fu-tsung. There is no record that the natal son married, and so it is possible that he died young. See also 12/3a, where Wen-chou has an adopted son and three natal sons. The natal sons are all younger than the adopted son; thus Wen-chou could have been childless at the time of the adoption. In addition, there is no record of the marriage of any of the natal sons, which lends credence to the suspicion that they may have died young. See also 15 *hsia*/17a, where Hsien adopted a son born in 1475. Although the genealogy unfortunately does not tell us when the child was adopted, it seems reasonable to assume that he was adopted before the birth of Hsien's own child, born when his father was 49. See also 5/5a, where Chuan is listed as having a natal son and an adopted son. The birth dates are not given, but it appears from the genealogy entry that the adopted child was older. This list as well could be extended ad infinitum.

57. Ibid., 15 *hsia*/8a.

58. *Hsin-an Ch'eng-shih t'ung-tsung shih-p'u,* 15 *hsia*/4a. For other examples, see 3/21b, where Kung-jung has four sons, one of whom is adopted out and one of whom marries uxorilocally. See also 15 *hsia*/5a, where I has four sons, two of whom are adopted out. The list could be extended ad infinitum.

59. Shiga Shūzō, *Chugoku kazoku hō no genri* (Tokyo: Sobunsha, 1968), p. 578.

60. Ibid., pp. 415–418.

61. See, for example, the *K'un Hsin liang-hsien hsü-hsiu ho-chih* (Taipei: Ch'eng-wen, 1970), 41/35b, where a Madame Chu adopts the son of her deceased husband's concubine.

62. See the discussion in Ann Waltner, "Widows and Remarriage in Ming and Early Qing China," *Historical Reflections* (Spring 1981), pp. 129–146.

63. *Hsin-an Ch'eng-shih t'ung-tsung shih-p'u* 15 *hsia*, 17b.

64. Ibid., 15 *hsia*, 16a–17a.

65. Ibid., 15 *hsia*, 24b–25a.

66. Ibid., 4/25b.

67. For a discussion of a posthumous adoption invented by the compiler of a genealogy for the purpose of insuring that a branch of the family does not die out, see Hu Hsien-chin, *The Common Descent Group in China and Its Functions* (New York: Viking Fund Publications in Anthropology, 1948), pp. 130–131.

68. For the adoption of a husband's younger brother, see, for example, *Chia-ting hsien-chih* (1605) 13/23a. For the adoption of a cousin, see *Ming shih* (Peking: Chung-hua shu-chü, 1974), *chüan* 303, biography of Hu Shih. See also *K'un Hsin*, vol. 2, 38/13a, p. 674.

69. *Hsin-an Ch'eng-shih t'ung-tsung shih-p'u*, 15 *hsia*, 29a–29b.

70. Ibid., passim.

71. Ibid., 16/1a.

72. Ibid., 17/3a.

73. Ibid., 4/5a.

74. Ibid., 4/7b.

75. Ibid., 4/14b.

76. Ibid., 16/3a.

77. Ibid., 5/4b.

78. Wu Hai, *Wu Ch'ao-tsung hsien-sheng wen-kuo-chai chi, TSCCCP*, vol. 475, *chüan* 1, p. 12. Patricia Buckley Ebrey, "The Early Stages of Descent Group Organization," in *Kinship Organization in Late Imperial China*, ed. Patricia Buckley Ebrey and James L. Watson (Berkeley and Los Angeles: University of California Press, 1986), p. 49.

79. Wu Hai, *Wu Ch'ao-tsung hsien-sheng wen-kuo-chai chi, chüan* 1, p. 3.

80. Jerry Dennerline, *The Chia-ting Loyalists: Confucian Leadership and Social Change in Seventeenth Century China* (New Haven, Conn.: Yale University Press, 1981), p. 144.

81. Wolf and Huang cite an article by Okamatsu Santaro that says that *tseng-tzu* (gift child) was a term used for adoption among affines. The existence of the term itself, as well as its more specific connotations, is intriguing. But Wolf and Huang suggest that they have been unable to document widespread use of the term, and I have not seen it in the materials I have examined. Wolf and Huang, *Marriage and Adoption*, p. 111.

82. *Ming shih, chüan* 159, p. 1919. Ch'in Hui-t'ien, *Wu-li t'ung-k'ao* (Taipei: Hsin-hsing shu-chü, 1971), 147/12a.

83. *Ming shih, chüan* 255, 2883.

84. *Sung-chiang fu-chih*, 55/66a, p. 1258.

85. *T'ai-ts'ang chou-chih* (1803), 31/186.

86. Ch'in Hui-tien, *Wu-li t'ung-k'ao*, 147/12a.

87. *Chia-ting Chou-shih chia-p'u*, n.p.

88. Dennerline, *Chia-ting Loyalists*, p. 144.

89. *Su-chou fu-chih*, 85/20b, p. 2062.

90. Dennerline, *Chia-ting Loyalists*, p. 145.

91. *Su-chou fu-chih*, 80/12b.

92. *K'uai-chi Ch'in-shih tsung-p'u* (manuscript held in National Central Library in Taiwan), n.p.

93. *T'ai-ts'ang chou-chih* (1803), 26/37a.

94. Ibid., 30/7a.

95. Shiga, *Hō no genri*, pp. 316–317.

96. Ch'in Hui-tien, *Wu-li t'ung-k'ao*, 147/13a.

97. Wolfram Eberhard, *Social Mobility in Traditional China* (Leiden: E. J. Brill, 1962), p. 159, writes that in the absence of agnatic nephews, a wife's relatives were preferred as adopted sons.

98. Feng Meng-lung, *Hsing-shih heng-yen* (Hong Kong: Ku-tien wen-hsüeh ch'u-pan-she, n.d.), *chüan* 20, pp. 401–402.

99. See Antonia Fraser, *Cromwell: Our Chief of Men* (New York: Granada, 1975), pp. 7–8. See also Jean-Louis Flandrin, *Familes in Former Times: Kinship, Household and Sexuality* (New York: Cambridge University Press, 1979), p. 15.

100. Ben Befu, *Worldly Mental Calculations: An Annotated Translation of Ihara Saikaku's Seken Munezan'yo* (Berkeley and Los Angeles: University of California Press, 1976), p. 60. See also William H. McCullough, "Japanese Marriage Institutions in the Heian Period," *Harvard Journal of Asiatic Studies* 27 (1967): 109 ff. McCullough makes a strong distinction between uxorilocal marriage, where the son-in-law resided with the wife's family but did not relinquish membership in his own clan, and adoption of a son-in-law into the wife's clan. He finds the former to be frequent and the latter infrequent.

101. S. J. Tambiah, "Dowry, Bridewealth and the Property Rights of Women in South Asia," in *Bridewealth and Dowry*, ed. Jack Goody and S. J. Tambiah (New York: Cambridge University Press, 1973), p. 66.

102. See, for example, Wolf and Huang, *Marriage and Adoption*, pp. 94–108; Margery Wolf, *Women and the Family in Rural Taiwan* (Stanford, Calif.: Stanford University Press, 1973), pp. 192–197; Stevan Harrell, *Ploughshare Village: Culture and Context in Taiwan* (Seattle: University of Washington Press, 1982), pp. 174–175. Harrell has noticed that in Ploughshare village, uxorilocal

marriage was relatively more common than it was in surrounding areas and that the adoption of males was less common than it was in those same areas. He thus suggests that there was seen to be a kind of equivalence between adopting a son and taking in a son-in-law.

103. See *Shih chi* (Peking: Chung-hua shu-chü, 1959), *chüan* 126, p. 3197.

104. Shiga, *Hō no genri*, p. 612.

105. *Ta Yüan t'ung-chih t'iao-ko* (Taipei: Hua-wen shu-chü, 1968), 4/9a.

106. *Ta Ming hui-tien*, 5 vols. (Taipei: Tung-nan shu-pao-she, 1963), vol. 1, 20/21a, p. 367.

107. Ibid.

108. Shiga, *Hō no genri*, p. 615; *Ta Ming hui-tien*, 20/21a, p. 367. The *Ta Yüan t'ung-chih t'iao-ko* (4/9b) explicitly states that most of the disputes involving uxorilocal marriage involved cases where there was no contract.

109. *Ta Yüan t'ung-chih t'iao-ko*, 4/8a.

110. *Ta Ming hui-tien*, vol. 1, 20/21a, p. 367.

111. Huang Liu-hung, *Fu-hui ch'üan-shu*, 20/12a. Djang Chu translation in *A Complete Book Concerning Happiness and Benevolence: A Manual of Local Magistrates in Seventeenth-Century China* (Tucson: University of Arizona Press, 1984), p. 452.

112. Shiga, *Hō no genri*, p. 617.

113. Wolf and Huang, *Marriage and Adoption,* p. 101; David Buxbaum, "A Case Study of the Dynamics of Family Law and Social Change in Rural China," in *Chinese Family Law and Social Change,* p. 243; Bernard Gallin, *Hsin Hsing, Taiwan: A Chinese Village in Change* (Berkeley and Los Angeles: University of California Press, 1966), pp. 155–157; Francis L. K. Hsu, *Under the Ancestors' Shadow,* rev. ed. (Stanford, Calif.: Stanford University Press, 1971), pp. 98–103; Wolf, *Women and the Family,* p. 192. Harrell, *Ploughshare Village,* pp. 176–180, however, finds there to be relatively little stigma attached to uxorilocal marriage in Ploughshare village. He offers two hypotheses: the fact that uxorilocal marriage is relatively common in Ploughshare village might increase acceptance of it, and second, the fact that lineage organization is relatively weak in Ploughshare village might reduce the pressure applied by the lineage group against this form of marriage. Burton Pasternak in *Guests of the Dragon: Social Demography of a Chinese District* (New York: Columbia University Press, 1983), too, finds there to be relatively little stigma attached to uxorilocal marriage in Chungshe, although uxorilocal marriage seems to be relatively uncommon there. He suggests that a primary motivation for uxorilocal marriage is the need for adult male laborers, rather than the need to continue the family line (pp. 3–4, 50).

114. P'u Sung-ling, "A-pao," *Liao-chai chih-i* (Peking: Chung-hua shu-chü, 1962), vol. 1, *chüan* 2, pp. 233–239. Translated by Giles as "Miss A-pao" in *Strange Stories,* pp. 115–121.

115. Feng Meng-lung, *Ku-chin hsiao-shuo, chüan* 27. Translated by Cyril Birch as "The Lady Who Was a Beggar" in *Stories from a Ming Collection* (Bloomington: Indiana University Press, 1958), pp. 19–36.

116. Ling Meng-ch'u, *Erh-k'e p'ai-an ching-ch'i* (Taipei: Kuei-kuan t'u-shu, 1984), *chüan* 6, p. 123.

117. *K'ang-hsi K'uai-chi hsien-chih* (Shaohsing, 1936), 7/3a.

118. Hsü Hsiang-ch'ing, *Hsü Yün-ts'un i-mou, TSCCCP,* vol. 167, forbids the taking in of a uxorilocal son-in-law (p. 7) and also forbids family members from marrying into other families uxorilocally (p. 5).

119. *Wang Shih-chin tsung-kuei* in *Hsün-su i-kuei* in Ch'en Hung-mou, *Wu-chung i-kuei, SPPY,* vol. 1548, 2/28b.

120. *Liu-pu ch'eng-yü chu-chieh,* ed. Naitō Kenkichi (Tokyo: Taian, 1962), p. 119.

121. Ho Ch'o (1661–1722), comp. *Fen-lei tzu-chin* (Taipei: Wen-yu shu-tien, 1967), 13/38b.

122. *Ta Yüan t'ung-chih t'iao-ko,* 4/8b.

123. Shiga, *Hō no genri,* p. 616.

124. Ibid., pp. 614–616.

125. *T'ai-tsang chou-chih* (1548), 7/20a.

126. *Hsiu-shui hsien-chih* (1596) (Taipei: Ch'eng-wen, 1970 rpt.), 6/43; *Hsiu-shui hsien-chih,* 1/361.

127. *K'un Hsin,* 38/4a, p. 669.

128. *Sung-chiang fu-chih* (1512), 54/32a, p. 1216.

129. *Ming shih, chüan* 303.

130. Cited by Paul Unschuld, *Medical Ethics in Imperial China* (Berkeley and Los Angeles: University of California Press, 1979), p. 59.

131. Cited in Unschuld, *Ethics,* p. 47. For other examples of *shih-i,* see Hsü Chun-fu, *Ku-chin i-t'ung,* pp. 31a–34a.

132. *K'un-shan jen-wu-chih,* 8/6a.

133. Ibid., 8/4a; *K'un-shan hsien-chih* (1538), 12/17a.

134. *K'un Hsin,* 38/5a, p. 670. *T'ai-ts'ang* (1644), 13/4a.

135. On female medical practitioners, see Victoria Cass, "Female Healers in the Ming and the Lodge of Ritual and Ceremony," *Journal of the American Oriental Society* 106:1 (Jan.–Mar. 1986): 233–240.

136. *Sung-chiang fu-chih,* 29/18a.

137. *Ming shih, chüan* 143.

138. *Pei-hsi tzu-i, TSCCCP,* vol. 1125, p. 60; Wing-tsit Chan, *Neo-Confucian Terms Explained (The Pei-hsi tzu-i)* (New York: Columbia University Press, 1986), p. 152.

139. *Wu-li t'ung-k'ao,* 147/12a.

140. *Chia-hsing fu t'u-chi* (1547–1549; rpt. 1916), 19/4b.

141. Ibid., 19/15a.

142. Christian Murck, "Chu Yün-ming and Cultural Commitment in Soochow" (Ph.D. dissertation, Princeton, 1978), pp. 39–40. For a discussion of the use of the supernatural by magistrates, see Alison Wayne Conner, "The Law of Evidence during the Ch'ing Dynasty" (Ph.D. dissertation, Cornell, 1979), pp. 160–167.

143. *Chu-shih chi-lüeh,* cited by Murck, p. 41 ff.

144. Ch'en Ching-mo, *Hai-ning Ch'en-shih chia-p'u* (revised 1882), cited and translated by Lo Hsiang-lin, "The History and Arrangement of Chinese Genealogies," in *Studies in Asian Genealogy,* ed. Spencer T. Palmer (Provo, Ut.: Brigham Young University Press, 1972), p. 18.

145. Ch'en Chi-yüan, *Yung-hsien-chai pi-chi* (Taipei: Wen-hai ch'u-pan-she, 1975), 1/1a, p. 3. Translated by Lo, "History and Arrangement," p. 19.

146. Hok-lam Chan, "Chang Hung," in *Dictionary of Ming Biography (DMB),* p. 85. *Ku-chin t'u-shu chi-ch'eng,* vol. 325, *chüan* 52, p. 16; *Ch'ang-shu hsien-chih,* vol. 2, p. 876; *Ming wai-shih,* preserved in Lou Tsu-k'uang, *Min-su ts'ung-shu,* Supplement 4, *Chia-fan p'ien,* no. 13, *Ch'u-chi yang-tzu* (Taipei: Chung-kuo min-su hsüeh-hui, 1979), pp. 398–399; *T'ai-ts'ang chou-chih* (1803), 26/4b. Although the other versions agree on the details of Chang Hung's birth and early adoption, the *Ming wai-shih* says that we don't know anything about his original family. The 1644 edition of the T'ai-ts'ang gazetteer (13/7b) says that his father died while traveling.

147. *Ming shih, chüan* 161. The appendix to the *chüan* tells us that K'uang's surname was Huang, but does not give details of the story. See Chaoyang Fang, "K'uang Chung," *DMB,* p. 751.

148. Yeh Meng-chu, *Yüeh shih p'ien* (Taipei: Wen-hai ch'u-pan-she, 1969), 4/22b, p. 400.

149. *T'ai-ts'ang hsien-chih* (1803), 26/11b.

150. *Ming wai-shih,* preserved in Lou Tsu-k'uang, *Min-su ts'ung-shu,* p. 395.

151. *K'un Hsin,* 38/13b.

152. Ch'in Hui-t'ien, *Wu-li t'ung-k'ao,* 146/22a, citing *Ming wai-shih. Ming shih, chüan* 292. The ambiguous phrase "adoptive grandmother and mother" (is the mother adoptive? or is she the biological mother?) occurs in the original. We know that the adoptive father could not have been a paternal uncle, because were that the case the "adopted grandmother" would have been the same as the biological grandmother, and the text clearly states that Wang supported his adoptive grandmother.

153. *Yung-chia hsien-chih* (1566), 7/38b.

154. Li Yü, *Tzu-chih hsin-shu,* part 1, 13/11a.

155. *K'un-shan jen-wu chih,* 6/5a; *Su-chou fu-chih,* 91/23b; *T'ai-ts'ang hsien-chih* (1644), 13/76a–76b.

Chapter 4

1. See, for example, the discussion in Katherine Carlitz, "Family, Society and Tradition in *Jin Ping Mei*," *Modern China* 10:4 (Oct. 1984): 388.

2. Li Yü, *Ch'iao t'uan-yüan*, in *Li Yü ch'üan-chi*, ed. Helmut Martin (Taipei: Ch'eng-wen Publishing House, 1970), vol. 11, *shang*/30a (p. 4653). Translation slightly modified from Eric P. Henry, *Chinese Amusement: The Lively Plays of Li Yü* (Hamden, Conn.: Archon Books, 1980), p. 72.

3. Feng Meng-lung, "Lü Ta-lang huan chin wan ku-jou," *Ching-shih t'ung-yen* (Hong Kong: Chung-hua shu-chü, 1978), *chüan* 5, p. 56.

4. Ling Meng-ch'u, *P'ai-an ching-ch'i* (Taipei: Shih-chieh shu-chü, 1975), *chüan* 17, pp. 313–314. Translated as "Der Abt und die Geborene Wu," in Tsung-tung Chang, *Chinesischer Liebesgarten* (Kunzelsau: Horst Erdman Verlag, 1964), p. 57. See also Dell R. Hales, "The *P'ai-an ching-ch'i:* A Literary Criticism" (Ph.D. dissertation, Indiana University, 1969), p. 64.

5. Katherine Newman Carlitz, *The Rhetoric of Chin p'ing mei* (Bloomington: Indiana University Press, 1986), p. 141.

6. *Hsing-shih heng-yen* (Hong Kong: Chung-hua shu-chü, 1978), *chüan* 3, p. 43. Translated as "The Oil Peddler Courts the Courtesan," by Lorraine S. Y. Lieu and editors Y. W. Ma and Joseph S. M. Lau in *Traditional Chinese Stories: Themes and Variations* (New York: Columbia University Press, 1978), p. 187.

7. *Hsing-shih heng-yen*, *chüan* 3, p. 43. Hsiao-chi was the crown prince to Wu-ting of the Shang dynasty (1339–1281 B.C.). Shen-sheng (d 654 B.C.) was the heir apparent to Duke Hsien of Chin. Both men suffered at the hands of their fathers' consorts.

8. Li Yü, "Ho-ying lou," in *Shih-erh lou* (Taipei: Chang-ko, 1975), p. 16. Translated by Nathan Mao as "The Reflections in the Water," in *Twelve Towers* (Hong Kong: Chinese University Press, 1975), p. 9.

9. Feng Meng-lung, *Hsing-shih heng-yen*, *chüan* 1, pp. 5, 7. Translated by William Dolby as "Two Magistrates Vie to Marry an Orphaned Girl," in *The Perfect Lady by Mistake and Other Stories* (London: Paul Elek, 1976), p. 122.

10. For an anthropologist's discussion of female adoption in contemporary Taiwan, see Bernard Gallin, *Hsin Hsing, Taiwan: A Chinese Village in Change* (Berkeley and Los Angeles: University of California Press, 1966), p. 161. Gallin says daughters were adopted for three reasons: because their families were too poor to support them, to "lead in" a son, and to serve as a future wife. To "lead in" a son refers to the belief that adopting a daughter would cause a couple to conceive a son. See also Arthur Wolf and Chieh-shan Huang, *Marriage and Adoption in China 1845–1945* (Stanford, Calif.: Stanford University Press, 1980), passim. See also Myron L. Cohen, *House United, House Divided: The Chinese Family in Taiwan* (New York: Columbia University Press, 1976), p. 32

ff. Cohen finds the belief that the adoption of a girl will "lead in" subsequent children to explain a number of cases. He also finds a number of the cases to be adoptions by a close kinsman which took place following the death of the girl's father. He finds there to be some evidence of "little daughter-in-law" adoptions, but does not find this form of female adoption to predominate in Yen-liao.

11. *Ch'iao t'uan-yüan*, act 3, *shang*/6a, p. 4605.

12. Arthur P. Wolf, "Childhood Association, Sexual Attraction, and the Incest Taboo: A Chinese Case," *American Anthropologist* 68 (4): 883–898; also his "Adopt a Daughter-in-law, Marry a Sister: A Chinese Solution to the Problem of the Incest Taboo," *American Anthropologist* 70 (5): 864–874. See also Margery Wolf, *Women and the Family in Rural Taiwan* (Stanford, Calif.: Stanford University Press, 1972), pp. 171–190 ("Girls Who Marry Their Brothers"). See also Wolf and Huang, *Marriage and Adoption.*

13. Hsü Hsiang-ch'ing, *Hsü Yün-ts'un i-mou*, TSCCCP, vol. 167, p. 5.

14. *Yü-li ch'ao-chuan;* trans. Herbert A. Giles in *Strange Stories from a Chinese Studio* (Hong Kong: Kelly and Walsh, 1936), p. 478.

15. Kuan Han-ch'ing, *Kan-t'ien tung-ti Tou O yüan* in *Kuan Han-ch'ing hsi-ch'ü chi* (Taipei: Hung-yeh shu-chü, 1973), p. 847, prelude, trans. Shih Chung-wen, *Injustice to Tou O* (Cambridge: Cambridge University Press, 1972), p. 47. Also Ching-hsi Perng, *Double Jeopardy: A Critique of Seven Yüan Courtroom Dramas* (Ann Arbor: Michigan Papers in Chinese Studies, 1975), p. 110.

16. Kuan Han-ch'ing, *Kan-t'ien tung-ti Tou O yüan, Kuan Han-ch'ing hsi-chü chi*, p. 848.

17. *Lettres édifiantes et curieuses de Chine par des missionnaires jésuites 1702–1776*, edited by Isabelle and Jean-Louis Vissière. (Paris: Garnier-Flammarion, 1979), p. 225. The information is contained in a footnote by Entrecolles.

18. Feng Meng-lung, *Ku-chin hsiao-shuo* (Peking: Jen-min wen-hsüeh ch'u-pan-she, 1979), *chüan* 27, p. 414. Translated as "The Lady Who Was a Beggar" by Cyril Birch in his *Stories from a Ming Collection* (Bloomington: Indiana University Press, 1958), p. 30.

19. *Ku-chin hsiao-shuo, chüan* 2, p. 60.

20. *Ching-shih t'ung-yen, chüan* 21, p. 302. Translated as "The Sung Founder Escorts Ching-niang One Thousand *Li*," by Lorraine S. Y. Lieu and the editors Ma and Lau, in *Chinese Stories*, p. 73.

21. P'u Sung-ling, "Nieh Hsiao-ch'ien," in *Liao-chai chih-i* (Peking:Chung-hua shu-chü, 1962), vol. 1, *chüan* 2. The first quotation comes from p. 165; the second from p. 166. Translated as "Nieh Hsiao-ch'ien" by Timothy A. Ross in Ma and Lau, *Chinese Stories*, p. 408.

22. Li Yü, "Ho-ying lou," in *Shih-erh lou*, pp. 19–20. Translated by Mao as "The Reflections in the Water," in *Twelve Towers*, p. 11.

23. Ling Meng-ch'u, *P'ai-an ching-ch'i, chüan* 17. Translated as "Der Abt und die Geborene Wu" by Tsung-tung Chang in *Chinesischer Liebesgarten*, p. 57.

24. *Chin p'ing mei* (Hong Kong: Kuang-chih shu-chü, 1955), chap. 69.

25. Ibid., chap. 32.

26. Ibid., chap. 42.

27. See Katherine Newman Carlitz, "The Role of Drama in the *Chin P'ing Mei:* The Relationship between Fiction and Drama as a Guide to the Viewpoint of a Sixteenth-Century Chinese Novel" (Ph.D. dissertation, University of Chicago, 1979), pp. 160–161, 300, and passim; idem, *Rhetoric,* p. 50. See also Paul Varo Martinson, "Pao, Order and Redemption: Perspectives on Chinese Religion and Society based on a Study of the Chin P'ing Mei" (Ph.D. dissertation, University of Chicago, 1973), pp. 176–189.

28. See the discussion of *ch'ing* in Hua-yuan Li Mowry, *Chinese Love Stories from* Ch'ing-shih (Hamden, Conn.: Archon Books, 1983), esp. the introduction, pp. 1–35.

29. Patrick Hanan, *The Chinese Vernacular Story* (Cambridge, Mass.: Harvard University Press, 1981), pp. 123–124.

30. Feng Meng-lung, *Hsing-shih heng-yen, chüan* 10. "The Two Brothers," in *The Courtesan's Jewel Box,* translated by Gladys Yang and Yang Hsien-yi (Peking: Foreign Languages Press, 1957), pp. 132–156. Although I have relied on the translation by Yang and Yang, I have frequently modified it.

31. See the discussion of this case in Charlotte Furth, "Androgynous Males and Deficient Females: Biology and Gender Boundaries in Sixteenth and Seventeenth Century China," *Late Imperial China* 9:2 (Dec. 1988): 22–23; and Judith Zeitlin, "Pu Songling's (1640–1715) 'Liaozhai zhiyi' and the Chinese Discourse on the Strange," (Ph.D. dissertation, Harvard, 1988), pp. 100–113.

32. *Hsing-shih heng-yen, chüan* 10, p. 199.

33. Ibid.

34. Ibid., p. 202.

35. Ibid., pp. 205–206.

36. Ibid., p. 206.

37. Ibid., p. 207.

38. Ibid., p. 210.

39. Ibid., p. 211.

40. Ibid., p. 213.

41. Ibid., p. 214.

42. Ibid., *chüan* 20.

43. Ibid., p. 399.

44. Ibid., p. 403.

45. Ibid., p. 407.

46. Ibid., p. 408.

47. Ibid., p. 409.

48. Ibid., p. 425.

49. Ling Meng-ch'u, *P'ai-an ching-ch'i, chüan* 33. See the discussion of this

plot in H. F. Schurmann, "On Social Themes in Sung Tales," *Harvard Journal of Asiatic Studies* 20 (1957): 253–261.

50. *P'ai-an ching-ch'i, chüan* 33, p. 619.

51. Ibid.

52. Ibid., p. 628.

53. Ibid., p. 630.

54. Keith McMahon, *The Gap in the Wall: Causality and Containment in Seventeenth Century Chinese Fiction* (Leiden: E. J. Brill, 1988),p. 172; Hanan, *Vernacular Story,* p. 172. On Li Yü in general, see Patrick Hanan, *The Invention of Li Yu* (Cambridge, Mass.: Harvard University Press, 1989); and Henry, *Chinese Amusement.*

55. Henry, *Chinese Amusement,* pp. 76–84.

56. Li Yü, "Sheng wo lou," *Shih-erh lou,* pp. 307–308.

57. Ibid., p. 309.

58. Ibid., p. 313.

59. Ibid., p. 322.

60. Ibid., p. 327.

61. Ibid., p. 328.

62. Li Yü, *Ch'iao t'uan-yüan, shang/*12b, p. 4618.

63. Ibid., *shang/*13a, p. 4619.

64. Ibid.

65. The two characters are similar: The character I is formed by adding the "man" radical to the character "Yin." I's jest is that if he sent a person over to the Yin family, the two surnames would be interchangeable, and hence the adoption would be correct.

66. Henry, *Chinese Amusement,* p. 70.

67. Li Yü, *Ch'iao t'uan-yüan, shang/*29b, p. 4652. I have followed Henry's translation for the last four lines.

68. Hanan, *Li Yu,* p. 102.

69. "Sheng wo lou," p. 326. I have followed the translation of Hanan, *Li Yu,* p. 102.

70. Henry, *Chinese Amusement,* pp. 61–62.

71. Li Yü, *Ch'iao t'uan-yüan, hsia/*51b, p. 4788.

72. P'u Sung-ling, "Chang Ch'eng," in *Liao-chai,* vol. 1, *chüan* 2, p. 252.

73. Feng Meng-lung, "Lü Ta-lang huan chin wan ku-jou," *Ching-shih t'ung-yen, chüan* 5, p. 55.

74. *Ching-shih t'ung-yen, chüan* 5.

75. Sarah Allan, *The Heir and the Sage* (San Francisco: Chinese Materials Center, 1981), passim.

Glossary

Terms

chao-fu 招夫
chao-hsü 招壻（婿）
chao hsü yang lao 招壻養老
chao-mu 昭穆
chen nü 眞女
ch'eng 誠
cheng ming 正名
ch'i 氣
chi 繼
chi-mu 繼母
chi-tzu 繼子
ch'i-yang 乞養
ch'i-yang kuo-fang 乞養過房
ch'i-yang wei-tzu 乞養爲子
chi yü 繼於
chia 假
chia-fu 假父
chia-hsün 家訓
chia mu 嫁母
chia-p'u 家僕
chia-tzu 假子
chien 賤
ch'ien 錢
chih 質
chin-shih 進士
ching 精

ch'ing 情
ch'ing-i 情意
ch'ing-ming 清明
ch'u chi 出繼
ch'u chui 出贅
chu hou 諸侯
chü jen 舉人
Chu jen mieh Tseng 莒人滅鄫
chüeh 絕
chui 贅
chui-fu 贅夫
chui-hsü 贅婿
chün-tzu 君子
chung 種
ch'ung-sheng fu-mu 重生父母

en 恩
en yang 恩養

fang 房
fei cheng 非正
fei lei 非類
fei tsu 非族
fen 分
fen yu ts'ai ch'an 分有財產
feng-shui 風水

187

feng-su 風俗
fu fu i t'i 夫婦一體
fu yang 撫養

henjō nanshi (Japanese) 變成男子
ho t'ung wen tzu 合同文字
hou 後
hsiang 象
hsiang-li 鄉里
hsiang wo 相我
hsiang-yin 鄉飲
hsiao 肖
hsien 賢
hsing 姓
hsüeh-pao 血抱
hsüeh-shih 學士
hu-chüeh 戶絕
hua-pen 話本
hun-tun 混沌

i 義
I (surname) 伊
i-ch'ih (strange and idiotic) 異癡
i-ch'ih (false teeth) 義齒
i chüeh 義絕
i-fu 義夫
i-hsing yang-tzu 異姓養子
i lei 異類
i-nan 義男
i-nü 義女
i te 異德
i-tzu 義子
ie (Japanese) 家

jen 仁
jen ch'ing 人情

ju-hua 入話
ju-mu 乳母

kan 感
kan-erh 乾兒
k'e-t'uo 可託
kuo-lou 蜾蠃
ku (grain) 穀
ku (father's sister) 姑
ku jou 骨肉
ku-sha 故殺
kuei 貴
k'un 鯤
kung 功
kung-kuo-ke 功過格
kuo 國
kuo-chi-tzu 過繼子
kuo-fang 過房
kuo-fang-tzu 過房子

lao t'ien 老天
lei 類
lei wo 類我
li (village; measure of distance) 里
li (ritual; correct behavior) 禮
li (substatutes) 例
li ch'i ch'u 立其出
liang (good, free status) 良
liang (measure of money) 兩
lien-tzu 連子
lü 律
luan 亂

mei yüan mei ku 沒緣沒故
mi 迷
mieh hsing 滅姓

min 民
ming 名
ming fen 名分
ming-ling nü-erh 螟蛉女兒
ming-ling-tzu 螟蛉子
ming-ling yu tzu/ shih ku ssu chih
　螟蛉有子，式穀似之
mo kuan 沒官
mu (wood) 木
mu (order of ancestral tablets) 穆

nei luan 內亂
neng 能
nu pi 奴婢

ou-sha 毆殺

pao-yang 抱養
p'eng 鵬
p'i 匹
piao (cousin) 表
piao (prostitute) 婊
piao-hsiung 表兄
p'in-chin 聘金
pu 卜
pu cheng 不正
pu hsien 不賢
P'u-i 濮議

shan 善
shan-jen 善人
shan-shu 善書
shen 神
sheng-jen 聖人
shih 氏
shih-i 世醫
shih-jen 矢人

shih-nü 石女
shih tai-fu 士大夫
shou yang 守養
shu-mu 庶母
sim-pua (Taiwanese) 媳婦仔
ssu 私
ssu-tzu 嗣子
sui 歲

ta-i 大義
ta-kung 大功
Ta li i 大禮議
ta ta 韃靼
t'ai chiao 胎教
tai fu 大夫
t'ai-tzu 太子
t'ai yang 胎養
t'an-tz'u 彈詞
te 德
ti 嫡
t'ien-huan 天宦
t'ien-yen 天閹
tou 斗
tsa-hu 雜戶
tsao-wu chih ch'iao 造物之巧
tseng-tzu 贈子
tsu 族
tsu-hsiung 族兄
tsung 宗
tsung-tsu 宗族
t'u feng 土蜂
t'uan-yüan 團圓
t'ung-hsing 同姓
t'ung-tsu 同族
t'ung-yang-hsi 童養媳
tz'u 慈

wai-sheng　外甥

wai-tsu　外族

wan wu　萬物

wei jen hou　爲人後

wei tzu　爲子

wen　文

wu　物

wu ch'ing　無情

wu hsing　五行

ya-t'ou　丫頭

yang (male principle)　陽

yang (to adopt, foster, nourish)　養

yang-fu　養父

yang fu mu　養父母

yang niu　養牛

yang-tzu　養子

yeh-jen　野人

Yin (surname)　尹

yin (hereditary privilege)　胤

yin (female principle)　陰

yin ssu　淫祀

yin te　陰德

yin-yüan　姻緣

yu ch'ing　有情

yu i　有義

yu wen hsüeh　有文學

yu yüan　有緣

yüan　元

yüan-fa　緣法

Titles of Texts

Texts listed in the bibliography are not included here.

"A-pao"　阿寶

Ch'an ching　產經

"Ch'an-pao tsa-lu"　產寶雜錄

"Chang Ch'eng"　張誠

"Chang T'ing-hsiu t'ao-sheng chiu fu"　張廷秀逃生救父

"Chang Yüan-wai i-fu ming-ling-tzu; Pao Lung-t'u chih-chuan ho-t'ung-wen"　張員外義撫螟蛉子，包龍圖智賺合同文

"Chao-kung"　昭公

"Chao T'ai-tsu ch'ien-li sung Ching-niang"　趙太祖千里送京娘

Ch'en Hsi-i hsin-hsiang pien　陳希夷心相編

"Ch'en Yü-shih ch'iao k'an chin ch'ai-tien"　陳御史巧勘金釵鈿

Chi-ssu chen-pao　己巳眞寶

"Chia-hsün yü-hsia p'ien"　家訓御下篇

"Chiang Hsing-ko ch'ung-hui chen-chu shan"　蔣興哥重會珍珠衫

"Chiao-no"　嬌娜

"Chieh-i"　借衣

Ch'ien chin yao fang　千金要方

"Chin yü"　晉語

"Chin Yü-nu pang-ta po-ch'ing-lang"　金玉奴棒打薄情郎

Ching ch'ai chi　荊釵記

Ching-shih shih-yung-pien hsü-chi　經世實用編續集

"Chiu te sung"　酒德頌

Chu-shih chi-lüeh　祝氏集略

"Ch'ü-ch'i pu ch'ü t'ung-hsing"　取妻不取同姓

"Ch'ü li"　曲禮

"Ch'uan chia pao"　傳家寶

"Chüeh-ssu"　絕嗣

Ch'un-ch'iu fan-lu　春秋繁露

Fa-yüan chu-lin　法苑珠林

"Fan li"　凡例

"Feng-hsien lou"　奉先樓

Fo-ting-hsin ta t'o-lo-ni ching　佛頂心大陀羅尼經

"Fu-kuei fa-chi ssu chih"　富貴發跡司志

Fu-lo-ch'ang　復洛娼

"Fu Te-ch'ien fu shih ming tzu hsü"　傅德謙復氏名字序

Hai-ning Ch'en-shih chia-p'u　海寧陳氏家譜

Hao ch'iu chuan　好逑傳

"Heng-niang"　恒娘

"Ho-ying lou"　合影樓

"Hsi kung"　僖公

"Hsi ming"　西銘

"Hsiang kung"　襄公

Hsiao ching　孝經

"Hsing"　姓

Hsing-an hui-lan　刑案匯覽

Hsing-ke t'iao-li　興革條例

"Hsiung Mien-an Pao-shan t'ang pu-fei-ch'ien kung-te-li"
　熊勉菴寶善堂不費錢功德例

"Hsü hsia"　恤下

Hsü San-chung chia-tse　徐三重家則

Hsün-su i-kuei　訓俗遺規

"Hsün-tzu yen"　訓子言

"Hu-chüeh"　戶絕

"Hua-teng chiao Lien-nü ch'eng fo chi"　花燈轎蓮女成佛記

Huang-ti nei-ching ling-shu　黃帝內經靈樞

I-hsin fang (Isshinpō)　醫心方

I-hsüeh ju-men　醫學入門

I-le-t'ang chi　一樂堂記

"Jen shih pu"　人事部

"Jen-wu i i wei ming"　人物以義爲名

Kan-t'ien tung-ti Tou O yüan　感天動地竇娥冤

"Kuan-shih-yin p'u-sa p'u-men-p'in"　觀世音菩薩普門品

"Kuei Yüan-wai t'u-ch'iung ch'an-hui"　桂員外途窮懺悔

Kung-kuo-ke　功過格

Le-ling hsien-chih　樂陵縣志

"Lei ts'ao"　雷曹

"Li Chiang-chün ts'o jen chiu; Liu shih nü kuei ts'ung fu"
李將軍錯認舅，劉氏女詭從夫

"Li K'o-jang ching ta k'ung-han; Liu Yüan-p'u shuang sheng kuei-
tzu"　李克讓竟達空函，劉元普雙生貴子

Li-ming p'ien　立命篇

"Liang hsien-ling ching-i hun ku-nü"　兩縣令競義婚孤女

Ling-shu ching　靈樞經

"Liu Hsiao-kuan tz'u-hsiung hsiung-ti"　劉小官雌雄兄弟

"Lü Ta-lang huan-chin wan ku-jou"　呂大郎還金完骨肉

"Lun tzu"　論子

"Mai-yu-lang tu-chan hua-k'uei"　賣油郎獨占花魁

"Meng-chiang-nü pien-wen"　孟姜女變文

Ming wai-shih　明外史

"Nan Meng-mu chiao-ho san-ch'ien"　男孟母教合三遷

"Nieh Hsiao-ch'ien"　聶小倩

Pai-i Kuan-yin ching 白衣觀音經
Pei-yu chi 北遊記
"Pien nü wei erh p'u-sa ch'iao" 變女爲兒菩薩巧
Po hu t'ung 白虎通

"San-yü lou" 三與樓
"Sang fu" 喪服
She-sheng tsung-yao 攝生總要
"Shen kuei pu" 神鬼部
"Sheng wo lou" 生我樓
Sheng yü 聖諭
"Shih-huo chih" 食貨志
"Su Sung erh fu t'ien-fu chih chung" 蘇松二府田賦之重
"Sung Hsiao-kuan t'uan-yüan p'o chan-li" 宋小官團圓破氈笠

"Ta Ming lü chih yin" 大明律直引
"T'u ou" 土偶
"Tuan-shih" 段氏
Tung-hsüan-tzu 洞玄子
Tung-ming pao-chi 洞冥寶記
"Tuo-chin lou" 奪錦樓
"Tzu ssu lun" 子嗣論

Wan-shih yü-ying chia mi 萬氏育嬰家秘
Wang Chung-shu ch'üan-hsiao ko 王中書勸孝歌
"Wang Kuei-an" 王桂菴
"Wang Shih-hsiu" 汪士秀
"Wang Ta-yin huo-fen Pao-lien ssu" 汪大尹火焚寶蓮寺
Wei Shu-tzu jih-lu 魏叔子日錄
Wen-hai p'i-sha 文海披沙
"Wu yin wu wei" 五音五味

"Yao tien" 堯典
"Yeh-ch'a kuo" 夜叉國
"Yü-kung" 禹貢
Yü-li ch'ao-chuan 玉曆鈔傳
Yüan-shih t'ien-tsun chi tu hsüeh-hu chen-ching 元始天尊濟度血湖眞經

Persons and Deities

Authors listed in the bibliography are not listed here. Neither are fictional characters, nor persons listed in genealogies.

Ao-jo 敖若

Chang Hsien 張仙
Chang Hung 張宏
Chang Shih 張栻
Chang Ts'ung 張聰
Ch'en Hsi-i 陳希夷
Ch'en T'ai 陳泰
Ch'eng I 程頤
Chia I 賈誼
Chih-hsü 智旭
Chou Ch'en 周忱
Chu Hao 祝顥
Chu Yu-tun 朱有燉
Chu Yün-ming 祝允明

Fan Ning 范寧
Fang Hsien-fu 方獻夫
Feng Ying-ching 馮應京

Ho Hsiu 何休
Hsien Huang-ti 獻皇帝
Hsiung Hung-pei 熊弘備
Hsü San-chung 徐三重
Hu Ssu-hui 忽思慧
Hu Ying-lin 胡應麟
Huang Pa 黃霸
Hung Chi 洪基

Ihara Saikaku (Japanese) 井原西鶴

Kao-mei 高禖
Kuan-yin 觀音
K'uang Chung (Huang Chung) 況鐘（黃鐘）
K'uang I-shih 況以實
Kuei O 桂萼

Lao K'an 勞堪
Li Kuei 李軌
Li T'ing 李梃
Lin Hsi-yüan 林希元
Liu Tsung-chou 劉宗周

Mao Ch'eng 毛澄

P'an Kuang-tan 潘光旦

Shao-wei 少微
Shih T'ien-chi 石天基
Shun 舜
Ssu-ma Ch'ien 司馬遷
Ssu-ma Kuang 司馬光
Sun Ssu-miao 孫思邈

T'ai Jen 太任
T'ien Kou 天狗
Tu Mu 都穆
Tung Ch'i-ch'ang 董其昌
Tung Chung-shu 董仲舒

Wan Ch'üan　萬全

Wang Meng-chi　王孟箕

Wang Ping　王冰

Wei Hsi　魏禧

Wen Wang　文王

Yang T'ing-ho　楊廷和

Yao　堯

Yen Shih-ku　顏師古

Yü　禹

Yün-ku　雲谷

Bibliography

Sources in Chinese and Japanese

Abbreviations

SKCS Ssu-k'u ch'üan-shu 四庫全書
SPPY Ssu-pu pei-yao 四部備要
SPTK Ssu-pu ts'ung-k'an 四部叢刊
TSCCCP Ts'ung-shu chi-ch'eng ch'u-pien 叢書集成初編

Asami Keisai 淺見絅齋. "Yōshi benshō" 養子辨証. In *Nihon Jurin susho* 日本儒林叢書. Edited by Seki Giichiro 關儀一郎. Tokyo: Tōyō tosho kankōkai, 1927–1929.
Chai Hao 翟灝. *T'ung-su pien* 通俗編. In *TSCCCP*. Vol. 226.
Chang Lu 張璐. *Chang-shih i-t'ung* 張氏醫通. Shanghai: Shanghai K'e-hsüeh chi-shu ch'u-pan-she, 1963.
———. *Sun Chen-jen pei-chi Ch'ien-chin fang* 孫眞人備急千金方. Shanghai: Chung-yüan shu-chü, 1930.
Chang Lu 張鹵. *Huang Ming chih-shu* 皇明制書. Edited by Yamane Yukio. Tokyo: Koten Kenkyukai, 1966–1967.
Chang Lü-hsiang 張履祥. *Yang-yüan hsien-sheng ch'üan-chi* 楊園先生全集. Taipei, 1968.
Ch'ang-shu hsien-chih 常熟縣志 (1539). Taipei 1965 reprint.
Chang Tsai 張載. *Chang-tzu ch'üan-shu* 張子全書. In *SPPY*. Vols. 1441–1443.
Chang Yü 張豫. *Erh-shih-erh tzu* 二十二子. Chiang-su shu-chü, 1874–1877.
Che-yü kuei-chien 折獄龜鑑. Compiled by Cheng K'o 鄭克. In *TSCCCP*. Vol. 134.
Ch'en Chi-ju 陳繼儒. *Chen-chu ch'uan* 珍珠船. In *TSCCCP*. Vol. 134.
Ch'en Ch'i-yüan 陳其元. *Yung-hsien-chai pi-chi* 庸閒齋筆記. Taipei: Wen-hai ch'u-pan-she, 1975.
Ch'en Ch'un 陳淳. *Pei-hsi tzu-i* 北溪字義. In *TSCCCP*. Vol. 112.
Ch'en Hsüeh-li 陳學禮. *Kao-yu Feng-hsi Ch'en-shih chia-p'u* 高郵奉西陳氏家譜 (1627). Manuscript held by National Central Library of Taiwan, no. 3014.

Ch'en Hung-mou 陳宏謀. *Wu-chung i-kuei* 五種遺規. In *SPPY*. Vols. 1547–1554.

Ch'en Ku-yüan 陳顧元. "Chui-hsü chih-tu k'ao" 贅壻制度考. *Ching shih* 1:8 (1935):34–37.

Ch'en Tzu-ming 陳自明. *Fu-jen liang-fang* 婦人良方. Taipei: Shang-wu yin-shu-kuan, 1977.

Ch'en Yao-wen 陳耀文. *T'ien chung chi* 天中記. Taipei: Shang-wu yin-shu-kuan, 1981.

Cheng K'o. See *Che-yü kuei-chien*.

Cheng T'ai-ho 鄭太和. *Cheng-shih kuei-fan* 鄭氏規範. In *TSCCCP*. Vol. 167

Cheng-t'ung tao-tsang 正統道藏. Taipei: I-wen, 1962.

Ch'i Chung-fu 齊仲甫. *Nü-k'o pai-wen* 女科百問. Shanghai: Shanghai ku-chi shu-tien, 1983.

————. *Nü-k'o pai-wen* 女科百問. Chü-chin t'ang, 1795.

Chia I 賈誼. *Chia I hsin-shu* 賈誼新書. In *SPPY*. Vol. 1422.

Chia-hsing fu t'u-chi 嘉興府圖記 (1549).

Chia-ting Chou-shih chia-p'u 嘉定周氏家譜.

Chia-ting hsien chih 嘉定縣志 (1605).

Chia-ting hsien chih 嘉定縣志 (1673).

Chiang-p'u hsien chih 江浦縣志 (1616).

Chien-teng hsin-hua 剪燈新話. Shanghai: Ku-tien wen-hsüeh ch'u-pan-she, 1957.

Chin-hua hsien chih 金華縣志.

Ch'in Hui-t'ien 秦蕙田, comp. *Wu-li t'ung-k'ao* 五禮通考. Taipei: Hsin-hsing shu-chü, 1971.

Chin p'ing mei 金瓶梅. Hong Kong: Kuang-chih shu-chü, 1955.

Ch'ing ming chi. See *Meikō shohan seimei shō*.

Ch'ing-pai lei-ch'ao 清稗類鈔. Compiled by Hsü K'o 徐珂. Taipei: Shang-wu yin-shu-kuan, 1967.

Ch'ing shih 清史. Taipei: Kuo-fang yen-chiu yüan, 1961.

Ching-shih t'ung-yen. See Feng Meng-lung.

Chu Chen-heng 朱震亨. *Ch'an-pao pai-wen* 產寶百問. Ming edition of Yüan original held at U.S. Library of Congress.

Chu Hsi 朱熹. *Chu-tzu ta-ch'üan* 朱子大全. In *SPPY*. Vols. 1458–1517.

Ch'ü Yu 瞿佑. *Chien-teng hsin-hua* 剪燈新話. Shanghai: Ku-tien wen-hsüeh ch'u-pan-she, 1957.

Ch'un-ch'iu Ku-liang chuan Fan-shih chi-chieh 春秋穀梁傳范氏集解. In *SPPY*. Vols. 53–56.

Ch'un-ch'iu Kung-yang chuan Ho-shih chieh-ku 春秋公羊傳何氏解詁. In *SPPY*. Vols. 47–52.

Ch'un-ch'iu Tso-shih chuan Tu-shih chi-chieh 春秋左氏傳杜氏集解. In *SPPY*. Vols. 35–46.

Chung-wen ta tz'u-tien 中文大辭典. 10 vols. Taipei: China Academy, 1971.

Fa-yen 法言. In *SPPY*. Vols. 1419–1420.

Feng Meng-lung 馮夢龍. *Ching-shih t'ung-yen* 警世通言. Hong Kong: Chung-hua shu-chü, 1978.

——. *Hsing-shih heng-yen* 醒世恒言. Hong Kong: Ku-tien wen-hsüeh ch'u-pan-she, n.d.

——. *Ku-chin hsiao-shuo* 古今小說. Peking: Jen-min wen-hsüeh ch'u-pan-she, 1979.

——. *Shan-ko* 山歌. Shanghai: Chung-hua shu-chü, 1962.

Feng-su t'ung-i 風俗通義. Peking: Centre Franco-chinois d'etudes sinologiques, 1943.

Fu I-ling 傅衣凌. *Ming Ch'ing nung-ts'un she-hui ching-chi* 明清農村社會經濟. Hong Kong: Shih-yung shu-chü, 1972.

Hai Jui 海瑞. *Hai Jui chi* 海瑞集. Peking: Chung-hua shu-chü, 1962.

Han shu 漢書. In *SPPY*. Vols. 440–471.

Ho Ch'o 何焯. *Fen-lei tzu-chin* 分類字錦. Taipei: Wen-yu shu-tien, 1967.

Hosono Kōji 細野浩二. "Minmatsu shinsho no okeru doboku kankei" 明末清初のおける奴僕關係, *Tōyō gakuho* 東洋學報 50:3 (Dec. 1967).

Hou Han shu 後漢書. In *SPPY*. Vols. 472–501.

Hsi-yu chi 西遊記. Peking: Jen-min wen-hsüeh ch'u-pan-she, 1972.

Hsiao Yung 蕭雍. *Ch'ih-shan hui-yüeh* 赤山會約. In *TSCCCP*. Vol. 127.

Hsin-an Ch'eng-shih t'ung-tsung shih-p'u 新安程氏統宗世譜. Compiled by Ch'eng Hui-min. Held at National Central Library, Taiwan.

Hsing-shih heng-yen. See Feng Meng-lung.

Hsieh Chao-che 謝肇淛. *Wu tsa-tsu* 五雜俎. Peking: Chung-hua shu-chü, 1959.

Hsiu-shui hsien chih 秀水縣志 (1596). Taipei: Ch'eng-wen, 1970 reprint.

Hsü Ch'un-fu 徐春甫. *Ku-chin i-t'ung ta-ch'üan* 古今醫統大全. 1570 edition held at the University of California at Berkeley.

Hsü Hsiang-ch'ing 許相卿. *Hsü Yün-ts'un i-mou* 許雲邨貽謀. In *TSCCCP*. Vol. 167.

Hsü Hsüeh-mo 徐學謨. *Kuei yu-yüan ch'en-t'an* 歸有園麈談. In *TSCCCP*. Vol. 72.

Hsüeh Yün-sheng. See *Tu-li ts'un-i*.

Huang Chang-chien. See *Ming-tai lü-li hui-pien*.

Huang Liu-hung 黃六鴻. *Fu-hui ch'üan-shu* 福惠全書. (1879?)

Huang Ming yung-hua lei-pien 皇明詠化類編. 8 vols. Taipei: Kuo-feng ch'u-pan she, 1965.

Hui-chou fu-chih 徽州府志 (1566). Taipei: Taiwan hsüeh-sheng shu-chü, 1965 reprint.

(Ch'eng ting-pen hsin-chüan ch'üan-pu hsiu-hsiang) Hung lou meng 程丁本新鐫全部繡像紅樓夢. Taipei: Kuang-wen shu-chü, 1977.

Hung Mai 洪邁. *Jung-chai sui-pi* 容齋隨筆. In *SPTK* hsü-pien. Vols. 329–332.

Hung P'ien 洪楩. *Ch'ing-p'ing shan-t'ang hua-pen* 清平山堂話本. Shanghai: K'u-t'ien wen-hsüeh ch'u-pan-she, 1957.

I-li Cheng-chu 儀禮鄭注. In *SPPY*. Vols. 19–26.

I-lin 意林. In *SPPY*. Vols. 1417–1418.

I-shuo 醫說. Compiled by Chang Kao 張杲. Taipei: Hsin-wen-feng ch'u-pan Kung-ssu, 1983.

Jen-ch'iu Pien-shih tsu-p'u 任邱邊氏族譜 (1772).

Ju-lin wai-shih 儒林外史. Peking: Tso-chia ch'u-pan-she, 1956.

Jung-chai sui-pi. See Hung Mai.

K'ang Sheng 康生. "Chung-kuo chi-ch'eng chih-tu te yen-chiu" 中國繼承制度的研究, *Hsin sheng ming* 新生命 1:11 (Nov. 1928).

Kao Chü. See *Ta Ming lü chi-chieh fu-li*.

Kao-yu Feng-hsi Ch'en shih chia p'u. See Ch'en Hsüeh-li.

Ku-chin hsiao-shuo. See Feng Meng-lung.

Ku-chin t'u-shu chi-ch'eng 古今圖書集成. First published 1726; reprinted, Shanghai: Chung-hua shu-chü, 1934.

Ku-liang chuan. See *Ch'un-ch'iu Ku-liang chuan Fan-shih chi-chieh*.

Ku Yen-wu 顧炎武. *Jih chih lu chi-shih* 日知錄集釋. In SPPY. Vols. 1621–1632.

———. *T'ien-hsia chün-kuo li-ping shu* 天下郡國利病書. N.p.p.: T'u-shu chi-ch'eng chü, 1901.

Ku Ying-t'ai 谷應泰. *Ming-shih chi-shih pen-mo* 明史紀事本末. Taipei: San-min shu-chü, 1963.

K'uai-chi Ch'in-shih tsung-p'u 會稽秦氏宗譜. Manuscript held in National Central Library of Taiwan.

K'uai-chi hsien chih 會稽縣志 (1575).

(K'ang-hsi) K'uai-chi hsien-chih 康熙會稽縣志. Shao-hsing, 1936.

Kuan Han-ch'ing 關漢卿. *Kuan Han-ch'ing hsi-ch'ü chi* 關漢卿戲曲集. Taipei: Hung-yeh shu-chü, 1973.

K'un Hsin liang-hsien hsü-hsiu ho-chih 崑新兩縣續修合志. 2 vols. Taipei: Ch'eng-wen 1970.

K'un-shan hsien-chih 崑山縣志 (1538).

K'un-shan hsien-chih 崑山縣志. Ch'ien-lung edition.

K'un-shan jen-wu-chih 崑山人物志. (Chia-ching).

Kung-yang chuan. See *Ch'un-ch'iu Kung-yang chuan Ho-shih chieh-ku*.

Kuo yü 國語. In *SPPY*. Vols. 1112–1117.

Kurihara Keisuke 栗原圭介. "Dosei fukon no rei kihanka" 同姓不婚の禮規範化, *Nihon chugoku gakkai ho* 日本中國學會報 27:(1975):17–33.

Li-chi Cheng-chu 禮記鄭注. In *SPPY*. Vols. 27–34.

Li Heng-mei 李衡梅. "Wo-kuo yüan-shih she-hui hun-yin hsing-t'ai yen-chiu" 我國原始社會婚姻形態研究, *Li-shih yen-chiu* 歷史研究 1 (1986):95–109.

Li Hsing-tao 李行道. *Pao Tai-chih chih chuan hui-lan chi tsa-chü*

包待制智賺灰闌記雜劇. In *Yüan ch'ü hsüan* 元曲選. Compiled by Tsang Mao-hsün 臧懋循. Peking: Wen-hsüeh ku-chi k'an-hsing she, 1955. Pp. 1107–1129.

Li Shih-chen 李時珍. *Pen-ts'ao kang-mu* 本草綱目. Peking: Jen-min wei-sheng ch'u-pan-she, 1975.

Li Yü 李漁. *Ch'iao t'uan-yüan* 巧團圓. In *Li Yü ch'üan-chi* 李漁全集. Edited by Helmut Martin. Taipei: Ch'eng-wen, 1970, vol. 11. Pp. 4577–4790.

———. *Shih-erh lou* 十二樓. Taipei: Chang-ko, 1975.

———. *Tzu-chih hsin-shu* 資治新書. Shanghai: Tu-shu chi-ch'eng yin-shu-chü, 1894.

———. *Wu sheng hsi* 無聲戲. Edited by Helmut Martin. Taipei: Chin-hsüeh shu-chü, 1969.

Liang Ch'i-tzu 梁其姿 (Angela Ki-che Leung). "Ming-mo Ch'ing-ch'u min-chien tz'u-shan huo-tung te hsing-chi—i Chiang Che ti-ch'ü wei li" 明末清初民間慈善活動的興起—以江浙地區為例, *Shih huo yüeh k'an* 食貨月刊 15:7–8 (Jan. 1986):304–331.

———. "Shih-ch'i, shih-pa shih-chi Ch'ang-chiang hsia-yu chih yü-ying-t'ang" 十七十八世紀長江下游之育嬰堂. In *Chung-kuo hai-yang fa-chan shih-lun wen-chi* 中國海洋發展史論文集. 3 vols. Taipei: Chung-yang yen-chiu yüan san-min chu-i yen-chiu-so, vol. 1 (1984). Pp. 90–130.

Ling Meng-ch'u 凌濛初. *Erh-k'e p'ai-an ching-ch'i* 二刻拍案驚奇. Taipei: Kuei-kuan t'u-shu, 1984.

———. *P'ai-an ching-ch'i* 拍案驚奇. Taipei: Shih-chieh shu-chü, 1975.

Liu Ch'ing-po 劉清波. *Yang-nü ch'ung-hun t'ung-chien chih yen-chiu* 養女重婚通姦之研究. Taipei: Shang-wu yin-shu-kuan, 1969.

Liu Hsiang 劉向. *Lieh nü chuan pu-chu* 列女傳補註. Ch'ang-sha: Shang-wu yin-shu kuan, 1938.

Liu Hsing-t'ang 劉興唐. "Chui-hun chih-tu te liang-ke hsing-shih" 贅婚制度的兩個形式, *Tung-fang tsa-chih* 東方雜誌 33:15 (1936):99–103.

Liu-pu ch'eng-yü chu-chieh 六部成語註解. Edited by Naitō Kenkichi. Tokyo: Taian, 1962.

Liu Tsung-chou 劉宗周. *Jen p'u lei chi* 人譜類記. Taipei: Kuang-wen shu-chü, 1971.

Lou Tzu-k'uang 婁子匡. *Min-su ts'ung-shu* 民俗叢書. Supplement 4, *Chia fan p'ien* 家範篇, no. 13, *Ch'u-chi yang-tzu* 出繼養子. Taipei: Chung-kuo min-su hsüeh-hui, 1979.

Lü Ch'eng-chih 呂誠之. *Chung-kuo hun-yin chih-tu hsiao-shih* 中國婚姻制度小史. Shanghai: Lung-hu shu-tien, 1935.

Lü-shih ch'un-ch'iu chiao-shih 呂氏春秋校釋. Taipei: Chung-hua ts'ung-shu wei-yüan-hui, 1950.

Lu Ts'an 陸粲. *Keng-ssu pien* 庚巳編. Shanghai: Commercial Press, 1937.

Lun-yü chu-shu 論語注疏. In *SPPY*. Vols. 173–175.

(Hsiu-hsiang) Lung-t'u kung-an 繡像龍圖公案. Taipei: T'ien-i ch'u-pan-she, 1974.

Ma Tsung 馬總. See *I-lin*.

Mao shih chiang-i 毛詩講義. In *SKCS*. Vols. 233–238.

Meikō shohan seimei shū 名公書判清明集. Tokyo: Koten kenkyu kai, 1964.

Meng-tzu chu-shu 孟子注疏. In *SPPY*. Vols. 176–179.

Min-shang-shih hsi-kuan tiao-ch'a pao-kao-lu 民商事習慣調查報告錄. Taipei: Chin-hsüeh shu-chü, 1969.

Ming lü chi-chieh fu-li. See *Ta Ming lü chi-chieh fu-li*.

Ming shih 明史. Peking: Chung-hua shu-chü, 1974.

Ming Shih-tsung shih-lu 明世宗實錄. Taipei: Academia Sinica, 1966–1968. Vols. 70–91.

Ming-tai lü-li hui-pien 明代律例彙編. Compiled by Huang Chang-chien 黃彰健. 2 vols. Taipei: Academia Sinica, 1979.

Niida Noboru 仁井田陞. "'Seimei shū ko kon mon' no kenkyū" 清明集戶婚門の研究, *Tōhō gakuhō* 東方學報 4 (1933):115–189.

———. *Shina mibun hōshi* 支那身分法史. Tokyo: Zayu baikan kokai, 1943.

———. *Tōrei shūi* 唐令拾遺. Tokyo: Tōhō bunka gakuin Tokyo kenkyujo, 1933.

Ning-po fu-chih 寧波府志. Taipei: Chung-hua ts'ung-shu wei-yuan hui, 1957.

P'u Sung-ling 蒲松齡. *Liao-chai chih-i* 聊齋志異. Peking: Chung-hua shu-chü, 1962.

Shang-chün-shu chien-cheng 商君書箋正. Taipei: Kuang-wen shu-chü, 1975.

Shang shu K'ung chuan 尚書孔傳. In *SPPY*. Vols. 4–6.

Shang-yü Shih-shih chia-p'u 上虞施氏家譜. Manuscript copy in National Central Library of Taiwan, no. 3024.

Shen Kua 沈括. *Meng-hsi pi-t'an* 夢溪筆談. In *TSCCCP*. Vol. 56.

Shen Te-fu 沈德符. *Wan-li yeh huo pien* 萬曆野獲編. 5 vols. Taipei: Wei-wen t'u-shu ch'u-pan-she, 1976.

Shiga Shūzō 滋賀秀三. *Chugoku kazoku hō no genri* 中國家族法の原理. Tokyo: Sobunsha, 1968.

Shih chi 史記. Peking: Chung-hua shu-chü, 1959.

Shui hu chuan 水滸傳. Taipei: Ku-hsiang wen-hua ch'u-pan-she, 1977.

Ssu-yu chi 四遊記. Edited by Yü Hsiang-tou 余象斗. Shanghai: Ku-tien wen-hsüeh ch'u-pan-she, 1956.

Su-chou fu-chih 蘇州府志 (1960 reprint).

Su Mao-hsiang 蘇茂相. *Hsin-k'e ta Ming lü-li lin-min pao-ching* 新刻大明律例臨民寶鏡 (1632). Held at the University of California at Berkeley.

Sung-chiang fu-chih 松江府志 (1512).

Sung hsing-t'ung 宋刑統. Peking: Kuo-wu-yüan fa-shih chü, 1918.

Sung shih 宋史. Peking: Chung-hua shu-chü, 1977.

Sung-shih chi-shih pen-mo 宋史紀事本末. Peking: Chung-hua shu-chü, 1978.

Sung Tz'u 宋慈. *Hsi yüan lu* 洗冤錄. Taipei: Wen-hai ch'u-pan-she, 1968.

———. *Hsi yüan lu hsiang-i* 洗冤錄詳義. Shan-tung shu-chü, 1886.

Sung Yüan hua-pen chi 宋元話本記. Taipei: Chang-ko, 1975.

Ta Ch'ing lü-li hui-t'ung hsin-ts'uan 大清律例會通新纂. Taipei: Wen-hai ch'u-pan-she, 1964.

Ta Ming hui-tien 大明會典. 5 vols. Taipei: Tung-nan shu-pao-she, 1963.

Ta Ming lü chi-chieh fu-li 大明律集解附例. Edited by Kao Chü 高舉. 5 vols. Taipei: T'ai-wan hsüeh-sheng shu-chü, 1970.

Ta-sheng Miao-fa lien-hua ching 大乘妙法蓮華經. Hong Kong: Fo-ching liu-t'ung chu, 1988.

Ta Yüan t'ung-chih t'iao-ko 大元通制條格. 2 vols. Taipei: Hua-wen shu-chü, 1968.

T'ai-p'ing yü-lan 太平御覽. Shanghai: Shang-wu yin-shu-kuan, 1935.

T'ai-ts'ang chou-chih 太倉州志 (1548).

T'ai-ts'ang chou-chih 太倉州志 (1644).

T'ai-ts'ang chou-chih 太倉州志 (1803).

Tai Yen-hui 戴炎輝. *Chung-kuo shen-fen-fa shih* 中國身分法史. Taipei: Ssu-fa hsing-cheng-pu, 1959.

Takahashi Yoshiro 高橋芳郎. "Minmatsu shinshoki dohi yatoi kojin mibun no saihen to tokushitsu" 明末清初期、奴婢、雇工人身分の再編と特質, *Toyoshi kenkyū* 東洋史研究 41:3 (Dec. 1982): 60–85.

Tan-yang hsien-chih 丹陽縣志. Revised 1885; reprinted 1927.

T'ang-lü shu-i 唐律疏義. Shanghai: Commercial Press, 1934.

T'ang-yin pi-shih 棠陰比事. Compiled by Kuei Wan-jung 桂萬榮. In *SPTK hsü-pien*. Vol. 321.

T'ao Tsung-i 陶宗儀. *Ch'o-keng-lu* 輟耕錄. In *TSCCCP*. Vol. 44.

Tetsui Yoshinori 鐵井慶紀. "Kobai no kigen ni tsuite no ichi shiron" 高禖の起源についての一試論, *Tōyō shokuhō* 30 (Oct. 1967): 20–34.

T'ien I-heng 田藝蘅. *Liu-ch'ing jih-cha* 留青日札. Taipei: Kuang-wen shu-chü, 1969.

Tso chuan. See *Ch'un-ch'iu Tso-shih chuan Tu-shih chi-chieh*.

Tu-li ts'un-i ch'ung-k'an pen 讀例存疑重刊本. Edited by Hsüeh Yün-sheng 薛允升. 5 vols. Taipei: Ch'eng-wen ch'u-pan-she, 1970.

(Wan-li) T'ung-chou chih 萬曆通州志.

T'ung-su pien. See Chai Hao.

T'ung-tien 通典. *Ssu-k'u shan-pen ts'ung-shu ch'u-pien* 四庫善本叢書初編. Vols. 227–286.

Wang Chung-min 王重民, ed. *Tun-huang pien-wen chi* 敦煌變文集. 2 vols. Peking: Jen-min wen-hsüeh ch'u-pan-she, 1957.

Wang K'en-t'ang 王肯堂. *Nü-k'o chun-sheng* 女科準繩. Taipei: Hsin-wen-feng ch'u-pan kung-ssu, 1974.

Wei shu 魏書. Peking: Chung-hua shu-chü, 1974.

Wen hsüan 文選. In *SPPY*. Vols. 2293–2314.

Wu Hai 吳海. *Wu Ch'ao-tsung hsien-sheng wen-kuo-chai chi* 吳朝宗先生聞過齋集. In *TSCCCP*. Vol. 475.

Yang Chi-sheng 楊繼盛. *Yang Chung-min kung i-pi* 楊忠愍公遺筆. Ch'ang-sha: Shang-wu yin-shu-kuan, 1939.

Yao Shun-mu 姚舜牧. *Yao-yen* 藥言. In *TSCCCP*. Vol. 168.

Yeh Meng-chu 葉夢珠. *Yüeh shih pien* 閱世編. Taipei: Wen-hai ch'u-pan-she, 1969.

Yeh Te-hui 葉德輝. *Shuang-mei ying-an ts'ung-shu* 雙梅景闇叢書 (1907).

Yen Chih-t'ui 顏之推. *Yen-shih chia-hsün* 顏氏家訓. In *TSCCCP*. Vol. 167.

Yin-shan cheng-yao 飲膳正要. In *SPTK hsü pien*. Vols. 326–328.

Yü-chiao-li 玉嬌梨. Shanghai: Kuang-i shu-chu, 1933.

Yüan Huang 袁黃. *Hsün-tzu yen* 訓子言. In *TSCCCP*. Vol. 168.

Yüan Ts'ai 袁采. *Yüan-shih shih-fan* 袁氏世範. In *Chih-pu-tsu-chai ts'ung-shu* 知不足齋叢書. Vol. 130.

Yung-chia hsien-chih 永嘉縣志 (1566).

Sources in Western Languages

Ahern, Emily (Martin). *The Cult of the Dead in a Chinese Village*. Stanford, Calif.: Stanford University Press, 1973.

Alabaster, Ernest. *Notes and Commentaries on Chinese Law*. London: Luzac, 1899.

Allan, Sarah. *The Heir and the Sage*. San Francisco: Chinese Materials Center, 1981.

The Arts of the Ming Dynasty: An Exhibition Organized by the Arts Council of Great Britain and the Oriental Ceramic Society. London: Charles F. Ince and Sons, 1958.

Baker, Hugh. *Chinese Family and Kinship*. New York: Columbia University Press, 1979.

———. *A Chinese Lineage Village: Sheung Shui*. Stanford, Calif.: Stanford University Press, 1968.

Baller, Frederic W. *The Sacred Edict with a Translation of the Colloquial Rendering*. 2 vols. Shanghai: American Presbyterian Mission Press, 1898.

Beattie, Hilary. *Land and Lineage in China: A Study of T'ung-ch'eng County, Anhwei, in the Ming and Ch'ing Dynasties*. Cambridge: Cambridge University Press, 1979.

Befu, Ben. *Worldly Mental Calculations: An Annotated Translation of Ihara Saikaku's Seken Munezan'yo*. Berkeley and Los Angeles: University of California Press, 1976.

Befu, Harumi. "Corporate Emphasis and Patterns of Descent in the Japanese Family." In *Japanese Culture: Its Development and Characteristics*. Edited by R. J. Smith and R. K. Beardsley. London: Metheuen, 1963. Pp. 34–41.

Bell, Clair Hayden. "The Call of the Blood in the Medieval German Epic," *Modern Language Notes* 37:1 (1922): 17–26.

Birch, Cyril, trans. *Stories from a Ming Collection*. Bloomington: Indiana University Press, 1958.

Bodde, Derk, and Clarence Morris. *Law in Imperial China: Exemplified by 190 Ching Dynasty Cases*. Cambridge, Mass.: Harvard University Press, 1968; reprinted by University of Pennsylvania Press, 1973.

Boswell, John Eastburn. "*Exposito* and *Oblatio:* The Abandonment of Children and the Ancient and Medieval Family," *American Historical Review* 89:1 (Feb. 1984): 10–33.

Boulais, Guy. *Manuel du code chinois*. Shanghai: Imprimerie de la Mission Catholique, 1924.

Brady, Ivan. *Transactions in Kinship: Adoption and Fosterage in Oceania*. Honolulu: University of Hawaii Press, 1976.

Brokaw, Cynthia. "Yüan Huang (1533–1606) and the Ledgers of Merit and Demerit," *Harvard Journal of Asiatic Studies* 47:1 (June 1987): 137–195.

Brook, Timothy James. "Gentry Dominance in Chinese Society: Monasteries and Lineages in the Structuring of Local Society 1500–1700." Ph.D. dissertation, Harvard, 1984.

Burckhardt, V. R. *Chinese Creeds and Customs*. 2 vols. Hong Kong: South China Morning Post, 1954.

Burns, I. R. "Private Law in Traditional China (Sung Dynasty): Using as a Main Source of Information the Work *Ming-kung shu-p'an Ch'ing-ming chi.*" Ph.D. dissertation, Oxford, 1973.

Bush, Susan, and Christian Murck. *Theories of the Arts in China*. Princeton, N.J.: Princeton University Press, 1983.

Buxbaum, David, ed. *Chinese Family Law and Social Change*. Seattle: University of Washington Press, 1978.

Bynum, Caroline Walker. *Holy Feast and Holy Fast: The Religious Significance of Food to Medieval Women*. Berkeley and Los Angeles: University of California Press, 1987.

Carlitz, Katherine N. "Family, Society and Tradition in *Jin Ping Mei,*" *Modern China* 10:4 (Oct. 1984): 387–413.

———. *The Rhetoric of Chin p'ing mei*. Bloomington: Indiana University Press, 1986.

———. "The Role of Drama in the *Chin P'ing Mei:* The Relationship between Fiction and Drama as a Guide to the Viewpoint of a Sixteenth Century Chinese Novel." Ph.D. dissertation, University of Chicago, 1979.

Carroll, Vern, ed. *Adoption in Eastern Oceania.* Honolulu: University of Hawaii Press, 1970.

Cartier, Michel. *Une reforme locale en Chine au XVIe siècle: Hai Jui a Chun'an.* Paris: Mouton, 1973.

Cass, Victoria B. "Female Healers in the Ming and the Lodge of Ritual and Ceremony," *Journal of the American Oriental Society* 106:1 (Jan.–Mar. 1986): 233–240.

Chan, Albert. *The Glory and Fall of the Ming Dynasty.* Norman: University of Oklahoma Press, 1982.

Chan, Wing-tsit. *Neo-Confucian Terms Explained (The* Pei-hsi tzu-i). New York: Columbia University Press, 1986.

———. *A Sourcebook in Chinese Philosophy.* Princeton, N.J.: Princeton University Press, 1963.

Chang, Tsung-tung. *Chinesischer Liebesgarten.* Kunzelsau: Horst Erdmann Verlag, 1964.

Chen, Fu-mei Chang. "Private Code Commentaries in the Development of Ch'ing Law." Ph.D. dissertation, Harvard, 1970.

Chiu, H. P. "The Origin and Purpose of Adoption," *China Law Review,* no. 3 (Feb. 1930): 79–88.

———. "Questions Concerning the Adoption of Children," *Chinese Law and Government,* Spring 1961, pp. 60–63.

Chow Tse-tsung. "The Childbirth Myth and Ancient Chinese Medicine: A Study of Aspects of the *wu* Tradition." In *Ancient China: Studies in Civilization.* Edited by David T. Roy and Ts'uen-hsuin Tsien. Hong Kong: The Chinese University Press, 1978. Pp. 43–89.

Chu, Djang, trans. *A Complete Book Concerning Happiness and Benevolence: A Manual for Local Magistrates in Seventeenth-Century China.* Tucson: University of Arizona Press, 1984.

Ch'u T'ung-tsu. *Law and Society in Traditional China.* Paris: Ecole pratique des hautes études, 1961.

Clarke, G. W., trans. "The *Yü-li* or Precious Records," *Journal of the Royal Asiatic Society, North China Branch* 28:2 (1894): 233–400.

Cohen, Myron L. *House United, House Divided: The Chinese Family in Taiwan.* New York: Columbia University Press, 1976.

Comber, Leon. *The Strange Cases of Magistrate Pao.* Rutland, Vt.: Charles Tuttle, 1964.

Conner, Alison Wayne. "The Law of Evidence during the Ch'ing Dynasty." Ph.D. dissertation, Cornell, 1979.

Crook, J. A. *Law and Life of Rome.* Ithaca, N.Y.: Cornell University Press, 1967.

Dardess, John W. "The Cheng Communal Family: Social Organization and Neo-Confucianism in Yüan and Early Ming China," *Harvard Journal of Asiatic Studies* 34 (1974): 7–52.

————. *Confucianism and Autocracy: Professional Elites in the Founding of the Ming Dynasty*. Berkeley and Los Angeles: University of California Press, 1983.

Day, Clarence Burton. *Chinese Peasant Cults*. Taipei: Chung-wen, 1974.

de Bary, William Theodore. *Self and Society in Ming Thought*. New York: Columbia University Press, 1970.

————. *Sources of Chinese Tradition*. 2 vols. New York: Columbia University Press, 1960.

de Groot, J. J. M. *Sectarianism and Religious Persecution in China*. Amsterdam: Johannes Muller, 1903–1904.

Dennerline, Jerry. *The Chia-ting Loyalists: Confucian Leadership and Social Change in Seventeenth Century China*. New Haven, Conn.: Yale University Press, 1981.

Despeux, Catherine. *Prescriptions d'acuponcture valant mille onces d'or: Traite d'acuponcture de Sun Simiao du VIIe siècle*. Paris: Guy Tredaniel, 1987.

Dickson, Arthur. *Valentine and Orson: A Study in Late Medieval Romance*. New York: Columbia University Press, 1929.

Dolby, William. *The Perfect Lady by Mistake and Other Stories*. London: Paul Elek, 1976.

Donzelot, Jacques. *The Policing of Families*. New York: Pantheon, 1979.

Doolittle, Justus. *Social Life of the Chinese*. 2 vols. New York: Harpers, 1865.

Dubs, Homer. *The History of the Former Han Dynasty*. 3 vols. Baltimore: Waverly Press, 1938–1955.

Dudbridge, Glen. *The Hsi-yu chi: A Study of Antecedents to the Sixteenth-Century Chinese Novel*. Cambridge: Cambridge University Press, 1970.

Dunstan, Helen. "The Late Ming Epidemics: A Preliminary Survey," *Ch'ing-shih wen-t'i* 3:3 (Nov. 1975): 1–59.

Duyvendak, J. J. L. trans. *The Book of the Lord Shang*. London: Arthur Probsthain, 1928.

Eberhard, Wolfram. *Guilt and Sin in Traditional China*. Berkeley and Los Angeles: University of California Press, 1967.

————. *Social Mobility in Traditional China*. Leiden: E. J. Brill, 1962.

Ebrey, Patricia Buckley. "Conceptions of the Family in the Sung Dynasty," *Journal of Asian Studies* 43 (Feb. 1984): 219–245.

————. "The Early Stages of Descent Group Organization." In *Kinship Organization in Late Imperial China*. Edited by Patricia Buckley Ebrey and James L. Watson. Berkeley and Los Angeles: University of California Press, 1986. Pp. 16–61.

————. *Family and Property in Sung China: Yüan Ts'ai's Precepts for Social Life*. Princeton, N.J.: Princeton University Press, 1984.

————. "Women in the Kinship System of the Southern Song Upper Class." In *Women in China*. Edited by Richard Guisso and Stanley Johannesen. New York: Philo Press, 1981. Pp. 113–128.

Ebrey, Patricia, and James L. Watson, eds. *Kinship Organization in Late Imperial China 1000–1940*. Berkeley and Los Angeles: University of California Press, 1986.

Egerton, E. Clement. *The Golden Lotus*. 4 vols. London: Routledge, 1939.

Elvin, Mark. *The Pattern of the Chinese Past*. Stanford, Calif.: Stanford University Press, 1973.

Fischer, Carney T. "The Great Ritual Controversy in the Age of Ming Shih-tsung," *Bulletin: Society for the Study of Chinese Religion*, no. 7 (Fall 1979): 71–87.

———. "The Great Ritual Controversy in Ming China." Ph.D. dissertation, University of Michigan, 1977.

Flandrin, Jean-Louis. *Families in Former Times: Kinship, Household and Sexuality*. New York: Cambridge University Press, 1979.

Forster, Robert, and Orest Ranum. *Ritual, Religion and the Sacred*. Baltimore: Johns Hopkins University Press, 1982.

Francis, H. T., and E. J. Thomas. *Jataka Tales*. Cambridge: Cambridge University Press, 1916.

Franke, Herbert. "Zu einem apokryphen Dharani-sutra aus China," *Zeitung der deutschen morgenlandischen Gesellschaft* 134:2 (1984): 318–336.

Franke, Herbert, and Dieter Eikemeyer. *State and Law in East Asia*. Wiesbaden: Otto Harrasowitz, 1981.

Franke, Herbert, and Wolfgang Bauer. *The Golden Casket: Chinese Novellas of Two Millennia*. Translated by Christopher Levenson. London: Penguin, 1966.

Franke, Wolfgang. *An Introduction to the Sources of Ming History*. Kuala Lumpur: University of Malaya Press, 1968.

Fraser, Antonia. *Cromwell: Our Chief of Men*. New York: Granada, 1975.

Freedman, Maurice. *Family and Kinship in Chinese Society*. Stanford, Calif.: Stanford University Press, 1970.

———. *The Study of Chinese Society: Essays*. Selected and introduced by G. William Skinner. Stanford, Calif.: Stanford University Press, 1979.

Fung, Tat-hang. *Die schöne Konkubine und andere chinesische Liebesgeschichten aus der Ming-Zeit*. Tübingen: H. Erdmann, 1966.

———. *Neuer chinesischer Liebesgarten: Novellen aus den berühmtesten erotischen Sammlungem der Ming-Zeit*. Tübingen: H. Erdmann, 1968.

Furth, Charlotte. "Androgynous Males and Deficient Females: Biology and Gender Boundaries in Sixteenth and Seventeenth Century China," *Late Imperial China* 9:2 (Dec. 1988): 1–31.

———. "Blood, Body and Gender: Medical Images of the Female Condition in China 1600–1850," *Chinese Science* 7 (1986): 43–66.

———. "Concepts of Pregnancy, Childbirth and Infancy in Ch'ing Dynasty China," *Journal of Asian Studies* 46:1 (Feb. 1987): 7–35.

Gallin, Bernard. *Hsin Hsing, Taiwan: A Chinese Village in Change.* Berkeley and Los Angeles: University of California Press, 1966.

Généstal, R. *Histoire de la légitimation des enfants naturels en droit canonique.* Paris: Bibliothèque de l'École des Hautes Études, Sciences Religeuses, 1905.

Giles, Herbert A. *Strange Stories from a Chinese Studio.* Hong Kong: Kelly and Walsh, 1936.

Girardot, N. J. *Myth and Meaning in Early Taoism: The Theme of Chaos* (huntun). Berkeley and Los Angeles: University of California Press, 1983.

Gonnet, Paul. *L'adoption Lyonnaise des orphelins légitimes (1536–1797).* Paris: Librarie Générale de Droit et de Jurisprudence, 1935.

Goodrich, Anne Swann. *The Peking Temple of the Eastern Peak.* Nagoya: Monumenta Serica, 1964.

Goodrich, L. Carrington, and Chaoyang Fang. *Dictionary of Ming Biography.* 2 vols. New York: Columbia University Press, 1976.

Goody, Jack. *The Development of the Family and Marriage in Europe.* Cambridge: Cambridge University Press, 1983.

———. *Production and Reproduction: A Comparative Study of the Domestic Domain.* Cambridge: Cambridge University Press, 1976.

Goody, Jack, and S. J. Tambiah. *Bridewealth and Dowry.* New York: Cambridge University Press, 1973.

Granet, Marcel. *Fêtes et chansons anciennes de la Chine.* Paris: E. Leroux, 1929.

The Graphic Arts of Chinese Folklore. Taipei: National Museum of History, 1977.

Grove, Linda, and Christian Daniels. *State and Society in China: Japanese Perspectives on Ming-Qing Social and Economic History.* Tokyo: University of Tokyo Press, 1984.

Hales, Dell R. "The *P'ai-an ching-ch'i:* A Literary Criticism." Ph.D. dissertation, Indiana University, 1969.

Hanan, Patrick. *The Chinese Short Story: Studies in Dating, Authorship and Composition.* Cambridge, Mass.: Harvard University Press, 1973.

———. *The Chinese Vernacular Story.* Cambridge, Mass.: Harvard University Press, 1981.

———. *The Invention of Li Yu.* Cambridge, Mass.: Harvard University Press, 1988.

Hanley, Susan and Arthur Wolf, eds. *Family and Population in East Asian History.* Stanford, Calif.: Stanford University Press, 1985.

Harrell, Stevan. *Ploughshare Village: Culture and Context in Taiwan.* Seattle: University of Washington Press, 1982.

———. "The Rich Get Children: Segmentation, Stratification and Population in Three Chekiang Lineages, 1550–1850." In *Family and Population in East Asian History.* Edited by Susan Hanley and Arthur Wolf. Stanford, Calif.: Stanford University Press, 1985. Pp. 81–109.

Hawkes, David, trans. *The Story of the Stone.* 5 vols. Bloomington: Indiana University Press, 1979–1987.

Hayden, George A. "The Judge Pao Plays of the Yüan Dynasty." Ph.D. dissertation, Stanford, 1971.

Hazelton, Keith Duane. "Lineages and Local Elites in Hui-chou, 1500–1800." Ph.D. dissertation, Princeton, 1984.

Hegel, Robert, and Richard Hessney. *Expressions of Self in Chinese Literature.* New York: Columbia University Press, 1985.

Henderson, John B. *The Development and Decline of Chinese Cosmology.* New York: Columbia University Press, 1984.

Henry, Eric P. *Chinese Amusement: The Lively Plays of Li Yü.* Hamden, Conn.: Archon Books, 1980.

Herzer, Rudolf. "Der Streit über das Grosse Rituel: Ein Hofkontroverse der frühen Chia-ching Zeit," *Oriens Extremis* 19:2 (Dec. 1972): 65–83.

Hoang, Pierre. *Le mariage chinois au point de vue légal.* Shanghai: Imprimerie de la Mission Catholique Orphelinat de t'ou se wei, 1898.

Hom, Marlon Kau. "The Continuation of Tradition: A Study of Liaozhai Zhiyi." Ph.D. dissertation, University of Washington, 1979.

Hsiao T'ung. *De la succession et de l'adoption en droit chinois.* Shanghai: Imprimerie de l'Orphelinat de t'ou se wei, 1927.

Hsu, Francis L. K. *Under the Ancestors' Shadow.* Revised edition. Stanford, Calif.: Stanford University Press, 1971.

Huang, Ray. *Taxation and Government Finance in Sixteenth-Century Ming China.* Cambridge: Cambridge University Press, 1975.

Hu Hsien-chin. *The Common Descent Group in China and Its Functions.* New York: Viking Fund Publications in Anthropology, 1948.

Idema, Wilt, and Stephen H. West. *Chinese Theater 1100–1450: A Sourcebook.* Wiesbaden: Franz Steiner Verlag, 1982.

Johnson, David, Andrew J. Nathan, and Evelyn S. Rawski, eds. *Popular Culture in Late Imperial China.* Berkeley and Los Angeles: University of California Press, 1985.

Johnson, Wallace. *The T'ang Code.* Princeton, N.J.: Princeton University Press, 1979.

Joubert, Laurent. *Erreurs populaires et propos vulgaires touchant la médicine et la regime de santé.* Bordeaux: S. Millanges, 1579. University of California, San Francisco, medical library.

Kasoff, Ira. *The Thought of Chang Tsai (1020–1077).* New York: Cambridge University Press, 1984.

Kuhn, Franz, trans. *Eisherz und Edeljaspis oder die Geschichte einer glucklichen Gattenwahl,* Leipzig: Inselverlag, 1947.

———. *Kin-ku ch'i-kuan.* Zurich: Manesse Verlag, 1960.

———. *Kin P'ing Meh, oder die abenteuerliche Geschichte von Hsi Men und seinen sechs Frauen.* Leipzig: Insel Verlag, 1930.

Larsen, Joy. "Family Law Reform in Postwar Japan: Succession and Adoption." Ph.D. dissertation, University of Colorado at Boulder, 1983.

Legge, James, trans. *The Chinese Classics.* 5 vols. Oxford: Oxford University Press, 1935.

———. *Li Chi: Book of Rites.* 2 vols. New Hyde Park, N.Y.: University Books, 1967.

Lettres édifiantes et curieuses de Chine par des missionnaires jésuites 1702–1776. Edited by Isabelle and Jean-Louis Vissière. Paris: Garnier-Flammiron, 1979.

Leung, Angela Kiche. "Autour de la naissance: La mère et l'enfant en Chine aux XVIe et XVIIe siècles," *Cahiers internationaux de sociologie* 76 (1984): 51–69.

Levenson, Christopher, trans. *The Golden Casket: Chinese Novellas of Two Millennia.* London: Penguin, 1966.

Levy, André. *Inventaire analytique et critique du conte Chinois en langue vulgaire.* 2 vols. Paris: Memoires de l'Institut des Hautes Études Chinois, 1978–.

Li Chi. *The Travel Diaries of Hsu Hsia-k'o.* Hong Kong: The Chinese University of Hong Kong Press, 1974.

Linck, Gudula. *Zur Sozialgeschichte der chinesischen Familie im 13.Jahrhundert: Untersuchungen am* Ming-gong shu-pan qing-ming-ji. Stuttgart: Franz Steiner, 1986.

Littrup, Leif. *Sub-bureaucratic Government in China in Ming Times: A Study of Shandong Province in the Sixteenth Century.* Oslo: Universitetsvorlaget, 1981.

Liu, Hui-chen Wang. *The Traditional Chinese Clan Rules.* Locust Valley, N.Y.: J. J. Augustin, 1959.

Liu, Ts'ui-jung. "The Demography of Two Chinese Clans in Hsiao-shan, Chekiang, 1650–1850" in *Family and Population in East Asian History.* Edited by Susan Hanley and Arthur Wolf. Stanford, Calif.: Stanford University Press, 1985. Pp. 13–61.

Lo, Hsiang-lin. "The History and Arrangement of Chinese Genealogies." In *Studies in Asian Genealogy.* Edited by Spencer T. Palmer. Provo, Ut.: Brigham Young University Press, 1972. Pp. 13–37.

Ma, Y. W., and Joseph S. M. Lau, eds. *Traditional Chinese Stories: Themes and Variations.* New York: Columbia University Press, 1978.

McCullough, William H. "Japanese Marriage Institutions in the Heian Period," *Harvard Journal of Asiatic Studies* 27 (1967): 103–167.

McGough, James Pierce. "Marriage and Adoption in China with Special Reference to Customary Law." Ph.D. dissertation, Michigan State University, 1976.

McKnight, Brian. *The Washing Away of Wrongs*. Ann Arbor: University of Michigan Press, 1981.

McMahon, Keith. *Causality and Containment in Seventeenth Century Chinese Fiction*. Leiden: E. J. Brill, 1988.

———. "The Gap in the Wall: Containment and Abandon in Seventeenth Century Chinese Fiction." Ph.D. dissertation, Princeton, 1984.

McMullen, I. J. "Non-Agnatic Adoption: A Confucian Controversy in Seventeenth and Eighteenth Century Japan," *Harvard Journal of Asiatic Studies* 35 (1975): 130–189.

Mair, Victor. "Language and Ideology in the Written Popularization of the *Sacred Edict*." In *Popular Culture in Late Imperial China*. Edited by David Johnson, Andrew Nathan, and Evelyn Rawski. Berkeley and Los Angeles: University of California Press, 1985. Pp. 325–359.

Mandeville, Elizabeth. "Kamano Adoption," *Ethnology* 20:3 (July 1981): 231–234.

Mao, Nathan. *Li Yü's Twelve Towers*. Hong Kong: Chinese University Press, 1975.

Mao, Nathan, and Liu Ts'un-yan. *Li Yü*. Boston: Twayne World Author's Series, 1977.

Marks, Robert B. *Rural Revolution in South China: Peasants and the Making of History in Haifeng County, 1570–1930*. Madison: University of Wisconsin Press, 1984.

Martin, W. A. P. "Native Tract Literature in China," *Hanlin Papers*. Shanghai: Kelly and Walsh, 1894. Pp. 304–326.

Martinson, Paul Varo. "Pao, Order and Redemption: Perspectives on Chinese Religion and Society Based on a Study of the *Chin P'ing Mei*." Ph.D. dissertation, University of Chicago, 1973.

Maspero, Henri. *Melanges posthumes sur les religions et l'histoire de la Chine*. Paris: Civilizations du Sud, S.A.E.P., 1950.

Mayne, John Dawson. *Treatise on Hindu Law and Usage*. London: Stevens and Haynes, 1898.

Monier, Raymond. *Manuel elementaire de droit romain*. 2 vols. Paris: Editions Domet Montchrestien, 1947.

Montaigne, Michel de. *Essays*. Baltimore: Penguin Books, 1958.

Moore, R. A. "Adoption and Samurai Mobility in Tokugawa Japan," *Journal of Asian Studies* 29:3 (May 1970): 617–632.

Mowry, Hua-yuan Li. *Chinese Love Stories from Ch'ing shih*. Hamden, Conn.: Archon Books, 1983.

Mulligan, Jean. *The Lute: Kao Ming's P'i P'a Chi*. New York: Columbia University Press, 1980.

Murck, Christian. "Chu Yün-ming and Cultural Commitment in Soochow." Ph.D. dissertation, Princeton, 1978.

Murray, Julia K. "Representations of Hariti, the Mother of Demons, and the Theme of 'Raising the Alms Bowl' in Chinese Painting," *Artibus Asiae* 43:4 (1981–1982): 253–268.

Nakane, Chie. *Japanese Society.* London: Weidenfield and Nicholson, 1970.

Nylan, Michael. "Ying Shao's *Feng-su t'ung-yi:* An Exploration of Problems in Han Dynasty Political, Philosophical and Social Unity." Ph.D. dissertation, Princeton, 1982.

O'Hara, Albert. *The Position of Women in Early China.* Taipei: Mei Ya Publications, 1971.

Oyama Masaaki. "Large Landownership in the Jiangnan Delta Region during the Late Ming–Early Qing Period." In *State and Society in China: Japanese Perspectives on Ming-Qing Social and Economic History.* Edited by Linda Grove and Christian Daniels. Tokyo: University of Tokyo Press, 1984. Pp. 101–163.

Palmer, Spencer T., ed. *Studies in Asian Genealogy.* Provo, Ut.: Brigham Young University Press, 1972.

Parsons, James B. *Peasant Rebellions of the late Ming Dynasty.* Tucson: University of Arizona Press, 1970.

Pasternak, Burton. *Guests of the Dragon: Social Demography in a Chinese District.* New York: Columbia University Press, 1983.

————. "On the Causes and Demographic Consequences of Uxorilocal Marriage in China." In *Family and Population in East Asian History.* Edited by Susan Hanley and Arthur Wolf. Stanford, Calif.: Stanford University Press, 1985. Pp. 309–334.

Peri, Noel. "Hariti la mère de demons," *Bulletin de l'Ecole Française d'Extrême Orient* 17:3 (1917): 1–103.

Perng, Ching-hsi. *Double Jeopardy: A Critique of Seven Yüan Courtroom Dramas.* Ann Arbor: Michigan Papers in Chinese Studies, 1975.

Presser, Stephen B. "The Historical Background of the American Law of Adoption," *Journal of Family Law* 11 (1971): 443–516.

Prévost, Marcel Henri. *Les adoptions politiques à Rome sous la Republique et le Principat.* Paris: Recueil Sirey, 1949.

Prusek, Jaroslav. *Chinese History and Literature.* Prague: Czechoslovak Academy of Sciences, 1970.

Ritter, Philip L. "Adoption on Kosrae Island: Solidarity and Sterility," *Ethnology* 20:1 (Jan. 1981): 45–61.

Sakai, Tadao. "Confucianism and Popular Educational Works." In *Self and Society in Ming Thought.* Edited by William Theodore de Bary. New York: Columbia University Press, 1970. Pp. 331–366.

Schneider, David M. *American Kinship.* New York: Prentice Hall, 1968.

————. *A Critique of the Study of Kinship.* Ann Arbor: University of Michigan Press, 1984.

Schurman, H. F. "On Social Themes in Sung Tales," *Harvard Journal of Asiatic Studies* 20 (1957): 239–261.

Seaman, Gary. *Journey to the North: An Ethnohistorical Analysis and Annotated Translation of the Chinese Folk Novel* Pei-yu chi. Berkeley and Los Angeles: University of California Press, 1987.

Serruys, Paul. "Les cérémonies du mariage," *Folklore Studies* 3:1 (1944): 73–154.

Shiga Shūzō. "Family Property and the Law of Inheritance in Traditional China." In *Chinese Family Law and Social Change.* Edited by David Buxbaum. Seattle: University of Washington Press, 1978. Pp. 109–175.

Shih Chung-wen. *The Golden Age of Chinese Drama:* Yüan tsa chü. Princeton, N.J.: Princeton University Press, 1976.

————. *Injustice to Tou O.* Cambridge: Cambridge University Press, 1972.

Smith, Arthur Henderson. *Proverbs and Sayings from the Chinese.* Shanghai: American Presbyterian Mission Press, 1914.

Smith, R. J., and R. K. Beardsley. *Japanese Culture: Its Development and Characteristics.* London: Methuen, 1963.

So, Kwan-wai. *Japanese Piracy in Ming China during the Sixteenth Century.* East Lansing: Michigan State University Press, 1975.

Spence, Jonathan. *Ts'ao Yin and the K'ang-hsi Emperor, Bondservant and Master.* New Haven, Conn.: Yale University Press, 1966.

Spence, Jonathan, and John E. Wills. *From Ming to Ch'ing.* New Haven, Conn.: Yale University Press, 1970.

Steele, John, trans. *The I-li or Book of Etiquette and Ceremonial.* 2 vols. Taipei: Ch'eng-wen, 1966.

Sturtevant, A. H. *A History of Genetics.* New York: Harper & Row, 1965.

Sundarajan, Kuen-wei Lu. "Chinese Stories of Karma and Transmigration." Ph.D. dissertation, Harvard, 1979.

Swann, Nancy Lee. *Food and Money in Ancient China.* New York: Octagon Books, 1974.

Taylor, Romeyn. *Basic Annals of Ming T'ai-tsu.* San Francisco: Chinese Materials and Research Aids Center, 1976.

Tch'en Si-tan. *L'adoption en droit chinois.* Shanghai: Imprimerie de l'Orphelinat de t'ou se wei, 1924.

Telford, Ted. "Survey of Social Demographic Data in Chinese Genealogies," *Late Imperial China* 7:2 (Dec. 1986): 118–148.

Teng Ssu-yu, trans. *Family Instructions for the Yen Clan.* Leiden: E. J. Brill, 1968.

Tju Som Tjan, trans. *Po Hu T'ung: The Comprehensive Discussions in the White Tiger Hall.* Leiden: E. J. Brill, 1949–1952.

Topelmann, Cornelia. *Shan-ko von Feng Meng-ling: Eine Volksliedersammlung aus der Ming-Zeit.* Wiesbaden: Franz Steiner, 1973.

Topley, Marjorie. "Cosmic Antagonisms: A Mother-Child Syndrome." In *Religion and Ritual in Chinese Society.* Edited by Arthur Wolf. Stanford, Calif.: Stanford University Press, 1974. Pp. 233–250.

Tsugaru Fusamaro. *Die Lehre von der Japanisher Adoption.* Berlin: Mayer and Miller, 1907.

Tu Wei-ming. *Centrality and Commonality: An Essay on the* Chung-yung. Honolulu: University of Hawaii Press, 1976.

———. *Confucian Thought: Selfhood as Creative Transformation.* Albany: State University of New York Press, 1985.

———. "The Idea of the Human in Mencian Thought." In *Theories of the Arts in China.* Edited by Susan Bush and Christian Murck. Princeton, N.J.: Princeton University Press, 1983. Pp. 57–73.

Unschuld, Paul. *Medical Ethics in Imperial China.* Berkeley and Los Angeles: University of California Press, 1979.

———. *Medicine in China: A History of Ideas.* Berkeley and Los Angeles: University of California Press, 1985.

———. *Medicine in China: A History of Pharmaceutics.* Berkeley and Los Angeles: University of California Press, 1986.

———. *Pen-Ts'ao: 2000 Jahre traditionelle pharmazeutische Literatur Chinas.* München: Heinz Moos Verlag, 1973.

van Gulik, Robert. *Parallel Cases from under the Pear Tree.* Leiden: E. J. Brill, 1956.

———. *Sexual Life in Ancient China.* Leiden: E. J. Brill, 1974.

von Möllendorf, P. G. "The Family Law of the Chinese, and its Comparative Relations with that of other Nations," *Journal of the Royal Asiatic Society, North China Branch,* 1879. N.s. 13:99–121.

Waley, Arthur, trans. *The Analects of Confucius.* New York: Random House, 1938.

———. *Ballads and Stories from Tun-huang.* London: George Allen and Unwin, 1960.

———. *Monkey.* New York: Grove, 1958.

Waltner, Ann. "Adoption of Children in Ming and Early Ch'ing China." Ph.D. dissertation, University of California at Berkeley, 1981.

———. "The Loyalty of Adopted Sons in Ming and Early Qing China," *Modern China* 10:4 (Oct. 1984): 441–459.

———. "Widows and Remarriage in Ming and Early Qing China," *Historical Reflections* (Spring 1981): 129–146.

Wang, C. C. *Traditional Chinese Tales.* New York: Columbia University Press, 1944.

Wang Yi-t'ung. "Slaves and Other Comparable Social Groupings during the

Northern Dynasties (386–618)," *Harvard Journal of Asiatic Studies* 16:3–4 (Dec. 1953): 293–364.

Watson, Burton. *Chuang-tzu: Basic Writings.* New York: Columbia University Press, 1965.

———. *Courtier and Commoner in Ancient China: Selections from the History of the Former Han.* New York: Columbia University Press, 1974.

Watson, James L. "Agnates and Outsiders: Adoption in a Chinese Lineage," *Man* 10:2 (June 1975): 293–306.

Watson, Rubie. *Inequality among Brothers.* New York: Cambridge Universit' Press, 1985.

Watt, John. *The District Magistrate in Late Imperial China.* New York: Columbia University Press, 1977.

Wechsler, Howard. *Offerings of Jade and Silk: Ritual and Symbol in the Legitimation of the T'ang Dynasty.* New Haven, Conn.: Yale University Press, 1985.

Wiens, Mi Chu. "The Origins of Modern Chinese Landlordism." In *Festschrift in Honor of the Eightieth Birthday of Professor Shen Kang-po.* Taipei: Lien Ching, 1976. Pp. 289–344.

Wilhelm, Richard, trans. *Frühling und Herbst des Lü Pu-wei.* Jena: E. Diederichs, 1928.

Wolf, Arthur. "Adopt a Daughter-in-law, Marry a Sister: A Chinese Solution to the Problem of the Incest Taboo," *American Anthropologist* 70 (5): 846–874.

———. "Childhood Association, Sexual Attraction, and the Incest Taboo: A Chinese Case," *American Anthropologist* 68 (4): 883–898.

———. *Religion and Ritual in Chinese Society.* Stanford, Calif.: Stanford University Press, 1974.

Wolf, Arthur, and Chieh-shan Huang. *Marriage and Adoption in China, 1845–1945.* Stanford, Calif.: Stanford University Press, 1980.

Wolf, Margery. *Women and the Family in Rural Taiwan.* Stanford, Calif.: Stanford University Press, 1972.

Wright, Arthur, and Denis Twitchett. *Confucian Personalities.* Stanford, Calif.: Stanford University Press, 1962.

Wu, Nelson. "Tung Ch'i-ch'ang." In *Confucian Personalities.* Edited by Arthur Wright and Denis Twitchett. Stanford, Calif.: Stanford University Press, 1962. Pp. 260–293.

Yamamura, Kozo. *A Study of Samurai Income and Entrepreneurship.* Cambridge, Mass.: Harvard University Press, 1974.

Yang, Gladys, and Yang Hsien-yi, trans. *The Courtesan's Jewel Box.* Peking: Foreign Languages Press, 1957.

———. *Selected Plays of Kuan Han-ching.* Shanghai: New Art and Literature Publishing House, 1958.

Yu, Anthony, trans. and ed. *Journey to the West.* 4 vols. Chicago: University of Chicago Press, 1977–1983.

Zeitlin, Judith. "Pu Songling's (1640–1715) 'Liaozhai zhiyi' and the Chinese Discourse on the Strange." Ph.D. dissertation, Harvard, 1988.

Zurndorfer, Harriet. "The *Hsin-an ta-tsu chih* and the Development of Chinese Gentry Society," *T'oung Pao* 67:3–5 (1981): 154–215.

Index

Short stories are listed by their Chinese title and by the titles of well-known English translations. In addition, for the convenience of the reader, they are grouped together under the title of the collection in which they appear.

About the Author

Ann Waltner holds a doctorate in Chinese history from the University of California, Berkeley. She is currently an associate professor of history at the University of Minnesota. Among her recent publications are "From Casebook to Fiction: Varieties of *Kung-an* in Late Imperial China" and "The Moral Status of the Child in Late Imperial China: Childhood in Ritual and Law." She is at work on a book-length study of T'an-yang-tzu, a female religious teacher who lived in the sixteenth century.

Production Notes
This book was designed by Paula Newcomb.
Composition and paging were done on the
Quadex Composing System and typesetting
on the Compugraphic 8400 by the design
and production staff of University of
Hawaii Press.
The text typeface is Sabon and the
display typeface is Goudy Old Style.
Offset presswork and binding were done by
Maple-Vail Book Manufacturing Group. Text
paper is Glatfelter Offset Vellum, basis 50.